ELUSIVE
TREASURE

Of Florida .

A cheife Herowans wyfe of Pomeoc .
and her daughter of the age of .8. or .
10. yeares .

ELUSIVE TREASURE

*The Story of Early Archaeologists
in the Americas*

Brian Fagan

BOOK CLUB ASSOCIATES

For Diane, with love
Because of friendship, the Ben Jonson, and many
shared Deanly experiences

CONTENTS

AUTHOR'S NOTE

The photographic research for this book revealed
an astonishing richness and diversity of material,
much of it little known except to specialists. It was
difficult to select a useful balance of contemporary
portraits, lithographs, artifacts, and site photographs. Anyone contemplating an excursion
into this fascinating material would do well to
consult the Museum of the American Indian in New
York, whose archives are an incredible treasure
house of fine photography, some of it dating from as
early as the 1880s. The American Museum of Natural
History, the Peabody Museum, and the Smithsonian
Institution are also fine sources of information and
rare photographs. So are the National Museum of
Anthropology in Mexico City and the various museums of the Southwest. Fascinating lithographs of

early sites in the Southwest are contained in the early military reports in *The Congressional Record*. Catherwood's watercolors and drawings are well known and need no introduction; equally useful, if less celebrated, is the delicate art of John White. In illustrating the chapters on the Mound Builders I relied heavily on the original monograph by Squier and Davis, which is comprehensively illustrated with plans that reveal the amazing industry of the early archaeologists.

I have followed common archaeological practice in omitting accents from Spanish place names but retaining them for personal names. Spellings of geographic locations are those adopted by *The Times Atlas of the World*.

This book is not fully referenced and footnoted as some readers might prefer. *Elusive Treasure* is designed as a synthesis of the early history of archaeology in America for the lay person and as such, references on any scale are inappropriate. Interested readers can easily investigate the technical literature more fully by consulting the sources at the end of the book.

ACKNOWLEDGMENTS

Only those who have worked over a period of years with the same sympathetic and knowledgeable editor understand the debt that I owe to Patricia Cristol of Charles Scribner's Sons. This book was her idea in the first place. Her sage comments at all stages of the work have been invaluable. I am grateful, too, to the production staff of Scribners who created order and beauty out of a complicated manuscript. Many friends and colleagues have read all or parts of this work. In particular, E. Willys Andrews V, Barbara St. John, Bernard Fontana, Robert Porter, and Barbara Voorhies corrected many errors and stylistic horrors at rough-draft stage. The debt I owe them is enormous. Many museums and research institutions have provided illustrations; individual acknowledgments to them are made elsewhere. The maps are the work of Je Goolsby.

My greatest debt is to those who have worked on the specific problems of American archaeological history and written admirable syntheses of their work. I want to acknowledge the important contributions of Robert Brunhouse on the Maya, Robert Silverberg on the mounds, and Jeremy A. Sabloff and Gordon Willey on the subject as a whole, which were fundamental sources for my general synthesis.

PREFACE

This book is an attempt to distill a narrative from the enormous body of literature on the major controversies of American archaeology from the time of the conquistadores to about 1900. As such it makes no new contribution to the technical literature on Maya archaeology, the mound sites of the eastern United States, or the Indians of the Southwest. Everything described here has appeared in print before, either in archaeologists' and travelers' accounts or in academic publications intended for a relatively small audience. I seek to identify some of the major controversies that have surrounded the history of the American Indian, not to describe that history itself. Many nineteenth-century controversies are far from settled. Nor have people lost their taste for escapism through archaeology. The

Ancient Astronauts of today are the successors to the Great Mound Builders and Atlanteans of yesterday. I hope that these pages will put the archaeological achievements of today in a meaningful historical context. Readers interested in delving more deeply into this fascinating story are urged to consult the sources listed at the end of this book and to explore further for themselves.

Santa Barbara, California   BRIAN M. FAGAN
1976

PART ONE

The Lure of Gold and Souls

"Much have I travell'd in the realms of gold,
And many goodly states and kingdoms seen."

JOHN KEATS

1 "Marvel You Not at the . . . Population of America"

"After the discovery of America, the minds of the learned and ingenious were much exercised to account for its habitation by men and animals," wrote the wise and sober antiquarian Samuel Haven in 1856. These words were penned nearly four hundred years after Christopher Columbus had encountered his first "Indians," well-built men "of very handsome bodies and fine faces." Haven described over three centuries of wild speculation, frenzied archaeological excavation, and changing attitudes toward the American Indian. All this was part of a massive intellectual adjustment to what one historian called the greatest event in the history of the Old World, the opening up of a whole new dimension in human diversity and achievement through the discovery of America. In part philosophical, in

Columbus landing in the Indies.
The frontispiece to Giuliano Dati's *Lettera*, 1493.

part religious, and stemming in large measure from plain human curiosity, the search for the origins of the American Indian is also one of the most colorful chapters in the history of archaeology.

Apparently Columbus himself was not surprised to find humans in the newly discovered lands. Since he had been looking for China, he naturally assumed that he had landed on some offshore islands near the Asian mainland. He had no idea that his ships had reached a wholly unknown world, separated from China by thousands of miles of open sea. In his time there was no reason to marvel at new men from a new world, for neither were thought to be new. Ferdinand Magellan's around-the-world voyage in 1519–21 was the achievement that finally convinced geographers that the Americas were truly a "new world," a term apparently coined by that vivid writer and controversial explorer Amerigo Vespucci. One of his printed letters, *Mundus Novus* ("New World"), is a brief account of "what we may rightly call a New World . . . a continent more densely peopled and abounding in animals than Europe or Asia or Africa." He was one of the first explorers to be at all explicit about the native inhabitants of the new continent. After describing their nudity and "excessive lust," always an appealing topic for a sixteenth-century audience, Vespucci claimed he had lived among them for twenty-seven days. "They have no laws or faith," he reported, "and live according to nature. . . . they have no boundaries of kingdoms and princes, and no king." It was a barbarian world of cannibalism and strange, pastoral simplicity that Vespucci described.

Those who were interested enough to think about the "Indians" were deeply puzzled by them. As long as Vespucci's New World was still thought to be part of Asia, even if it was not China, the strange inhabitants of the Americas were merely an intellectual curiosity. They lived apparently simple, uncomplicated lives in what often appeared to be a paradise of plenty, as though in a contemporary Garden of Eden: "Very handsome, and goodley people, and in their behavior as mannerly, and civil,

Die figur anzaigt vns das volck vnd insel die gefunden ist durch den cristenlichen künig zů Portigal. oder von seinen vnderthonen. Die leüt sind also nackent hübsch. braun wolgestalt von leib. ir heübter halß. arm. scham. füß. frawen vnd mann ain wenig mit federn bedeckt. Auch haben die mann in iren angesichten vnd brust vil edel gestain. Es hat auch nyemantz nichts sunder sind alle ding gemain. Vnd die mann habendt weyber welche in gefallen. es sey mütter. schwester. oder freündt. darjnn haben sy nit vnderschayd. Sy streyten auch mit ainander. Sy essen auch ainander selbs die erschlagen werden. vnd hencken das selbig fleisch in den rauch. Sy werden alt hundert vnd fünfftzig iar. Vnd haben kain regiment.

as any of Europe," observed one early visitor to Virginia. "The soile is the most plentifull, sweete, fruitfull and wholesome of all the world," enthused Elizabethan sea captain Arthur Barlowe in 1584.

In most places the indigenous population rapturously received the English, Portuguese, or Spanish explorers, who were often thought to be gods from heaven, to be worshipped as immortals. "We were entertained with all love and kindness," remembered Barlowe, "and with as much bounty, after their manner, as they could possibly give. Wee found the people most gently, loving and faithfull, void of all guile and treason, and such as lived after the manner of the golden age. The earth bringeth foorth all things in aboundance, as in the first creation, without toile or labour." But this period of peaceful coexistence, of warm hospitality and honest trading, did not last long. The colonists who followed the pioneer explorers were hungry for gold and copper, land and slaves. The Indians of the New World were no longer regarded with benevolent eyes but were depicted as lazy, treacherous, and guilty of cannibalism. Subjection and conversion of the Indians were accepted as Christian duties.

The conquistadores who conquered Mesoamerica in a few stirring years after 1519 were not scholarly men. Their interests were entirely commercial; their motives, frenzied greed. Gold was the objective, a tangible form of wealth as highly prized in the sixteenth century as it is today. The unlimited supplies of gold that the New World seemed to promise had eluded the conquistadores in Hispaniola and Cuba. But as they explored the mainland they heard rumors of mighty rulers in the interior whose capital cities were paved with gold. Hernando Cortés and his men, outnumbered, traveling in environments that inhibited the use of firearms and cavalry, traversed the rain forests of Vera Cruz and emerged on the Mexican highlands, where they encountered the incredible Aztec.

The last survivor of that expedition, Bernal Díaz del Castillo, lived to the ripe old age of eighty-nine, and years after the great campaigns were over he wrote his own firsthand account of this remarkable time. *The History of the Conquest of New Spain* is an enduring and workmanlike masterpiece that vividly portrays the incredible events and personalities of the first encounter between a prehistoric American state and European society. The passage of years in no way diminished the powerful effect that the marvels of the Aztec state had on Cortés and his captains. The four hundred Spaniards were greeted at the threshold of the city of Tenochtitlan by Montezuma himself, "magnificently clad, in [Aztec] fashion," in sandals, "the sides of which were of gold and the upper parts ornamented with precious stones." Montezuma's feet were not allowed to touch the ground; "noblemen with averted eyes" laid cloaks in front of him wherever he went. Cortés

Aztec priests sacrificing
human victims to
Huitzilopochtli.
From the Codex
Magliabecchiano.
Library of Congress

described Tenochtitlan, built on a swamp, as being
as large as Seville or Cordova. It was two leagues in
radius, and four causeways joined it to the mainland.
A huge, orderly market flourished in the city. Each
category of merchandise was assigned a section to itself, merchandise so varied that Díaz despaired of
ever describing it all. But he was careful to describe
the gold dust "placed in the thin quills of the great
geese of that country, which are so white as to be
transparent."

The temples were gruesome, reeking with the
stench of human sacrifice; the altars, adorned with
terrible figures, witnessed the carnage of helpless
victims. But the temples were also impressive. The
Aztec war god Huitzilopochtli "had a very broad

8

face and huge terrible eyes. And there were so many precious stones, so much gold, so many pearls and seed pearls stuck to him with a paste . . . that his whole body and head were covered with them." Carvings, ornaments, elaborate cloaks and robes, great furnished courtyards, and huge public works dazzled the conquistadores. The savage decadence of the Aztec religion appalled them, while the unbelievable wealth of Tenochtitlan aroused their cupidity.

Soon Montezuma was in captivity, the conquistadores were searching for gold, and the terrible sequence of events that led to the siege and fall of the city had begun. Within a few months the entire political and religious fabric of the Aztec state had collapsed in the face of a small expeditionary force of soldiers with firearms. The spoils were enormous, the carnage almost beyond endurance, as Díaz saw his captured companions sacrificed in front of his own eyes and dismembered in cannibal orgies. Bloodthirsty in their methods of governance, the Aztec were far from popular with the regional population as a whole. Other chiefs came to the aid of the Spaniards but were soon disillusioned by the conquistadores' ruthless exploitation of their new Mesoamerican possessions. Within a few generations the great ceremonial centers and precincts of Tenochtitlan were in ruins. A scattered rural population lived on; the drama of Aztec life was but a folk memory.

Everything that could be carried away became the spoils of war. Scattered artifacts and ornaments were presented to the Spanish court or preserved as curiosities. Gold dust was squirreled away in huge quantities or gambled for property, sometimes lost in games of chance. No one has any idea how much gold was removed from the New World. Until the Mexican archaeologist Alfonso Caso opened the famous undisturbed Mixtec tomb at Monte Alban, Oaxaca, in 1932, nobody had an inkling of what gold and jewelry the Aztec might have possessed. Only a few startling insights have been found in history.

Perhaps the most famous comes from the cele-

9

Two Indians with jug and plate.

The first known pen drawings of American Indians, which were executed in Europe by German artist Christopher Weiditz in 1529. He saw the Indians on a visit to the court of Charles I of Spain. Cortés had brought the strangers to the court as a present for the king in 1528. Apparently they delighted everyone with their juggling and skillful games.

brated artist Albrecht Dürer. His diary records a visit to a goldsmith in Brussels during August 1520, where he saw some of Cortés's loot ready for presentation to the king of Spain. "I have also seen objects brought to the King from the new Land of Gold," he wrote. "A Sun all in gold, as much as six feet in diameter and a moon all in silver. . . . there were two chambers full of armour used by these people, and all kinds of weapons, cuirasses, wondrous shields, strange clothing, bed-clothes, and all manner of curious objects for various purposes, more exquisite than any marvels. All these things were so costly that they are estimated at 100,000 gold florins in value." As far as is known, all these magnificent objects were dispersed or melted down. As one of the most remarkable and vigorous of American Indian states passed into oblivion, the fruits of its labors produced an extraordinary lust for gold, jewels, and wealth as hundreds sought their fortune in the New World. The consequences for the American Indian were tragic.

Initially, the Indians fascinated the Europeans. A handful of imported hostages and chiefs were displayed at Henry VIII's court, and the Spanish monarchs were treated to elaborate triumphal parades in which recently returned explorers and their Indian servants were prominently featured. A whole string of literary figures enlisted as public officials in Virginia: people like William Strackey, who wrote a *Historie of Travell into Virginia Britania*, knew Shakespeare, and provided the inspiration for the latter's *Tempest* by his account of a winter spent on Bermuda after a shipwreck. *The Tempest*, with its songs of the sea, Caliban, the savage owner of the island, and Prospero, the superior person who takes over, is an almost symbolic replay of what happened when European civilization had its first impact on the primitive societies of the New World. Caliban seemed overwhelmed by his visitor, who showed him how "to name the bigger light, and how the less that burn by day and night." His avidity to learn about the newcomer was like that of the Indians, who taught the Pilgrim fathers

The only woman in the party wearing a brightly feathered cape.

A juggler.

11

Aztec featherwork shield, probably sent to Europe by Hernando Cortés. This is one of the few objects sent to the Old World by the conquistadores that has survived the centuries. Formerly in the Hapsburg royal collections, it is now in the Museum für Volkerkunde, Vienna. The coyote depicted on the shield is a version of the Aztec fire god. The fire god is outlined in flame while the tufted border signifies flames.
Museum für Volkerkunde, Vienna

how to plant maize and where to fish and who helped them through the first lean years.

Even after bitter experiences with white man after white man, the Indians never seemed to learn how vast was the gulf between their attitudes toward life and those of the newcomers. So Caliban, even after alcoholic insults and much suffering, still entreats the drunken Trinculo to be his god: "I'll show thee every fertile inch o' th' island: / and I will kiss thy foot: I prithee, be my god."

The same work reflects the idyllic view of American Indian life, the notion of a pastoral Garden of Eden, that was already taking hold in the popular mind. The people of Shakespeare's island were living in a paradise and had gentility to match: "Their manners are more gentle-kind than of / Our human generation you shall find / Many, nay, almost nay," reported Gonzalo. This idyllic land led him to speculate on the ideal state of nature, a wonderland where "all things in common nature should produce without sweat or endeavour." Shakespeare himself seems to have been deeply cynical about this paradisiacal view of the New World, *The Tempest* perhaps being his way of commenting on a popular philosophy. But to most people American Indians seemed to be the very embodiment of the uncomplicated pastoral existence that they expected of simple societies.

Those who came into lengthier contact with the Indians were soon disillusioned, however, and were often driven to brutality. But the myth lived on, to be immortalized in the drawings of the Virginia pioneer John White and in travelers' tales of the New World that unashamedly catered to the public tastes of the day. As the astonishing diversity of mankind was revealed to European eyes from the sixteenth century onward, so speculations about the nature of savagery mounted. The eighteenth-century philosopher Thomas Hobbes had a jaundiced view of primitive society; he thought that Indians lived in a constant state of strife and turmoil. More pervasive was the romantic view, fostered by Captain Cook's astounding revelations about Tahiti and the South

Sea islanders in the eighteenth century. Jean Jacques Rousseau glorified savage life, depicting primitives as happy creatures prancing in uncomplicated pastoral groves. Thus arose the concept of the Noble Savage, who "entered the study and drawing room of Europe in naked majesty, to shake the preconceptions of morals and politics," as historian J. C. Beaglehole once remarked. Even if disillusionment about the natural state of the Indian soon took hold in the New World itself, the pastoral idylls of European literature helped satisfy curiosity about the origins and history of the American Indian.

Quite apart from untold wealth and pastoral fantasies, the discovery of the Aztec, and, indeed, of the Inca in Peru raised all sorts of intellectual questions. Columbus had encountered relatively unsophisticated savages, and the natives of Virginia were living in small villages with few signs of elaborate social or religious practices. But the huge temples and palaces of the Aztec were quite a different matter. Cortés himself had compared Tenochtitlan with Salamanca in Spain, to the latter's disadvantage. Montezuma obviously ruled over a highly sophisticated society the splendor and wealth of which took the Spaniards by surprise. Debates as to whether or not the Aztec were human were obviously irrelevant; they were only too human for comfort. The pressing question was from where had they come.

At first the Indians, being inhabitants of what was assumed to be Asia, were naturally considered as merely another Asian race. When the New World was finally recognized as such, this neat explanation could no longer suffice. The problem was this: European philosophers and intellectuals of the day automatically assumed that everyone on earth was descended from Adam and Eve. The biblical account of the Creation, dated by Archbishop James Ussher to 4004 B.C., was the only possible interpretation of human origins, defined and reinforced by religious dogma. To discount Genesis was to commit heresy—no light matter in sixteenth- and seventeenth-century society. The Garden of Eden itself was conventionally sited in the Near East, while Noah's

14

ark was supposed to have landed on high ground in
that same general area. Only eight people survived
the Flood; but the world's entire population was
descended from them, having spread out over the
land masses of Europe, Africa, and Asia in the six
thousand years separating the Elizabethans from the
Deluge.

As long as the world's continents were thought to
form a single land mass, there was no difficulty in
explaining how population movements had taken
place. But once Magellan crossed the Pacific and
proved that Central America was farther from Asia
than from Europe, land migrations seemed an im-
possibility. One of the classical debates of American
history was now joined, one that figures promi-

Ole Worm's Museum of
Curiosities in Copenhagen, from
Museum Wormianum, Leyden,
1653. The artifacts of American
Indians were prized items for
cabinets of curiosities whether
the Indians were considered
human or not.

15

nently in these pages: how had the American Indian crossed the Atlantic or Pacific to settle in the New World? Had there been, as some writers claimed, a second Adam created by God for the New World? But why were the animals of the Americas different as well? The immediate reaction was to fall back on the Scriptures, for, with only some six thousand years to play with, at least some degree of cultural uniformity between American and Old World societies had to be assumed, if Adam and Eve had truly existed.

But this uniformity was hard to detect. The exotic Indian artifacts that the early adventurers brought home looked quite unlike anything Europeans had seen before. Hundreds had flocked to see John Tradescant's Indian collection in the Ashmolean Museum at Oxford. Powhatan's ceremonial mantle of deerskin adorned with elaborate shell patterns lay beside wooden canoe paddles, necklaces, and girdles, artifacts that brought new words, such as *tobacco, canoe,* and *wampum,* into the Elizabethan vocabulary. Even more disturbing, the religious beliefs and practices of the Indians turned out to be highly distinctive and incompatible with Christian dogma. Furthermore, the Scriptures, then the ultimate key to all world history, made no mention of these strange practices.

According to the Scriptures, all human beings were descended from Noah—the Asians from Shem, the Africans from Ham, Europeans from Japheth. But it was impossible to decide who was responsible for the American Indians. By 1550 a mounting wave of literature about the Americas had focused more attention on the controversies about Indian origins. Soon more extravagant claims surfaced. It was alleged that an "unknown pilot" had preceded Columbus and that Europeans had discovered America centuries before and then forgotten about it. Spanish authors, eager to legitimize Spain's rights in the New World, were especially sensitive on this latter point.

In 1535 Gonzalo Hernández de Oviedo y Valdéz published his *Historia general* of the "Indian islands

The mantle of Powhatan.
*Department of Antiquities,
Ashmolean Museum, Oxford*

16

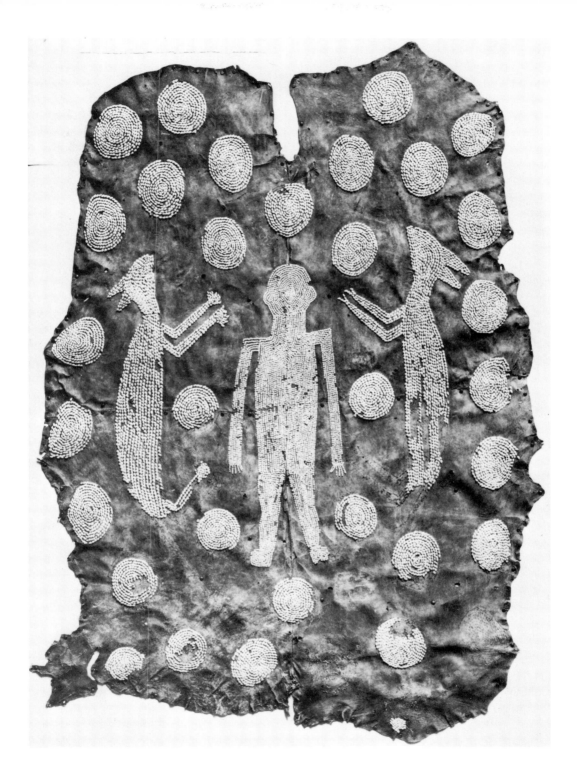

and mainland," an account of the New World based on both personal experience and an intimate knowledge of popular and scientific literature. He thought that the Indians had originally come from Carthage, introducing one of the most persistent of all theories about American Indian origins. The first Americans, he speculated, were descended from ancient Spaniards. The Carthaginian legend was derived from Aristotle's story about an island beyond the Pillars of Hercules, far distant in the western ocean, which Carthaginian merchants had visited in ancient times and which, they discovered, "abounded in all things that nature produced." The merchants settled there, promptly exiled by the Carthaginian senate, which forbade all access to the new land under pain of death. In even more far-reaching speculations Oviedo ascribed the earliest settlement of the Indies to Hespero, twelfth king of Spain, who conquered and settled the "Islas Hesperides" around 1600 B.C. The transatlantic links were broken soon after Hespero's death, the islands being given back to Spain only in 1492, through the voyage of Christopher Columbus. Most people rejected the Hespero theory, but the Carthaginian hypothesis, relatively little developed by Oviedo, satisfied many.

A far more pressing concern was the correct treatment of the Indians. Should they be converted forcibly or peacefully, should they be enslaved, or should they even be treated as humans? The debate between colonists and humanitarians, priests and administrators, raged furiously in the sixteenth century. Meanwhile the Indians of Mexico and Peru were being mercilessly exploited and hunted down in the name of God and of gold. Bartolomé de las Casas, the most celebrated Spanish humanist of the day, fought throughout his life for better treatment of the Indian. His books, *Apologetica historia* and *Historia de las Indias,* both written in the 1550s but published over three hundred years after his death, reveal him as an anthropologist of some note.

Las Casas rejected Oviedo's hypothesis as fictitious nonsense but remained noncommittal on the ultimate origin of the Indians. Perhaps he thought it

an insoluble problem, an event that had taken place
so long ago that the mystery would never be solved.
One curiously prophetic statement in his *Historia*
reveals some of his thinking: "I have seen in these
ruins of Cibao, a stadia or two in the virgin earth, in
the plains at the foot of some hills, burned wood and
ashes as if a few days ago a fire was made there. And

Bartholomé de las Casas.

19

for the same reason we have to conclude that in other times the river came near there, and in that place they made a fire, and afterwards the river went away. The soil brought from the hills by the rains covered it. And because this could not happen except by the passage of many years and most ancient time, there is not a great argument that the people of these islands and continent are very ancient." Unfortunately Las Casas never developed his "great argument." He wrote two hundred years before serious archaeological research began in the Americas, before people started digging for clues about Indian origins.

Few people were as restrained as the sympathetic Las Casas. Theories about lost continents became fashionable. In 1572 the Spanish writer Pedro Sarmiento de Garboa came out in favor of the existence of Atlantis, a vast, long, flooded continent that had extended from Cadiz to America. This land mass, he alleged, had been colonized by descendants of Noah, who also crossed into America. After the great inundation of 1320 B.C. only the American Indians were left. "Marvel you not at the thin population of America, nor at the rudeness and ignorance of the people," wrote Francis Bacon prettily, "for you must accept your inhabitants of America as a young people: younger a thousand years, at the least, than the rest of the world."

Another persistent theory claimed that the Aztec were one of the Ten Lost Tribes of Israel. This particular theory was unpopular among early Spanish chroniclers. It originated in the writings of an obscure Dutch theologian named Joannes Fredericus Lumnius in 1567. He argued that the ten tribes of Hebrews exiled by King Shalmaneser to various parts of the Assyrian empire (II Kings 17:6) escaped and spread all over the world. A later development of this theory had the Hebrews passing through Tartary on their way to the New World, where they acquired the custom of sun worship. There were many elaborations of the Ten Lost Tribes theory over the years, extravagant concoctions based on attempts to find cultural traits common to both the Hebrews and the Indians. Big noses, burial customs, timidity, and a penchant for ceremony were all cited as similarities. As the years passed the Lost Tribes theory became enmeshed in dogma and evangelism; it was linked to attempts to christianize the Indians and to wild claims that they were the descendants of the Jews.

The debate about Indian origins was soon one of pure intellectual curiosity, for it had long ceased to be of practical economic or theological importance. Official colonial policy revolved around the legal and religious conditions under which Indians were permitted to work. Indian origins were of vital importance only to certain racial, religious, or occultist interest groups that manipulated the tortuous and inadequate scientific literature for their own purposes—not that there was much to go on. Perhaps the sanest voice was that of Joseph de Acosta, a Jesuit missionary who served in Peru, and later Mexico, in the 1570s and 1580s. His great *Historia natural y moral de las Indias* was first published in 1589, the first attempt at an objective analysis of Indian origins and ancestry.

Acosta began by assuming that all humans, including Indians, were descended from Adam. The Indians had reached the New World; it was important to decide how they had got there. His ground rules for the early settlement of America rejected the Carthaginians and other exotic races. Although he thought it entirely possible that "men came to the Indies driven unwillingly by the wind," he conceived of their arrival in the same terms as that of the wild beasts that abounded in the Americas. They could not have arrived by boat but must have crossed from the Old World by a hitherto undiscovered land connection or narrow strait to the north or south of the known part of the New World.

These ground rules made it possible for Acosta to argue that the Indians had arrived in easy stages, reaching the new continent at a point where it lay closest to the Old World. The first inhabitants were "savage hunters driven from their homelands by starvation or some other hardship." Their successors

21

A cheife Herowans wyfe of Pomeoc. and her daughter of the age of .8. or. .10. yeares.

An Indian woman from Virginia
by John White.
British Museum, London

settled down and later developed their own agriculture and their own social and religious institutions, which could be seen at a remarkable pitch of development in the Aztec and Inca states.

Acosta's *Historia* was a work of enormous significance, a classic study read by every scholar interested in the New World, ignored, refuted, and praised. Its sober arguments were a welcome breath of fresh air among the theological and classical researches of the day. Acosta had argued for the cultural independence of the American Indian. This notion ran contrary to the researches of earlier investigators intent on looking at the problem in mainly theological terms, within a rigid framework of six thousand years of biblical history.

The cultural independence of the American Indian was an argument that Acosta himself never developed any further. He did not have the tools to do so, for archaeology did not emerge as an even vaguely significant tool for unveiling the prehistory of early Americans until the late eighteenth century, and only then under the shadow of vigorous controversy.

At a time when Acosta was taking a long, hard look at the origins of the American Indian, firsthand knowledge about the New World was still in short supply. But interest in Indian manners and customs was increasing. A veritable deluge of "Geographies," "Histories," and travelogues flooded scholarly libraries. The cartographers were busy integrating geographic information from dozens of voyages. Fray Bernardino Sahagun wrote twelve volumes about the Aztec between 1558 and 1569. Walter Raleigh and Richard Hakluyt wrote brilliant works on the North American Indians that were not only authoritative monographs but fine pieces of literature, too.

Raleigh and his associates were hungry for new knowledge. Their work was full of shrewd observations. They were fascinated by the remarkable diversity of plants, animals, and people that unfolded before their colonizing eyes. Thomas Hariot's *Brief and true Report of the new found land of Vir-*

22

Theire sitting at meate.

ginia, for example, was soon recognized as a model of scientific reporting. Hariot worked closely with the artist John White to collect a mass of information about the Indians of Roanoke, Virginia—much of it, alas, lost in a hurricane. Only a small fragment of Hariot's work and a few of White's drawings survive to give us an insight into two expert observers' views of sixteenth-century American Indian society. Their methods of agriculture, fishing techniques, properties of soils, manners, and customs are carefully described in dispassionate order. What a

John White's drawing of Virginia Indians eating. *British Museum, London* masterpiece of anthropological research would have resulted had these men been able to collaborate over a longer period of time! As it is, as historian D. B. Quinn has pointed out, "we know the Indians of the Carolina Sounds as well in some respects as we know the contemporaries of the Tudor Englishmen who drew and studied them." And White's paintings of the people became the conventional representation of American Indians to Europeans for over a century.

The American Indian did not, initially at any rate, pose a philosophical conundrum or a pressing intellectual problem to Europeans. These strange people impressed themselves on the Renaissance mind through travelers' accounts, hearsay, and a handful of artifacts—necklaces, shells, and ornaments—brought home by the returning voyagers. Then there were the occasional Indians who were brought to European courts, among them the celebrated Pocahontas. She created such a lasting impression in Europe that several now famous public houses were named after her.

Noble savages, flattering portraits, scattered artifacts, and the rare exotic face were the foundations of initial intellectual attitudes toward the American Indian. Religious and secular considerations that often had little to do with reality later influenced these attitudes. Mere speculation, however, could not answer many of the apparently insoluble questions about the origins of the Indian posed by Acosta. Some of the answers lay in the material possessions of the native Americans that the conquistadores coveted. This book is the story of how the study of American prehistory began and about the attitudes that surrounded it.

Pocahontas (1597–1619). She was taken to England by John Rolfe, duly baptized, and dressed in the English fashion of the time. This "unbeeleeving creature" was renamed Lady Rebecca by her hosts.
Radio Times Hulton Picture Library

Ætatis suæ 21. Aº. 1616.

Matoaks ats Rebecka daughter to the mighty Prince
Powhatan Emperour of Attanoughkomouck ats virginia
converted and baptized in the Christian faith, and
wife to the wor.ll Mr Tho: Rolff.

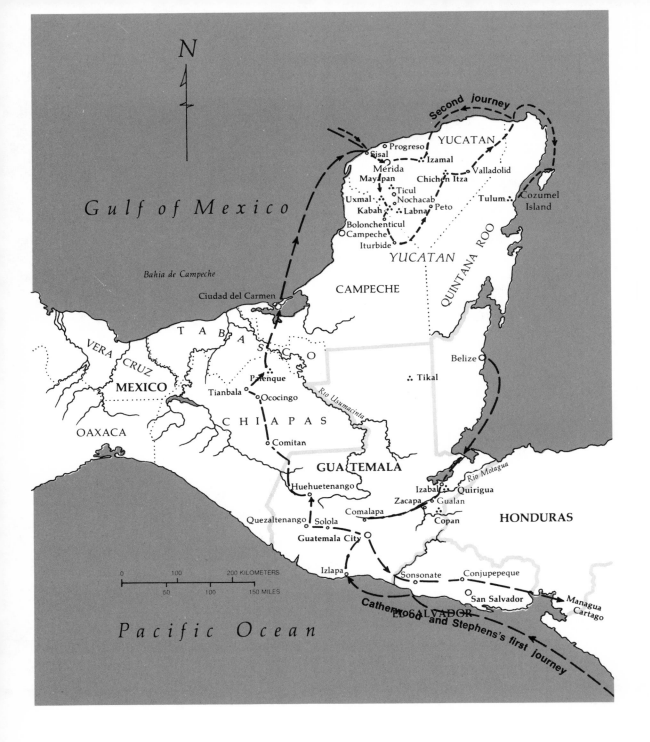

N

Gulf of Mexico

Second journey

YUCATAN

Progreso
Sisal
Izamal
Merida
Valladolid
Mayapan
Chichen Itza
Ticul
Uxmal
Nochacab
Kabah
Labna
Peto
Tulum
Cozumel Island
Bolonchenticul
Campeche
Iturbide
YUCATAN

QUINTANA ROO

Bahia de Campeche

Ciudad del Carmen

CAMPECHE

T A B A S C O

VERA CRUZ

Belize

Palenque

Tikal

MEXICO

Tianbala
Ococingo

Rio Usumacinta

C H I A P A S

OAXACA

Comitan

GUATEMALA

Rio Motagua

Huehuetenango

Izabal
Quirigua
Zacapa
Gualan
Comalapa
Copan
HONDURAS

Quezaltenango
Solola
Guatemala City

Izlapa
Sonsonate
Conjupepeque

SALVADOR
San Salvador
Managua
Cartago

Catherwood and Stephens's first journey

0   100   200 KILOMETERS
50   100   150 MILES

Pacific Ocean

2 "Abominable Lusts and Sins"

The Indians, wrote Vincent Palatino de Curzola, were people who observed neither "divine law, natural law, nor the laws of men, nor even . . . the law of the ferocious beasts." Such primitive and uncouth savages were regarded as the enemies of Christianity, or, at best, as Christians who had strayed from the mainstream of the faith. There was a strong case for readmitting the Indians, as descendants of Adam, to the Christian fold, and the Spaniards pursued the divinely guided task of converting them with extraordinary enthusiasm and ruthlessness.

The missionary zeal of the Spaniards reached its height when two companies of Franciscan friars arrived in Yucatan from Guatemala in 1545 and settled down to the enormous task of converting the three hundred thousand Indians estimated to live in

Archaeological sites in Central America, and Catherwood and Stephens's itineraries.

Fray Diego de Landa.
A contemporary portrait.

Yucatan at the time. Soon new priests were needed; Fray Nicolás de Albalate was sent to Spain two years later in search of more. He returned in 1549 with a company of six, among them Diego de Landa, soon to be famous as a zealous missionary and student of Indian life. It is to Landa that we owe a glimpse of the great temples of Mesoamerica just before they passed into four hundred years of oblivion.

Diego de Landa was born of "noble parents" in Cifuentes, Toledo, Spain, on November 12, 1524. Sixteen years later he entered the Franciscan order in Toledo, and at the age of twenty-five he joined Albalate's small party of friars. Almost immediately his strength of personality and fervent missionary instincts surfaced. He was soon appointed assistant to the guardian of the monastery of Izamal, a newly established foundation set up as an important center for missionary work among the Indians. Within a few years Landa's success as a teacher, administrator, and preacher led to his election to the post of guardian.

By this time Landa was surrounded by Indian students, one of a handful of missionaries in a huge, densely populated territory. Their first priority was to instruct native schoolmasters, to train them to spread the word of God throughout the hundreds of villages near Izamal. The Franciscans had already set themselves a formidable task by forbidding any ancient customs and religious practices, including human sacrifice, body tattooing, slavery, and selling daughters in marriage. Then they had to learn the Maya language. Landa was one of the most adept pupils. The early friars learned Indian dialects by using "signs and small stones." The native grammar was distilled from these simple beginnings, and a start was made on committing Christian doctrine to paper in Maya. Landa rapidly became fluent and was able to preach to his converts in their own tongue.

The friars centered their missionary efforts around their monasteries, where they recruited the children of the local rulers and of important noblemen, housing them in communal dormitories near the missions. Their eager converts, many rescued from

28

slavery, were only too happy, according to Landa, "to notify the priests of acts of idolatry or of drunken orgies that occurred." The large, scattered Indian population was difficult to convert, so the friars forced the people to gather in larger settlements, "settling them where they wished in places not so healthful nor suitable as those where they lived." Hundreds of local people were forcibly set to work on the construction of monastery or mission buildings. As each new guardian was appointed, the buildings multiplied according to the vanity of the new supervisor. Planting and harvesting seasons were ignored as the Indians were kept at work. Many starved, suffering under harsh punishments meted out under the guise of religious instruction. Within a few generations foreign diseases had decimated the Indian population, ancient villages were abandoned, and many traces of Maya civilization were erased from human vision and even memory.

When Landa first arrived in Yucatan there were abundant signs of impressive and magnificent ceremonial centers and temples. Even the earliest Spanish explorers had come across fine stone buildings that bore idols and strange carvings. "There are in Yucatan," wrote Landa, "many beautiful buildings. . . . They are all of stone very well hewn, although there is no metal in this country with which they could have been worked. These buildings are very close to one another and are temples; and the reason that there are so many of them is that the people changed their dwelling places many times; and in each town they built a temple. . . ." He went on to add, "These buildings have not been constructed by other nations than the Indians; and this is seen from the naked stone men made modest by long girdles which they called in their language ex as well as from other devices which the Indians wear."

Landa was in a remarkable position to study Maya civilization and its monuments at first hand, while much of the fabric of the indigenous civilization was still in existence. While preaching to the heathens and punishing them for their idolatries, he had

Indians ferrying two Spanish horses across a river
in Yucatan in a pair of canoes lashed together.

Indians mining for gold in a
Spanish-controlled works.

Indian carrying two baskets
on a pole.

Three woodcuts that were used to
illustrate the manuscript of
Gonzalo Hernández de Oviedo's
*Historia general y natural de las
Indias.*
Huntington Library

ample chance both to observe and to destroy their temples and works of art. His first opportunities for leisurely observation were at Izamal, where there were several fine stone temples, "all there without any recollection of the builders."

In 1549 the Indians "requested" the friars to build a monastery at Izamal, on the summit of the most conspicuous Maya pyramid. This monastery of San Antonio became one of the focal points of Christian endeavor, flourishing among the pagan temples and pyramids that stood "eight leagues from the sea, in a very beautiful situation and in a fertile land and well peopled region." Landa admired the largest pyramid at Izamal, "of such height and beauty that it astonished one." He described its many steps formed of large, cut stones, the plazas and staircases that led to a "beautiful chapel of well worked stone." The monastery was reached by over 150 ancient steps, built of stone taken from the ruins. Nearby, some stucco figures of what one writer described as "giants armed with their shields and helmets" caused Landa to wonder if the builders of the temples had been "superior and of very much greater size and strength" than contemporary Indians.

Thirteen leagues from Izamal lay the ruins of Tihoo, which had become the site of the Spanish city of Merida, so called, Landa tells us, "on account of the singularity and size of the buildings." The principal structure was "a square of great size, as it has an extent equal to two runs of a horse." A staircase led up the eastern side, the other sides being bound by stone retaining walls. The structure rose to a height that filled Landa with astonishment. The summit was covered with a complex of stone buildings divided into small cells, courts, and passageways. Nearby was a "large and beautiful mound" which was being quarried systematically for the buildings of Merida. It was so enormous that Landa doubted it would ever be entirely exhausted.

The quarrying of buildings and pyramids has continued unabated into modern times. Fragments of carved stones and worked Maya masonry can be seen incorporated into the walls of early Spanish buildings in many parts of Yucatan today. The idolatrous temples of the Indians were regarded simply as a convenient source of building stone; of the awful rites that had taken place in the ruined temples only lurid folklore remained, although human sacrifices still occurred in the bush. The summits of the temples were places where the devil had moved the Indians "with great superstitions and auguries and similar inventions of his." Cannibalism, worship of false idols, lust, and "abominable lusts and sins" led the same writer to "weep for the wretchedness of the Occidental Indians and for their consummate malice." He added that God's "Divine Goodness" had allowed the Indians to be discovered "so that they might deserve to be evangelized and brought to the worship of their true God at the time when their faults and sins had reached these extremes described."

The locals by no means appreciated the friars' efforts to convert them. Many were quite comfortable with their idols and traditional religious practices. Backsliders, "perverted by the priests whom they had at the time of their idolatry and by their chiefs," returned to their idols and human sacrifices. Matters came to a head in 1562 when fears of a native insurrection caused the Spanish authorities to investigate persistent rumors of idolatry. The convent of Mani was the target of an intense investigation that produced evidence of widespread regression.

By this time Landa was *provincial* of Merida. He authorized an ecclesiastical and secular investigation that soon implicated the local chiefs, magistrates, and teachers. A savage auto-da-fé in the classic traditions of the Inquisition was held at Mani. With zealous torture conducted with fiendish ingenuity, the friars sought to learn the hiding places of idols and the owners of false gods and to punish offenders. They sat comfortably and watched the guilty being scourged with a hundred or more lashes. Indians were suspended by their arms or feet, whipped, and spattered with burning wax tapers. Many were so ruthlessly tortured that they were too

A depiction of Spanish cruelty
to Indians that appeared
in Las Casas's book,
published in 1598.

weak to be subjected to the public whipping that was
to be their final penance. Victims were maimed or
killed by pouring water into their abdomens and
then standing on them, by twisting their limbs, or by
sadistic whipping. Some of the witnesses were
driven to suicide; others were imprisoned or
condemned to forced labor for the Church for years.
Many were forced to pay enormous tithes to the
Church. The mass of testimony on idolatry was both
impressive and terrifying. One witness, who was
subjected to only the mildest of torture, eventually

34

confessed to possessing no fewer than twenty-seven idols. The friars' response to these revelations was not only an orgy of torture and punishment, but also a systematic destruction of Maya codices and idols.

Maya codices in particular were highly prized by their owners. Landa examined many of these priceless documents: "These people also made use of certain characters or letters, with which they wrote in their books ancient matters and their sciences, and by these and other drawings and by certain signs in these drawings, they understood their affairs and made others understand them and taught them. We found a large number of books in these characters and, as they contained nothing in which there were not to be seen superstition and lies of the devil, we burned them all, which they regretted to an amazing degree, and which caused them much affliction." Archaeologists working four hundred years later have also bitterly regretted this wanton destruction. Ironically, the burning of the codices did not prevent

Some pages from the Dresden Codex, as illustrated by Lord Kingsborough in his *Antiquities of Mexico* (1831–48).

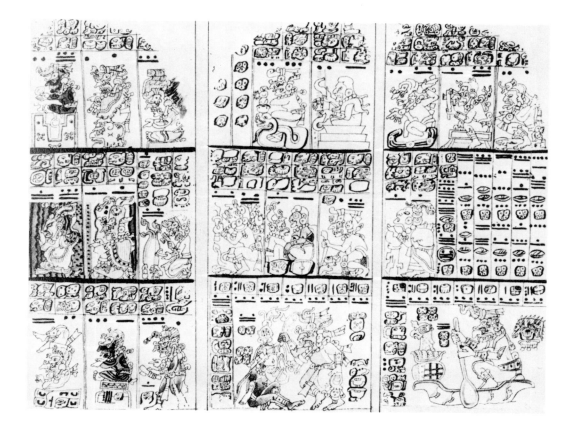

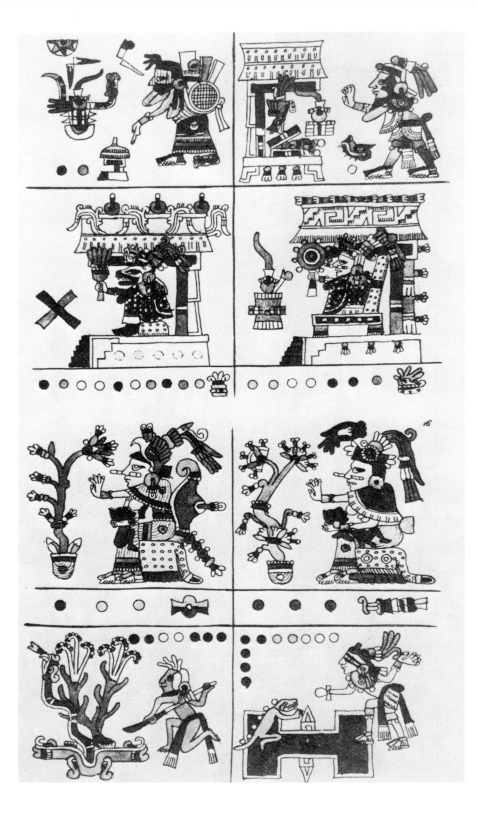

Facing page: The eccentric Lord Kingsborough reproduced this portion of the Codex Féjerváry in his monumental *Antiquities of Mexico*, published between 1831 and 1848.

Left: An early attempt at illustrating Indian writing. From Lorenzo Pignoria's *Imagini degli del indiani*, 1615.

Below: A copy of a Mexican codex by Pedro del Rios, 1566–89.

Landa from writing a description of Maya script that has been of some assistance to those who worked on the hieroglyphs several centuries later.

Apparently Landa caused as many codices as could be found at Mani to be collected and burned in batches. "Thus," wrote Bernardino de Lizana in 1633, "he collected the books and ancient writings and he commanded them burned and tied up. They burned many historical books of the ancient Yucatan which told of its beginning and history, which were of much value if, in our writing, they had been translated because today there would be something original. At best there is not great authority for more than the traditions of these Indians." Ironically, several friars had learned how to decipher and even to write the hieroglyphs. Yet the priceless codices were burned in a display of vicious and intolerant religious zeal. After all, religious doctrine held that the books were nothing but witchcraft and magic. The people were merely wayward savages, and nothing they had written down was worth recording anyhow. And so the details of the Maya calendar, religious practices, and a mass of data on plants, fauna, customs, and oral tradition was consigned to historical oblivion in a few short years. Today only three, perhaps four, Maya codices are known to survive.

At the same time as Maya literature was being enveloped in flames, the friars set to work on the idols. No one knows how much Maya statuary was smashed to pieces or thrown away during the Mani auto-da-fé or in subsequent years. The only estimates were compiled in 1805, but upon what authority it is not clear. According to a Jesuit priest, no fewer than 5,000 idols, of "different form and dimension," 13 altars, 27 rolls of signs and hieroglyphs on deerskins, and "197 vases of all sizes and shapes" were destroyed by the friars. The actual figures must have been far higher, for the depredations of the priests were accompanied by those of casual visitors to the ruins—souvenir hunters and people who quarried temples for building stone. The glories of Maya civilization discovered by the archaeologists of the nineteenth century were but a pale reflection of the incredible riches of antiquity that confronted the destructive friars of colonial Spain.

Diego de Landa himself is a curious enigma. His official portraits project the image of an austere man. His grim mouth and air of asceticism suggest that he was a man with whom it was unwise to cross swords. His is the face of a fanatic with a ruthless ambition to succeed in his God-given mission. Yet Landa was a surprisingly perceptive observer of Maya customs. His *Relación de las Cosas de Yucatan* remains the classic early account of the Maya. It was written from firsthand observations of the Indians and their traditional customs, using informants who spent many hours enlightening the studious Landa.

One of the friar's key sources was Juan Cocom, "a Christian, . . . a man of great reputation, learned in their affairs, and of remarkable discernment and well acquainted with native matters. He was very intimate with the author of this book . . . and told him many facts concerning the antiquities." Landa conveniently forgot to mention that his prize Maya student, himself a *cacique,* or governor, had been implicated in human sacrifices by independent testimony. Juan Cocom died "in church" in 1561, after several human sacrifices had been offered for his recovery, but to no avail. A year later his brother is known to have thrown three boys alive into the *cenote* at Chichen Itza.

Juan Cocom may have accompanied Landa to the magnificent temples which the prelate admired, at Chichen Itza, "surrounded by very fertile lands." He marveled at the famous Temple of Kukulcan and drew a highly inaccurate plan of it in his notebook.

Landa seems to have been interested in any rumors of ceremonies that were still held at the site. "From the court in front of these stages a wide and handsome causeway runs as far as a well which is about two stones' throw off," he recalled. "Into this well they have had, and then had, the custom of throwing men alive as a sacrifice to the gods, in time of drought. . . . They also threw into it a great

The first page of Landa's *Relación.* From the copy preserved in the Real Academia de la Historia, Madrid. This manuscript was discovered by Brasseur de Bourbourg in 1864. *Real Academia de la Historia, Madrid*

The Temple of Warriors
and the Temple of Kukulcan
at Chichen Itza.
Peabody Museum, Harvard University

many other things, like precious stones and things
which they prized." The *cenote* of Chichen Itza with
its deep, vertical sides and brownish green, murky
water was greatly revered by the Indians, who, according to Landa, held it "in the same veneration as
we have for the pilgrimages to Jerusalem and Rome."
Had there been gold in Yucatan, Landa speculated, it
would surely be found in the mysterious waters of

the *cenote*. It was not for 350 years that anyone probed its depths for treasure, acting on Landa's supposition. But the *cenote* itself became a place of mystery where the ghastly sacrificial rites of the Indians lived on in local folklore and legend.

Relación de las Cosas de Yucatan shows that Landa paid careful attention to even minute details of Indian life. Landa also accumulated an amazing collection of detail about archaeological sites and antiquities in general. Apart from recording with glee how Cortés had always replaced idols with crosses and complaining of "such a great quantity of idols that even those of their gods were not enough," he examined stelae at Mayapan, their painted glyphs worn away by heavy rain. The exotic human figures of "nude men, having their loins covered with long girdles," excited his interest. Excavations in Mani for a deep well revealed "a grave full seven feet long, full of very fresh red earth, and of human bones. And when they were taken out they were already nearly changed into stones." The limestone caves of Yucatan also yielded fine examples of sculpture and many ancient burials.

It is difficult to explain the anomaly of a man who with one hand punished the backward convert for his idolatry, while with the other he recorded the fine details of Maya cultural achievements. Perhaps a clue can be found in Landa's prayers that "having left the abode of my sensuality and the rule of my vices and sins, I can make a perfect example of serving thee. . . ." Perhaps "the perfect example" involved both prosecution of sin and documentation of the extent of it as well.

Not everyone agreed with Landa's methods of handling the wayward. When stories of the auto-da-fé at Mani, carried by Landa's many enemies, reached Spain he was recalled to stand trial for his excesses. He resigned as *provincial* of Merida in 1563 and embarked on what turned out to be a long and arduous journey to Spain. It took him eighteen months to reach Europe. He was shipwrecked and delayed by serious illness, writing to a friend in 1568 that he had "become old, full of white hairs and poorly

41

embellished with teeth and molars which give me pain." The long delays in the hearing of his case gave him time to write the *Relación*, apparently compiled mainly in 1566.

Three years later the *provincial* of Castile formally exonerated Landa. His ultimate rehabilitation was complete, for he was elected bishop of Yucatan in 1571 upon the death of a bitter rival. Taking his precious *Relación* with him, he served out the rest of his years in pastoral service and died in Merida on April 29, 1579, mourned, we are told, by all. The manuscript of the *Relación* was carefully preserved in the Franciscan convent at Merida, and copies were sent to Spain.

Diego de Landa was not the only friar to destroy idols and burn valuable codices. He is remembered for his missionary work and is perhaps labeled as more of an archaeological villain than his contemporaries simply because of his writings. But he is a symbol of an ecclesiastical intolerance and zeal for exploitation that consigned the Maya and their works to oblivion. With his death a silence descended on the temples of the Maya for two centuries.

The *Relación* was soon forgotten, as the ruins of Yucatan slowly crumbled and vanished under the damp canopy of the ubiquitous rain forest. It was not until 1864 that the French cleric and scholar Abbé Brasseur de Bourbourg came across the *Relación* and translated it for simultaneous publication in Spanish and French. Probably the only reason he could gain access to the secrets of the rare manuscripts in the Madrid archives and in Spanish America was that he was considered a good Catholic. The secrets of the Maya had remained securely locked up for three centuries; it was almost as if they had never been written.

The silence was broken only by the curiosity of the occasional priest or government official. In the mid-eighteenth century, for example, the curate of the town of Tumbala in Guatemala was told by his relatives that curious "stone houses were to be found near the settlement." The curate himself died without investigating the report; but years later, in 1773, a priest named Ramon Ordoñez, who had heard the story while a schoolboy, sent a party to look at the "houses." Their reports prompted him to pass the information on to his superiors. The president of the *Audiencia* of Guatemala was sufficiently intrigued to call for a full report on the ruins, now known to be near the small settlement of Santo Domingo de Palenque. The royal architect, Antonio Bernasconi, was charged to find out the age of the ruins and the origin of the peoples who had built the structures, and to describe the architecture and dimensions of Palenque. His report was a sketchy disappointment, but it was sufficiently interesting to cause the royal historiographer in Spain to ask for more specific information.

Bernasconi died soon after handing in his inadequate report, and the Royal Audiencia had to look for a new investigator. The president settled on an artillery officer named Antonio del Río. Captain del Río got the job mainly because he had a reputation for careful observation, but the authorities also took the precaution of sending an artist with him.

From the beginning the expedition proved to be a much larger undertaking than had been anticipated. On May 3, 1787, del Río arrived at Palenque accompanied by a party of Indians he had requisitioned as guides. The rain forest was so dense that they had to cut their way through undergrowth that rendered a person invisible fewer than six feet away. Palenque itself was entangled in vegetation, so seventy-nine more Indians were rounded up to clear the ancient buildings. Two weeks later del Río stood in the middle of a huge clearing, gazing at a ruined palace, a complicated maze of rooms and courtyards standing on a huge earthen and rubble platform measuring 300 by 240 feet. Elaborate stucco decorations adorned the walls of this curious structure that del Río labeled "uncouth." He was at a loss to explain the magnificent human figures executed in stucco relief and incorrectly described them as rulers and gods. Because his orders called on him to collect artifacts, he hastily dug trenches in the rooms of the

An engraving of a drawing of the Tablet of the Cross at Palenque by Jean Frédéric Waldeck. The original drawing was made on the del Río expedition and subsequently published in his *Description of the Ruins of an Ancient City.*

palace and burrowed into the solid base of its tower. Del Río emerged from what he called his "indisputably necessary" excavations with only a few exotic pieces—some fragments of bas-relief, a few hieroglyphs, and a scattering of pottery and stone implements. All thirty-two objects were eventually forwarded to the Grand Audiencia with the expedition report.

Del Río's report was mainly descriptive and benefited from a chance encounter with a friar from Merida, who told him that Palenque seemed to resemble the well-known ruins of Yucatan. Del Río seems to have been impressed by Palenque, for he compared the life of ancient times advantageously with that of his own. Accompanying the narrative was a folio of twenty-five illustrations executed by

44

the official artist, depicting some of the decoration and stucco work. Del Río submitted his work to his superiors in June 1787. Eventually the document was forwarded to Madrid and deposited in the official archives. That would have been the end of the matter had not a copy of the report been taken to England many years later by someone named Dr. McQuy. Quite how McQuy obtained the report no one knows, but he was sufficiently interested in the manuscript to contact a publisher. *Description of the Ruins of an Ancient City, Discovered near Palenque . . . from the Original Manuscript Report of Captain Don Antonio del Río* was published by London bookseller Henry Bothould in 1822—to the accompaniment of deafening silence from the critics.

The scholarly and literary world quietly ignored Palenque and del Río. Only one reviewer noticed the book, contemptuously dismissing it as a report "upon a certain mass of ruins in New Spain." A few scholars later dipped into the book for their own specialized purposes, but the outside world cared little about the Maya ruins until the remarkable and well-publicized discoveries of John Lloyd Stephens and Frederick Catherwood in the 1840s justified the commercial gamble of a small-time London publisher. For over three centuries the Maya ruins remained where the ecclesiastical authorities of sixteenth-century Mexico had intended them to be—in almost total physical and intellectual obscurity.

3 "The Nations Are Very Ancient and Were Formerly Very Numerous"

The Spanish government was amazed at the wealth of Mexico, at the magnificent gold ornaments and artifacts that came from Cortés's campaigns. In the seventeenth century there ensued a scramble for new territory and easily acquired wealth that engaged the efforts of hundreds of gentlemen-adventurers and soldiers of fortune. As more territory was opened up, the lust for gold intensified. Vast unknown land masses lay to the north and south of wealthy Mexico. Did these also contain fabulous wealth? Applicants willing to lead expeditions to North America importuned the government to find out.

Ponce de Leon was the the first Spaniard to explore what is now Florida. He landed near Palm Beach in 1513, to search for the mythical "Fountain

Archaeological sites in the eastern United States and approximate itinerary of de Soto.

The legendary
"Fountain of Youth,"
from a woodcut by the early
sixteenth-century artist
Hans Sebald Beham.

of Youth" that chroniclers insisted was to be found on an island north of Cuba. The quest for the aphrodisiac was fruitless; the Indians, fierce and unfriendly. Ponce de Leon was followed in 1519 by Alonso Alvarez de Pineda, who entered the Mississippi River estuary where he spent six weeks and visited many Indian villages. Neither of these expeditions, nor the strange venture of the sinister and red-bearded Pánfilo de Narváez who followed them, yielded the sort of riches that the Spaniards automatically associated with the New World.

Narváez's men traded for a few gold objects in Tampa Bay, merchandise that fired their greedy imaginations. Sending the five ships under his command in search of a better harbor, Narváez set out to march with his party of 260 men to the west. This crazy journey ended in disaster. The land party never made contact with the ships, and temporary boats had to be constructed for the perilous journey home. All but one foundered off the Mississippi. The last vessel was cast ashore near what is now

Galveston, Texas. At this point only a junior officer, Alvar Nuñez Cabeza de Vaca, two soldiers, and a black slave survived. After years of incredible hardship, the party succeeded in walking across Texas into Spanish Mexico. Accounts of this epic journey give little information about the Indians, except for an impression of poverty in a harsh, dry environment. Cabeza de Vaca admired the acute senses of the Indians. "They are great in hunger, thirst and cold, as if they were made for the endurance of these more than other men, by habit and nature." Although de Vaca's walk led to the Spanish exploration of New Mexico and the remote territories of the Southwest, there were no signs of enormous wealth like that found in Aztec and Inca treasuries.

In 1537 a wealthy conquistador named Hernando de Soto came home to Spain after making a small fortune under Pizarro in Peru. He set up house in a style befitting the son of an Andalusian gentleman who had risen from genteel poverty to great riches. But, like so many adventurers, de Soto was restless for further glory and wealth. When stories of the potential riches of Florida reached the Spanish court, de Soto was granted the governorship of Cuba and Florida. Within two years this remarkable adventurer had raised a force of 622 men and had landed in Tampa Bay, Florida. De Soto hoped to find a native kingdom fully as wealthy as that of Montezuma or Atahuallpa, the recently murdered ruler of the Inca in Peru. The only objectives of his expedition were gold, wealth, and colonization.

When the soldiers disembarked at Tampa they found "a town of seven or eight houses, built of timber, and covered with palm-leaves. The chief's house stood near the beach on a very high mount made by hand for defense; at the other end of the town was a temple, on the top of which perched a wooden fowl with gilded eyes." Many of the buildings, including the temple, were demolished. Temporary huts for the soldiers were erected at the village. Then a scouting expedition of forty horsemen and eighty infantrymen brought back a shipwrecked Spaniard who had lived among the In-

Sauvage en habit d'hiver.

An eighteenth-century French artist, A. de Batz, painted this Louisiana Indian in his winter dress. A buffalo-skin robe complete with tail and painted with intricate patterns on the inside keeps him warm. The mouse tucked into the loincloth was probably an ornament. *Peabody Museum, Harvard University*

dians for eight years. He gave de Soto depressing news about the surrounding country, which was swampy, desolate, and certainly devoid of gold. Some days later a deputation of Indians arrived to discover de Soto's intentions. They were asked if they knew of territory where gold or silver was to be found in abundance. To the Spaniards' delight, the Indians pointed to the west, where "the province of Cale" lay, the land of a warlike people "where there was so much gold, that when the people came to make war upon those of Cale, they wore golden hats like helmets."

Immediately de Soto set off westward, leaving a substantial garrison at his embarkation point. Progress was slow through the marshy country of Florida. As the party reached higher ground, they came on ripened fields of maize, which they immediately harvested for their own use. They took hostages at every village, seizing those who resisted to be porters or slaves. When one group of prisoners rebelled they were bound to a post in the middle of the camp and killed with arrows. The Indians bitterly resented the foreigners and their high-handed ways. The shrewder chiefs gave the Spaniards food and pointed to the west, where they said gold was abundant. But there were still no signs of it, although a young Indian pointed to the country of Yupalia, where he said that a woman ruled over a territory rich in metals.

The route to Yupalia lay through sparsely populated country, where the soldiers suffered greatly from hunger. After a week de Soto's guide was completely lost. "Fortunately for him, at the time, there was not another whom Juan Ortíz understood, or he would have been cast to the dogs." Food supplies ran so low that de Soto was obliged to slaughter some of the three hundred pigs that accompanied the party, the descendants of thirteen sows landed in Florida many months before. Those Indians not needed for carrying loads were abandoned.

Eventually a scouting party brought in a woman and a child who guided the Spaniards to a village some twenty miles away. The villagers denied all

50

knowledge of the settlement the Spaniards sought until "one of them was burned." Then they surlily directed the travelers to Cofachiqui, the capital of the great queen. A few days later the chieftainess greeted de Soto with a stately message. "With sincere hands," she said, "and purest good will I tender you my person, my lands, my people, and make you these small gifts." The gifts turned out to be clothing, shawls, and skins. She herself arrived in a shaded canoe, wearing a large string of pearls around her neck which she solemnly presented to de Soto "with many gracious words of friendship and courtesy."

The country on the South Carolina and Georgia sides of the Savannah River looked fertile and prosperous, and numerous abandoned villages testified to a long established Indian occupation of the region. There were few signs of gold, but the Spaniards were just as interested in the queen's pearls. The necklace presented to the governor had been an impressive bauble, "a large strand of pearls as thick as hazelnuts which encircled her neck three times and fell to her thighs." De Soto had presented her with a fine gold ring adorned with a ruby in exchange, a gift followed up with persistent inquiries about gold and silver.

The queen patiently explained that there were no mines in her country, for her people obtained their supplies by long-distance trading. Evidently terrified of the Spaniards, she issued orders that all yellow and white metals in her kingdom be laid before the foreigners. Large quantities of copper and brass were forthcoming, for the Indians, who had been shown gold ornaments to indicate what de Soto and his men wanted, were unable to distinguish these metals from gold. They also brought huge slabs of mica—of no interest to the greedy explorers. Pearls, too, were in short supply, for they were also imported into Cofachiqui territory.

When the Spaniards pressed the queen about pearls she directed them to "the upper part of the town," where a temple covered the burial place of long-dead chiefs and noblemen. She advised them to

A woman from Florida. Depicted by U. Aldrovandi in his *Ornithologia*, 1599.

51

A magnificent mica ornament depicting a human face found in a nineteenth-century excavation of a mound in Ohio.
Peabody Museum, Harvard University

loot these sepulchers before investigating another, much larger, mound in an abandoned town a few miles away. The greedy explorers hastened to the temple on this mound and opened the wooden chests inside, which contained the noble ancestors of the inhabitants. Nearby stood smaller chests that contained hundreds of freshwater pearls. Discolored pearls, 350 pounds of them, were weighed out and divided among the soldiers, despite de Soto's urging that they leave them until later and instead search for gold.

The abandoned village of Talomeco three miles away was a larger settlement with the usual artificial earth mounds upon which the temple and chief's house had formerly stood. Talomeco had been abandoned quite recently after an epidemic, but the temple was still standing, its contents undisturbed. The structure itself was over a hundred feet long and forty feet wide, with a steep roof of reeds and split cane decorated with large seashells. Garcilaso de la Vega, the celebrated Inca historian, "El Inca," described the interior of the shrine at second hand and in rather exaggerated terms. Twelve huge wooden statues mantled with pearls guarded the interior, and pearls were also strung from the rafters. Many chests of similar pearls lay on the floor—so many, he alleged, that the plunderers could not possibly remove them all in one load. Enormous bundles of skins and dyed clothes were stacked in the temple. The Spaniards wondered at the caches of copper-bladed weapons, battle-axes and clubs, that lay in the temple annexes near piles of delicately inlaid bows and arrows, wooden shields, and woven cane shields, all of the finest workmanship.

Even the veterans of the Mexican and Peruvian campaigns were amazed at the wonders of the temple, although the riches were nowhere near the scale of the incredible treasures of the Aztec and Inca. These pearls too were mostly discolored by cooking to extract them from the mussel shells. Again de Soto refused to carry away large quantities. But we can be certain that much of the contents of this abandoned shrine joined the looted graves of the Cofachiqui nobles in the baggage train of the governor and his soldiers.

The lust for gold still preoccupied de Soto himself, however. "Being an inflexible man, and dry of word," records a contemporary eyewitness, "the Governor determined to march further westwards in search of the gold-rich territory that the queen had hastened to assure him, lay some twelve days march ahead." His soldiers would have been content to stay where they were, amid apparently friendly people and abundant food supplies. But de Soto was adamant. On May 3, 1540, the expedition moved on, taking the friendly queen along as an unwilling guide. A few days later she escaped, leaving the Spaniards to press westward over what is now Tennessee into the Blue Ridge Mountains.

But there were no signs of gold or of the fabulous wealth promised at Cofachiqui. The countryside became drier and less hospitable. Choctaw braves ambushed the column as it made its way southwestward. De Soto was forced to attack their stronghold to recover his baggage which had been stolen by the Indian porters. Over 150 men were killed or wounded in the assault, including de Soto himself. The crippled expedition wintered near the Yazoo River in Mississippi, where the Spaniards encountered "fine looking" Indians in a fleet of canoes that "appeared like a famous armada of galleys." Their lust for gold unabated, the soldiers wandered through the Ozarks into eastern Oklahoma to the edge of the Plains. There they heard stories of "many cattle" whose skins the local Indians gave them in abundance as bed covers. But they never set eyes on the buffalo; they turned back toward more densely populated country where food supplies were more plentiful.

Finally de Soto realized that the gold-laden kingdoms sedulously mentioned by the Indians did not exist except in his own vivid imagination, so he gave up the search and headed southeast toward the Gulf of Mexico. The journey was a harsh one, through unfriendly territory occupied by suspicious Indians. The governor himself was fatally stricken

53

with a fever at the Mississippi and was buried with great ceremony, his dreams unrealized. Luís de Moscoso, one of de Soto's most competent and experienced lieutenants, brought the expedition back to Cuba after an abortive attempt to reach Mexico overland. Amazingly, half of the 622 men who had set out survived the long expedition. The many Indian slaves who had suffered through the long marches were simply left to their fate on the banks of the Mississippi.

De Soto's expedition had resulted in the first known plundering of an archaeological site in the United States. The Indians of the Southeast had had a taste of the vicious ways of white foreigners which must have lingered in folk memory for many generations. But apart from two abortive French expeditions to Florida in the 1560s, the Mississippi Valley and the Southeast were left in peace for over a century. There was no gold or silver to lure fresh expeditions through the ghastly swamps of Florida. Nor did the freshwater pearls of Cofachiqui, mostly spoiled by having been boiled in hot water, appeal to adventuresome speculators. Yet the curtain had been lifted briefly on some of North America's most conspicuous archaeological sites, the great earthen mounds that were to be found along the Mississippi, extending all the way from eastern Texas to Florida.

At the time de Soto visited the South, many mounds were still in use as shrines and burial places, some of them only recently abandoned. The Inca historian Garcilaso de la Vega explicitly linked the mounds to the local population in his almost

Etowa Group, Georgia: the Great Mound. *Peabody Museum, Harvard University*

54

lyrical description of de Soto's expedition. El Inca knew of the North American Indian only by hearsay and at second hand. But his own Indian ancestry caused him to write of them as people with rather more romantic and chivalrous characteristics than they actually possessed.

El Inca was biased in his views. His somewhat romanticized view of North America helped build up the image of the Noble Savage, the godlike being gamboling in pastoral groves that so entranced European observers of the American scene in the sixteenth and seventeenth centuries. The image was helped, too, by the few pictures of the American Indians of Florida to be published in Europe. Jacques Le Moyne de Morgues was an artist attached to a French expedition to Florida in 1564–65. He executed some watercolors of Indian life, of farming and marriage ceremonies, and of a chief's funeral. Most

Spaniards attacking a Florida village. Engraving by de Bry taken from a painting by Jacques Le Moyne.

of the actual watercolors are lost, but engravings taken from them were published by the Flemish publisher de Bry in 1591. They are romantic depictions of the Indians at work and at play, with the usual mixture of romantic posturing and fairly accurate observation.

The artist and his engraver exercised great liberties with their subjects. In one picture a group of Indians is shown seated around a low mound, not more than a few feet high, encircled by arrows. A large shell is on the summit. Le Moyne himself wrote below his painting, "Sometimes the deceased king of this province is buried with great solemnity, and his great cup from which he was accustomed to drink is placed on a tumulus with many arrows set about it."

The Indian chief Outina
on a military expedition.
A de Bry engraving, 1591.

56

Le Moyne's tiny mound is a far cry from the vast mounds of Cahokia in Illinois or the earthworks to be seen in the Ohio Valley. The chief's burial place could hardly be called a mound at all. It would never have been thought of as such had it not been for the discovery of a burial by the celebrated nineteenth-century archaeologist Cyrus Thomas near Naples, Illinois, in 1881.

Thomas opened a large burial mound which yielded a skeleton buried in an upright position. There were no grave goods with the body except "a single sea-shell resting on the earth just over the head, and a number of . . . bone awls . . . sticking in the sand around the skeleton." Thomas speculated that the seated body surrounded with the awls had been covered with sand. When the head was six inches below the summit, a large shell was placed on the top of the mound before the laborious process of completing the earthwork was continued. Ultimately, the mound was 132 feet long, 98 feet wide, and 10 feet across. Cyrus Thomas reproduced Le

An Indian burial in Florida, showing the small shell resting on a low mound. From an engraving by de Bry, itself a copy of a painting by Jacques Le Moyne, sixteenth century.

Two sketches made by
Le Page du Pratz during his
expedition to the Natchez.

A captive set up in an execution
frame.

Moyne's engraving next to his report on the Naples mound. "It is quite probable," he conjectured, "that Le Moyne figures the mound at the time it reached the point where the shell cup was to be deposited, when, in all likelihood, certain ceremonies were to be observed and a pause in the work occurred." Many people believe that Le Moyne's burial mound was but the foundation of a far larger edifice that for centuries marked—and perhaps still does today—the site of a chiefly burial.

After the French left Florida a long silence descended over the Southeast. The lasting shock of de Soto's ravages and the strange diseases that the foreigners brought with them are thought to have had a permanent effect on the Indian population, resulting possibly in epidemics and in the development of new religious cults that emphasized death and fear of the unknown. Most of the southern tribes de Soto visited dropped out of written history for

over a century. But between 1698 and 1732 a group of Frenchmen lived among the Natchez people, a group of about four thousand Indians whose seven small villages were built around a large earthen mound, thirty-five feet high, that covered an area of seven acres.

In 1720 Le Page du Pratz visited the colony and struck up a friendship with Tattooed-serpent, a famous chieftain who had welcomed the French to his villages. Both the chief's house and his temple were built on earthen mounds. Le Page was taken to see the temple, "which is about thirty feet square, and stands on an artificial mound about eight feet high, by the side of a small river." When a chief died his house was destroyed and a new mound erected for his successor's dwelling. No chief was allowed to live on his predecessor's tumulus. Tattooed-serpent died while Le Page was in Natchez country, and the explorer wrote a vivid account of the elaborate ceremonies of the funeral. He described the despair that gripped the villagers when the chief's counselor "uttered a fearful cry, that was instantly repeated by all the people of the villages. The chief's hearth was extinguished. He lay on his bed of state, dressed in his finest clothing, his face painted with vermilion, moccasined as if to go on a journey, and wearing his crown of white feathers mingled with red." His arms and pipes of peace lay by his side, and a large pole displayed his triumphs over his enemies. The extinguished fire and doleful cries made "all the Natchez tremble with reason . . . for who could guess the consequences of the despair in which we saw all plunged?"

Le Page described the burial preparations and the apparent unconcern of most of the sacrificial victims who were to be strangled at the rites, a group that included the chief's wife, chancellor, doctor, and pipe bearer. The French were able to witness the entire ceremony as well as the rehearsals and dances at which the sacrificial victims were prepared for their role. They ate a final meal with the chief's favorite wife who adjured them always to "be friends of the Natchez; trade with them, do not be too stingy with

Mort et Convoi du Serpent piqué

Temple.

Funeral ceremony among the Natchez. A temple on a mound is shown in the background. Tattooed-serpent is being carried on a litter while several retainers are executed to accompany the dead man.

59

your goods, and do not repel what they bring you, but treat them with gentleness."

On the day of the funeral the visitors were permitted to sit at the side of the temple where they could observe the ceremonies without intruding. "The Tattooed-serpent, having come out of his cabin in his state bed, as I have pictured it, was placed on a small litter with four poles, which four men carried." His corpse was carried in procession from his own house to the temple, followed by the funeral victims with red-daubed hair. Behind walked their executioners with reddened heads and red feathers in their hair. Eight male relatives served as the executioners for the victims, each assigned a role in the ceremony. One carried a war club, others the strangling cord and mats, others the tobacco pellets used as a stupefying drug. It was deemed a great honor to be selected as an executioner. At the temple the victims sat in an assigned order on their mats, their heads covered with skins. The tobacco pellets were administered, and in a few moments executioners tightened the strangling cord. Each victim died swiftly and painlessly. Then "the body of the Tattooed-serpent was placed in a great trench to the right of the temple in the interior. His two wives were buried in the same trench." The other victims were either deposited with the chief or carried away for interment in the village temples. "After this ceremony," ends Le Page, "the cabin of the deceased was burned according to custom."

This vivid account of a mound burial was all but forgotten until recent times. It is remarkable because it is the only eyewitness account of the elaborate rituals surrounding the erection, abandonment, and use of earthen mounds in North America. Unfortunately, the fine words of Tattooed-serpent's wife were to no avail; nine years later the Natchez rose against the French. After bloody massacres they were virtually exterminated; their mounds, abandoned and forgotten. The wooden temples on their summits were obliterated. The earthworks themselves were overgrown, eroded by rain and

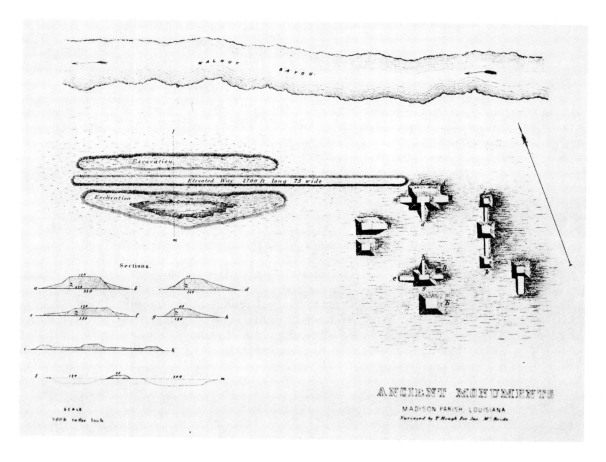

Sections.

ANCIENT MONUMENTS

MADISON PARISH, LOUISIANA

Surveyed by T Hough For Jas McBride

SCALE
500 ft to the Inch

wind. They became as much part of the landscape as the natural levees of the Mississippi.

Earlier the French had pressed inland from the Saint Lawrence River to the Great Lakes and then to the upper reaches of the Mississippi in the late seventeenth and early eighteenth centuries. They found the banks of the great river deserted. This was the heart of mound country. Yet the abandoned earthworks had melted into the landscape and looked like natural embrasures on the riverbanks. Explorers like Louis Joliet and Jacques Marquette, who passed down much of the river in 1672–73, made no mention of artificial mounds. Trading,

"Ancient Monuments in Madison Parish, Louisiana." A plan by Squier and Davis, published in their classic work on American mounds, 1848. The plan shows an elevated walkway and temple mounds. Sites such as this one were unobserved by de Soto and other early explorers.

61

souls, and furs were more on the explorers' minds than archaeology. But farther to the south, the peoples of the Yazoo River were "dispersed over the country upon mounds of earth made with their own hands" in the early eighteenth century, when the Natchez still flourished. We know this from the writings of Bernard de La Harpe, one of the last Europeans to see the mounds in use.

While Harpe was inferring that "these nations are very ancient and were formerly very numerous," the settlers of the thirteen colonies to the east began to turn their land-hungry eyes to the unknown wild country in the far interior of the vast continent. By 1750 the British were settling in the Ohio Valley. A decade later France had yielded control of North America east of the Mississippi to Britain, except for an enclave around New Orleans, which passed to Spain. Soon settlers were moving westward into the vast territory that had seen thousands of years of mound building. A new myth, that of the Mound Builders, was about to move to the center of the archaeological stage.

4 "A Faire Citie . . . Builded in Order"

Alvar Nuñez Cabeza de Vaca, one of the few survivors of the ill-fated Narváez expedition, appeared in Mexico in 1536. Officials heard his astonishing tales of a harsh and strange land to the north with interest. The gold-hungry colonial government had long wondered what lay to the north of Mexico. No one knew who lived on that vast continent.

But they ignored Vaca's tales of suffering. His stories of buffalo, the first eyewitness account of these animals to reach civilization, caused little interest. Vaca described them as cows "the size of those in Spain. Their horns are small, like those of Moorish cattle; the hair is very long, like fine wool and like a pea jacket." People were bored when he described dozens of Indian tribes with different lifestyles, living in environments of widely contrasting severity. The trouble was that Vaca had returned empty handed, with nothing more than the skins he wore.

Ever since Cortés and Pizarro had plundered Mexico and Peru, people had expected someone to find a fabulous El Dorado teeming with gold and silver in the New World. Perhaps this El Dorado would be the famed Seven Cities of Cibola, cities founded as long ago as the eighth century by a legendary bishop who fled westward from Lisbon in fear of the Moors and Islam. By the time Cortés arrived in Mexico the Seven Cities were part of tavern gossip. Within a few generations Indian legends had embroidered the story beyond all recognition. The Seven Cities were there for the finding, a mysterious symbol of untold wealth open to the first taker. But all Vaca could contribute were a few persistent rumors of huge towns, crowded with people, rich in gold and silver, to console his questioners. So obsessed were the Spaniards with easy riches that some actually believed that Vaca had hidden the spoils of his expedition so that he could keep them for himself.

Although Vaca and his companions had seen nothing of these fabled cities—indeed they stressed that they were merely repeating the stories they had heard from the Indians—the viceroy of Mexico, Don Antonio de Mendoza, was undeterred. He decided that a special expedition should be mounted to look for the lost cities, one that would prepare the way for a more thorough investigation, and presumably exploitation, later on. He chose Fray Marcos of Niza, a well-known Franciscan, for the task, a man who "had great experience in the affairs of the Indians" and could be relied upon for an accurate and unbiased report. His guide was to be Estevaníco, the black man who had accompanied Vaca. He had begun his career as a slave and then had been freed.

They were a curious pair: the sober, eminent priest and the jaunty ex-slave with his vast experience of Indians and fluency in sign language. Estevaníco traveled in great style, fantastically dressed in feathers and ribbons. His new importance had gone

Archaeological sites in the Southwest and Coronado's approximate itinerary.

64

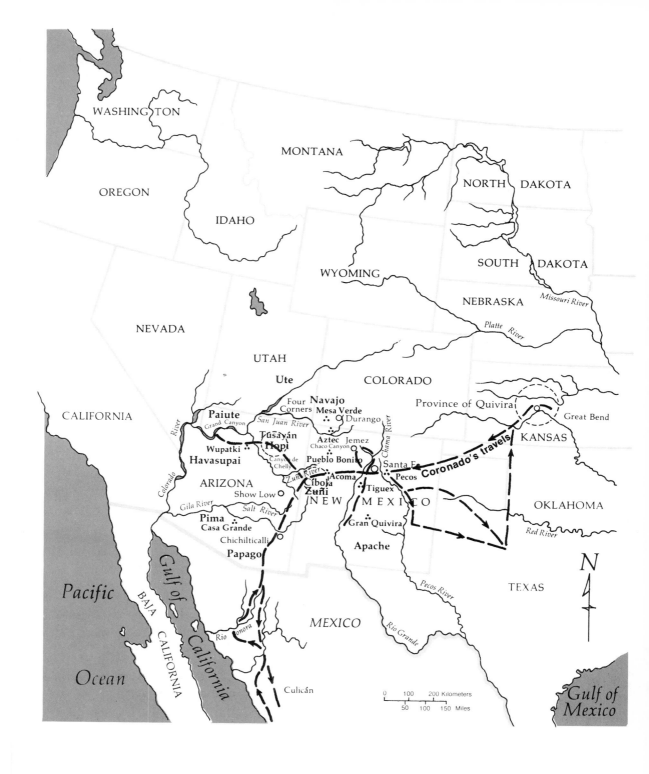

to his head, for his reputation as a medicine man among the Indians had preceded him. Within a few days of departure he had attracted a huge following and a personal harem, the latter a development that Fray Marcos and his priests viewed with great acerbity.

Soon the travelers heard tales of a "large and mightie plain" where there were many towns. Gold vessels and sheets were apparently in common use, and the "walles of their temples are covered therewith," said their informants.

As the guide, Estevaníco traveled with a smaller party ahead of Marcos and the main expedition. Friendly Indians, captivated by Estevaníco's antics, prepared fine camps and supplies of food. But as the expedition moved farther north, the distance between the two parties increased, Estevaníco prancing alertly into unknown territory, while a continuous stream of messengers brought back the latest information on the peoples whom they found ahead. Fray Marcos had arranged for a simple method of communication in the event that the advance guard arrived at the Seven Cities of Cibola. A messenger was to be dispatched with a white cross, the size of which would indicate the degree of importance of the lands ahead. If the cities "were but a meare thing, he should send me a white cross of one handfull long," wrote Fray Marcos later; "if it were any great manner one or two handfulls long; if it were a Country greater and better than Nueva España he should send me a great crosse."

Excitement mounted in the rear guard when Estevaníco began sending back a series of fantastic messages. Four days after his departure an Indian brandishing a huge cross turned up in camp. All manner of rumors began to circulate, stories fueled by later messengers who described great cities "thirtie days journie" away in the interior. The settlements were made up of great houses joined together, they said, houses whose gates were inlaid with "many Turques-stones cunningly wrought." Two days after Easter, Marcos left for the interior, following his advance guard, encouraged by yet

66

another huge "white crosse." Everywhere the Indians provided food for the party while Marcos was regaled with stories of the wealthy cities to be seen. More crosses arrived. Marcos was urged to march faster; the friar seems to have been in no hurry, for he kept arriving at hospitable villages where he was entertained royally. Many turquoises and ox hides were displayed for him, and the people willingly gave him information on the country ahead.

After a four-day passage through a desert, the rear guard traversed a valley "very well inhabited with people" who were familiar with the fabled cities. They described their fine adobe buildings and told stories of "very great houses of five stories high, wherein the chiefes of the citie assemble themselves at certain times of the year." Again the stories were of turquoise and wool, of gold and other riches. It was at this point that Marcos learned of a fifteen-day desert crossing that lay in front of him, a desert that Estevaníco had already entered with three hundred companions. The black man's eager messages continued to flow unabated as the priests traveled across the desert for twelve days, "being always well provided of victuals, of wild beasts, Hares and Partridge."

A village of Pima Indians on the Gila River painted by Seth Eastman. The watercolor was based on a sketch by John Russell Bartlett, a U.S. border survey commissioner in the 1850s. At that time the Pima were living in huts made of saplings and grass. *On deposit in the John Carter Brown Library from the Museum of Art of the Rhode Island School of Design*

67

Their appetites were spoiled on the twelfth day when an exhausted Indian who had accompanied Estevaníco in the advance party burst into camp in a great fright. One day out from the first "city," Estevaníco had sent ahead his "great mace made of a gourd," the symbolic gesture of peace that had previously assured his safe conduct. The head man of the town was incensed, gave orders that these strangers were notorious enemies, and ordered them to leave his territory posthaste. Estevaníco shrugged aside the message, was refused entry into the pueblo, and was shut up inside a large house outside the main settlement. All the trade goods accompanying the caravan were confiscated. The prisoners were given no food or drink. The messenger himself had escaped slaughter because while slipping undetected out of the makeshift prison to get a drink early in the morning he had seen Estevaníco and his companions being massacred, so he hid and then escaped into the desert.

Fray Marcos was appalled at the news. He divided his valuable trade goods up among the party, partly to appease the grief-stricken Indians who had lost many relatives in the slaughter. Then he slipped on to the hostile town, taking only a few Indians with him. Surreptitiously he gazed on the legendary settlement, undetected by its inhabitants. From his mountain perch he saw "a faire citie," many houses "builded in order . . . all made of stone with divers stories, and flatte roofs, as farre as I could discerne." The people were light skinned, possessed "emeralds and other jewels," and used "vessels of gold and silver, for they have no other metal, whereof there is greater use and more abundance than in Peru."

Marcos did not dare enter the settlement, rightly fearing for his life. He and his companions erected a huge pile of stones and a small wooden cross, lacking "means to make a greater." (How they did this without being detected by the local people is left to the reader's imagination.) The friar then solemnly took possession of the Seven Cities in the name of Spain and retreated as fast as he could. It was a

68

miracle that he had not been spotted; he returned with "more feare than victuals."

Fray Marcos's expedition has been surrounded with controversy ever since it returned in disorder. His report caused a sensation in Mexico City, for it confirmed the existence of seven great cities in the far north. In fact, the Seven Cities of Cibola were merely a group of Zuñi pueblos in New Mexico—substantial settlements indeed, but nothing as elaborate or wealthy as Spanish imagination painted them. Again the lust for gold overcame rational analysis of Marcos's reports. While many colonists in Mexico City believed everything Marcos had to say and more, others vilified him for cowardice and accused him of lying. They felt he should have gone ahead and investigated the pueblos at closer range in spite of the danger. Historians have generally made an even harsher judgment, for many feel there is strong reason to believe that his alleged eyewitness account of Cibola was a complete fabrication. In all probability Marcos never penetrated much farther north than the Gila River in southern Arizona, a far cry from the Zuñi country. Estevaníco, however, probably did reach the pueblos.

Marcos's report was magnified all out of proportion in Mexico City. The friar himself was a good storyteller and he embellished his official report on every possible occasion. The worthy Bishop Zumárraga wrote to a friend from Mexico City that the friar had told him of "other cities larger than this one of Mexico." Even Marcos's barber was regaled with stories of wealthy cities where the men wore "girdles of gold and white woollen dresses." The friar was elevated to the position of father-principal, over the heads of several candidates of longer service—a political appointment if ever there was one.

The people of Mexico City had been awaiting reports of a new land of fabulous wealth for years. Gold was still everyone's objective, but the supplies of it in Mexico and Peru had been greatly diminished. Marcos was hailed as a great pioneer who had made discoveries fully as important as those of Christopher Columbus or Pizarro. The viceroy himself was officially cautious, although eager to cash in on the friar's remarkable discoveries. He organized an expedition that would take possession of the Seven Cities on behalf of the king of Spain. The viceroy moved ahead on his own initiative—always a tricky decision with uncertain consequences in the hierarchical governmental system of Spain. Besieged with requests for permission to mount expeditions, the viceroy carefully selected a young military governor, Francisco Vásquez de Coronado, for the task of leading the next exploration into the fabled territories of the north.

Coronado was a *hidalgo* of noble birth who had entered Viceroy Antonio de Mendoza's service in 1535. Born in 1521, he had been a young courtier in the court of Charles V before joining the new viceroy's retinue. After a few months in Mexico the young Coronado was high in the viceroy's regard, acting as his secretary and chamberlain. Within two years he had made a brilliant marriage to Beatríz de Estrada, the daughter of a wealthy pioneer who was a cousin of the king of Spain. The viceroy soon appointed his young lieutenant as a member of Mexico City's town council. Coronado also played a leading role in the suppression of a revolt of black slaves against the Spaniards in 1536–37. The following year the viceroy appointed him to the newly vacant governorship of New Galicia on the west coast of Mexico, a province that was in considerable disorder.

Coronado had been in his new job but a year when he was summoned for another task: commanding the expeditionary force to investigate Cibola. Coronado himself apparently did not seek the appointment; rather he took it out of a sense of duty and loyalty to the viceroy. Myriad preparations culminated in a ceremonial review of the expedition at Compostela in New Galicia on February 22, 1540. There had been no difficulty in recruiting volunteers for the expedition; Mexico City was full of young bloods who had shipped out from Spain in search of wealth and fortune in the New World. Skillful with sword and horse, they idled away their time in Mexico City, living off the bounty of the locals. More than three hundred of them volunteered for the expedition without salary, and many of them paid their own way. On that memorable day in Compostela, 225 horsemen finally paraded before the viceroy, together with 60 foot soldiers with crossbows or crude firearms and a motley crowd of Negro slaves, servants, and Indian allies flamboyantly dressed in feathers and war paint. This large expeditionary force had one objective in mind: to discover and collect as much gold as possible. If at the same time a few souls were saved and some land partitioned among members of the expedition, so much the better. Fray Marcos and four friars accompanied Coronado, the former so excited that he had already set off for the north.

Progress was slow until Coronado reached Culiacan in northern New Galicia. There he dispatched a small advance party of seventy horsemen led by himself to reconnoiter. The route north was through harsh territory, a far cry from the fertile paradise Fray Marcos had described. But eventually Coronado's party reached the fertile upper valley of the Rio Sonora, by a route that is still debated.

Ahead lay the southern Arizona desert, a shimmering wilderness of breathless heat in the summer. Fortunately it was the time of the spring runoff and there was some forage for the horses. At the Gila River they watered their steeds and stopped at a place that Fray Marcos's report had described as a large settlement. But all the soldiers found was a roofless and deserted fortress with large earth walls. A short time before, a tribe of nomads had destroyed Chichilticalli. The discovery depressed Coronado, who had also been led to expect that he could see the sea from the site. Fray Marcos's reputation as an explorer began to diminish rapidly.

After a two-day rest near the ruins—an archaeological site, incidentally, that no one has been able to identify in recent times—food ran short. Coronado was forced to push on. The next stage of the journey was a horrible experience, as the horsemen struggled through the harsh ravines of the Colorado plateau. After five hundred arduous leagues the small party emerged from the wilderness at the "river of Cibola," a short distance from their El Dorado.

Zuñi country now lay ahead, to be approached by the well-trod trade routes that the prudent Coronado had followed all the way from Mexico. So far he had experienced little trouble with the Indians and had lost only a few men, to food poisoning. But his small force of Spaniards and Indians were weary and weakened by hardship, and they were disillusioned by the false stories they had discovered in Marcos's report. Word of Coronado's advance had, of course, preceded him, and both Indians and Spaniards were ready for trouble. Peaceful overtures by the locals did not deceive the general, who ordered a scouting party ahead to secure any likely spot for an ambush. They occupied a narrow defile just in time, because a large band of Indians had advanced for the same purpose. The Indians flung themselves at the Spaniards, were beaten off, and retired in good order. But it was evident that the Indians of Cibola were to be a formidable enemy for the weakened expeditionary force. Signal fires flickered in the hills ahead. The avenging of Estevaníco's murder and the occupation of Cibola with all its riches were not going to be easy matters.

The six Zuñi villages that lay ahead, known to have flourished on the upper reaches of the Zuñi River, were the Seven Cities of Cibola so beloved by the chroniclers. But the legend was soon to be shattered. Hawikuh, where Estevaníco had met his end, was the nearest settlement, the pueblo that Coronado and his soldiers sighted on July 7, 1540; the other five pueblos were in the nearby hills, where the Zuñi still live today. Coronado sighted Hawikuh early in the morning, but it was a disappointingly unimpressive sight. "It is a little, crowded village," wrote Pedro de Castañeda, Coronado's chronicler, "looking as if it had been crumpled all up together. There are haciendas in New Spain which make a better appearance at a distance. It is a village of about two hundred warriors, in three and four stories high,

with the houses small and having only a few rooms
and without a courtyard." Marcos's celebrated city
of gold and silver was little more than a glorified
village.

Coronado was disgusted and wrote to the viceroy
that Marcos "has not told the truth in a single thing
that he has said, but everything is the reverse of what
he has said, except the name of the city and the large
stone houses." Everyone denounced the friar. "Such
were the curses hurled at friar Marcos," wrote
Castañeda, "that I pray God may protect him from
them." As soon as he could, Marcos returned to
Mexico in disgrace. He lived out his days in dig-
nified poverty until he died in 1558.

But the soldiers had little time for recriminations,
for warriors from all the Zuñi settlements were in
battle order before the pueblo. The formal proclama-
tion of submission required of all Spanish expeditions occupying new territory was read and greeted
with jeers. A few minutes later battle was joined. Coronado restrained his soldiers as long as he dared,
hoping to take Hawikuh intact. When the shower of
arrows became intolerable, he gave the signal for a

Zuñi pueblo, the site of
Hawikuh. A photograph taken
in the late nineteenth
century.
*Photograph courtesy of the
Museum of the American
Indian, Heye Foundation*

73

charge, the impact of which scattered the Indians. The pueblo walls overhead were lined with fierce warriors, and the entrance was accessible only through a winding passage. Coronado resolved on strategy and stormed the walls under cover of a diversionary barrage, a stratagem that proved inadequate, as his musketeers were too fatigued to fire their heavy harquebusiers. The general himself was an easy target with his shining armor and was severely bruised by stones and arrows before he was carried to safety. But the defense was quickly weakened. Within an hour Hawikuh was in Spanish hands and its inhabitants melted away into the desert. The hungry soldiers made a beeline for the storehouses, where they found "much corn and beans, and fowl," booty more prized at that particular moment than all the gold and silver in the Indies. Of gold and precious stones there were no signs.

Within a few days Coronado had recovered sufficiently from his wounds to pay a visit to a neighboring pueblo of larger size. Matsaki boasted some

A general view of Zuñi depicted by F. H. Cushing, *My Adventures in Zuñi*, 1882–83.

buildings seven stories high, was well fortified, and would be difficult to invade. Coronado wisely emphasized the peaceful nature of his mission, made no move against the hostile inhabitants, and contented himself with exploring the surrounding country. He sent messengers back to his main force and dispatched a scouting force under Don Pedro de Tovar to investigate another group of pueblos said to lie seven days' travel away.

The people of Cibola had told glowing stories of the Tusayan settlements, now known to be a group of Hopi Indian pueblos. Perhaps gold would be found there. The scouting party was guided across the Painted Desert until a sandstone mesa, where the first Hopi village lay, loomed ahead. The pueblo consisted of a mass of terraced houses at the foot of the mesa. The soldiers approached the well-fortified settlement quietly after nightfall, hiding nearby,

Women grinding corn. From F. H. Cushing, *My Adventures in Zuñi*, 1882–83.

within earshot of the inhabitants. So confident were the Indians of their defense works that they had not bothered to post lookouts, even though they had heard of Cibola's capture "by very fierce people, who travelled on animals which ate people." When the scouting force was discovered, however, the Hopi did not panic but prepared to resist the newcomers. But once they saw that the Spaniards were formidable opponents and a few Indians had died in a skirmish, the chief sued for peace. Corn, a few dressed skins, some cotton cloths, even a few turquoises, were forthcoming. There were no precious metals to be seen, however, which was frustrating for the Spaniards because they were allowed to trade freely with all the Hopi pueblos.

As a result of Tovar's report another party was dispatched to visit a large river over twenty days' journey distant across a tract of desert. Don García López de Cárdenas and twelve companions had an arduous ride which took them to the cliffs overlooking the Grand Canyon. Far below them flowed the inaccessible Colorado, "which looked from above as if the water was six feet across, although the Indians said it was half a league wide." Another party ventured to the east, for Coronado was curious about a report of strange animals like cows but with hairy skins. Hernando de Alvarado was chosen for the task, and he journeyed as far as the pueblo at Acoma, New Mexico, and then into country named Tiguex in the upper Rio Grande, southwest of the present city of Santa Fe. From there he returned to the northeast, soon arriving at Pecos pueblo, where he met an Indian slave, probably a Pawnee, who came from far to the southeast. He was promptly nicknamed "the Turk" and was retained as a guide to show Alvarado the strange "cows," although he spent most of his time babbling about "the wealth of gold and silver" in his own country.

Meanwhile the soldiers wondered at the mound of Pecos, itself a remarkable settlement. It could field nearly five hundred warriors, an army to be feared over a wide region. The town "is square, situated on a rock, with a large court or yard in the middle,

76

containing the steam rooms," recalled Castañeda. "The houses are all alike, four stories high. One can go over the top of the whole village without there being a street to hinder." He described how there were "corridors going all around it at the first two stories, by which one can go around the whole village." The houses could be entered only by means of ladders from the roofs, with doors that led into the corridors. A freshwater spring inside the town gave the inhabitants additional security in time of war.

By 1540 Pecos had grown in size until it was the largest settlement of its type in what is now North America. Two great complexes of rooms rose from the mound, protected by the blank outer walls of the houses, stone walls, and a moat. It was a perfect defensive arrangement. The Spaniards did not, of course, know that Pecos was the largest pueblo they would ever see. They were given many turquoises that came from workings near the modern town of Los Cerrillos not too far away. Wisely, the people of Pecos guided the foreigners away from the mines.

Frustrated by the lack of gold in Pecos, Alvarado fell under the influence of the Turk's carefully woven tales. The party traveled several days east of Pecos onto the plains of New Mexico, where they soon found themselves surrounded by enormous herds of buffalo, "the most monstrous thing in the way of animals that has ever been seen or read about." Castañeda remarked on "their extremely large bodies and long wool," noticing that they were not afraid of rough country. The troopers had a difficult time hunting buffalo until they learned that it was safer for their horses if they used their pikes at a distance. But even buffalo could not grip the attention of gold-hungry Alvarado and his men. They hastened back to Tiguex, taking the Turk with them to inform the general of the good news.

Coronado had now moved his forces to Tiguex, for it seemed an admirable winter quarters, with relatively plentiful food supplies. There he found Alvarado and the Turk, who repeated his stories for the eager general, telling of a great river, huge fish, ceremonial canoes with figureheads. Everyone had metal vessels, he said, while jugs and bowls were made of gold.

The general was so impressed by the Turk's stories that he sent Alvarado after some gold bracelets that the men at Pecos had allegedly taken from him. The chief, a good friend of the Spaniards, denied all knowledge of the ornaments, was promptly taken prisoner, and was taken in chains back to Tiguex, where he remained for over six months. Alvarado had been stupid and lost the confidence of the Indians. The situation did not improve when Coronado demanded pieces of cloth from the Indians for winter clothing. Instead of trading for them, his soldiers seized all the cloth they could find at the twelve villages, even stripping it from onlookers. An incident between a soldier and a woman brought matters to the boiling point.

A nocturnal horse raid caused Coronado to take drastic action. All the pueblos were closed and barricaded when he arrived on the scene. He chose one village to set an example and ordered it to be taken by force. After fierce fighting the inhabitants were smoked out from their *kivas* until they surrendered. Don García López de Cárdenas, who was in charge of the attack, was determined to make an example of the miscreants, "so that the other nations would fear the Spaniards." Two hundred stakes were erected and the roasting of prisoners begun. When the uproar reached the ears of the other captives they began a desperate struggle that ended with the massacre of every Indian in sight. It took a great deal of hard fighting and much slaughter to restore peace. The villages of Tiguex were decimated and probably never recovered completely.

With Tiguex and Pecos in an uneasy state of peace, Coronado was now determined to set out eastward for Quivira, where the Turk still insisted there was gold. It was now April or May 1541, the cold weather was behind them, and the soldiers had to make a bridge to cross the Rio Pecos. Eight days after the crossing they came to buffalo country—flat, featureless plains that were without landmarks except for occasional lakes and buffalo wallows. For thirty-

78

seven days the army moved across the plains. The huge herds of sheep, goats, horses, and cattle that accompanied them obliterated all traces of their passage, so the soldiers piled up bones and cow dung to mark their route for the rear guard. Soon they came across Plains Indians, nomadic peoples dependent entirely on the buffalo for their livelihood. Their *travois* made trails on the ground that marked their constant pursuit of the herds. At one point in northwestern Texas the Spaniards came across a huge pile of buffalo bones by a salt lick that was "a crossbow shot long," about twelve feet high and eighteen feet across. The Indians of the region were expert hunters. They skinned their prey in a short time by slitting the carcass along the back and pulling the hide off over the legs, using a small, saw-edged stone tool. The skins served as clothing. Deer, wolves, and jackrabbits relieved the monotony of their diet and clothing.

The farther the army traveled, the less they liked the look of the country. By the time they had reached

A fanciful depiction of a Spanish attack on a pueblo painted by the Dutch artist Jan Mostaert about 1545. The Indians have long beards and are attacking the Spaniards on the ground and with rocks from above. Mostaert apparently based his picture on published accounts of the Coronado expedition.
Frans Halsmuseum, Haarlem

the Texas plains, the soldiers were frustrated and weary. A tornado and a hailstorm stampeded the horses and caused much damage. Clearly, drastic action was needed, and the general called a council. He was convinced by now that the Turk was lying, something that the Pecos guides had been trying to tell him for days. It was resolved that Coronado and a small party of thirty would strike out to the north in search of the elusive Quivira. The disgraced Turk was taken along in chains.

After forty-eight days of exhausting riding the small party reached Quivira, actually situated somewhere near Great Bend, Kansas. There they found the Wichita Indians living in grass lodges, but no sign of gold or copper. Juan Jaramillo, who accompanied the party, admired the country "with mesas, plains, and charming rivers with fine waters." There were excellent wild fruits and plenty of buffalo. Coronado had arrived at the moment of truth, for the quest for gold was evidently a will-o'-the-wisp. The Turk was forced to confess that he had lied, having been encouraged by the Tiguex Indians to lead the Spaniards far out on the plains where they would perish of thirst. He was garroted for his pains, a stone cross was erected, and the party turned back, reaching Pecos without incident after forty days.

The dream of untold riches had evaporated, and a costly summer of travel based on the lies of an Indian slave had achieved nothing. Deep despair enveloped the army. After wintering at Tiguex, Coronado led his dispirited troops back to New Galicia, a humiliating retreat that was complicated by mutinies and continual skirmishes with the Indians. In the fall of 1542 barely a hundred men marched into Mexico City, there to be disbanded with nothing to show for their efforts. The viceroy had spent sixty thousand ducats of his own money; Coronado, fifty thousand. The booty was a handful of Indian blankets and turquoises and a wealth of new geographical knowledge. But since this concerned goldless territory, no one was particularly interested. To the colonists it was a venture that had ended in failure. It was half a century before attempts were made to settle the American Southwest. Coronado himself did not live to see this happen. Censured and fired for ill-treating Indians and for other alleged misdeeds, he spent the rest of his brief life on his estates, serving as a member of Mexico City's town council. He died in 1554 at the age of forty-four, a respected servant of the king whose lack of results had at least been partially forgiven.

The objective had been gold. The results in treasure were negligible, but the geographical consequences were momentous. Coronado had carried out a careful reconnaissance of the Southwest and had penetrated deep into lands where people still lived by hunting big game. Coronado was a wise and sober commander, despite the ill-considered actions of his subordinates, and he kept his unruly gold seekers under a stern rein. The accounts of his expeditions provided archaeologists of later centuries with their earliest glimpse of one of the homelands of North American archaeology. There the riches have not been gold but critical historical information that set the prehistory of the American Indian on a firm footing for the first time.

The earliest confrontation between Western society and the archaeological sites of America occurred because of the gold lust of early colonists. At the heart of this lust lay the character of the Spanish gentlemen who sought wealth and fame in the Indies. The young Spanish adventurers came from a harsh mountain environment, from a country where the weak perished. Historian A. Grove Day described them as "hardy, ascetic, alert, active, and courageous. . . . wealth was to be won through freebooting, gambling, or the acquisition of large holdings worked by slaves. . . . a reputation for cruelty sprang from a hardened insensibility to suffering either in himself or in others." And it was these characteristics and the fanaticism of the Franciscans that led to the first ravaging of archaeological sites in the New World.

PART TWO

Lost Civilizations

"Antiquities are history defaced, or some remnants
of a history that have casually escaped the shipwreck
of time."

FRANCIS BACON

5 "They Are of Considerable Notoriety among the Indians"

"Cibola is composed of seven pueblos. . . . the houses, as a rule, are three and four stories high. . . . this land is a valley between sierras that rise like boulders. . . . the Indians plant in holes, and the corn does not grow tall." The vignettes of Indian life in the Southwest and on the Great Plains contained in the writings of Spanish authors raised little interest in a society more concerned with gold than with colonization or even with Christianity. It was fifty years after Coronado's troops had stumbled back into Mexico City before conversion of the Indians of the Southwest was attempted on any scale.

The story of the Spanish colonization of New Mexico and Arizona is emblazoned with the names of memorable prelates, priests like Father Kino, who founded a network of missions in Sonora and brought a new era of colonization and exploitation to the Southwest. The introduction of horses and wheat soon wrought enormous changes in Indian life. The close-knit pueblos were, however, past their peak of power and prosperity and were beset with increasing water shortages that made it difficult for the centuries-old systems of cereal agriculture and irrigation to survive. Abandoned pueblos were forgotten as they melded imperceptibly with the harsh desert landscape of browns and grays.

In like manner the stirring narratives of Marcos, Castañeda, and others were buried in the archives of Madrid and New Spain, practically forgotten by Spanish historians and beyond the ken of British or French scholars. The Far West of North America was another world, seemingly a desolate and unproductive region without mineral wealth, its only remarkable features some glorious landscape and the pueblos of mud that had promised so much to the pioneer explorers. It was harsh, sparsely populated by missionaries and traders, a hispanic world that was totally alien to the hard-working pioneers of the thirteen colonies thousands of miles to the east.

The colonies themselves were peopled by Anglo-Saxon farmers and merchants with a harsh work ethic, a commitment to self-sufficiency rather than self-indulgence, and a constant hunger for agricultural land. To the north lay French Canada, a network of pioneer settlements on the Saint Lawrence from which the delicate tentacles of the fur trade extended far into the interior, to the shores of the Great Lakes and beyond. Everywhere one looked a vast, unexplored continent stretched toward the west, known only from Spanish and French explorations up the Mississippi and through Spanish and British expeditions up the west coast in the sixteenth and seventeenth centuries.

This New World took pride in its European culture and historical heritage, a heritage that bore no resemblance to the values or culture of the Indian hunters and farmers whose lands were annexed in Virginia, New York, Connecticut, and elsewhere. An uneasy familiarity with the "Red Indian" had taken

86

hold in Europe during the sixteenth century, based on knowledge of a few captive hostages and scattered collections of cloaks, weapons, and other trophies assembled by explorer and colonist. The American Indian, romanticized by painter John White and others, then became the pastoral dream of those who speculated about human diversity. But this romantic image did not last long in the realistic world of the colonies. The Indians' welcome assistance and hospitality soon turned sour on both sides, as the confrontations between Christian and pagan, superior technology and simple adaptation, accelerated. Unfamiliar European diseases and the colonists' ever escalating demands for farming land decimated the Indian population, and it slowly evaporated, almost without a trace. There were few signs of their former ownership of the land, as if their possession of America had been as transitory as their dealings with the white man.

The more scholarly colonists were puzzled. It is characteristic of most colonial societies to seek justification of their colonization in historical precedent. The very primitiveness of the American Indians compounded puzzlement over their origins. The North American landscape was devoid of any conspicuous monuments of antiquity, of any lasting memorials of ancient civilizations that had preceded the Indian or lived alongside them. The Spanish assumption that all humans had descended from Adam and Eve was as much a part of the Anglo-Saxon Protestant dogma as it was of the Catholic. Thus, most people looked to the Old World civilizations for inspiration, to lands where mighty pyramids and great temples stood as tangible evidence of antiquity. Egypt had the pyramids of Gizeh and the temples of Luxor and Karnak that had been standing since time immemorial. The world's oldest civilization on the Nile was matched by the architectural achievements of classical Athens with its Parthenon and the stereotyped public buildings of the mighty Roman Empire. Even the ancient Britons had Stonehenge, that mysterious circle of stones on the Wiltshire downs that sent antiquarians into

A mounted Spanish soldier attacking a band of California Indians. A typical Indian house is seen at the left. Their houses are "digged round within the earth, and have from the uppermost brimmes of the circle, clefts of wood set up, and joyned close together at the top." A drawing by José Cardero, an artist with a Spanish scientific expedition that visited Monterey in 1771. *Museo Naval, Madrid*

ecstasies of enthusiastic speculation. But there were no signs of ancient civilizations in North America. Nor had any monuments of colonists from Mediterranean lands survived for those of antiquarian bent to examine. Reports from unexplored territory were disappointing, too. Everywhere the native Americans lived in simple settlements. Sir Francis Drake had met only primitive hunter-gatherers in California, people with simple canoes and a diet based on shellfish. Their houses were "digged round within the earth, and have from the uppermost brimmes of the circle, clefts of wood set up, and joyned close together at the top, like our spires on the steeple of a church. . . ." These simple people with their thatched huts were a far cry from the Aztec or Inca. The colonists' antiquarian curiosity had to be satisfied by collecting Indian artifacts from living tribes and by a few casual diggings in recent burial grounds that yielded few treasures of interest or value.

In the mid-eighteenth century intellectual curiosity about the American countryside proliferated in a spate of books and explorations. After the Anglo-French war and its settlement in 1756 a vast tract of territory between the colonies and the Mississippi, hitherto traversed only by missionaries and trappers, was opened for settlement as it fell under British control. A new and significant stage in American archaeology was about to begin.

As wagon trains of pioneer farmers and missionaries climbed over the mountains and descended into the Midwest and the great Ohio River Valley, the landscape showed many more signs of ancient human activity. The fertile tracts of plain and woodland were dotted with earthen mounds that followed the floodplain of the Ohio. Over ten thousand of these mounds were to be found in the Ohio Valley in future years; some were enormous accumulations of soil; others, mere bumps on the plain.

When first discovered the mounds were densely overgrown with woodland and undergrowth. But they stood out clearly as farming operations stripped off the regenerated vegetation of centuries. Once the settlers fanned out over the Midwest, across the Alleghenies and into the Mississippi Valley, even more tumuli appeared, some of them enormous, like the complex of mounds at Cahokia, Illinois, on the east bank of the Mississippi near Saint Louis. The largest mound at Cahokia was over one hundred feet high and covered sixteen acres. An enormous area of the Midwest and South was dotted with these mounds. Many of them, it was true, were of relatively small size. Some stood in solitary grandeur; others were grouped in impressive clusters, testifying to a long period of mound-building activity. East of the Alleghenies the mounds stretched out from western New York along the southern shores of the Great Lakes into Wisconsin and as far west as Nebraska. The major rivers of the American heartland—Missouri, Illinois, Indiana, and Ohio—were lined with thousands of mounds. In the South de Soto's men had passed through country dotted with tumuli that extended from Florida into eastern Texas.

To the new colonists, ignorant of Spanish and French explorers' writings and finding few Indians living in their homeland, the mounds seemed to be the work of a long-vanished race that bore little resemblance to the modern inhabitants. When bones, agricultural implements, and weapons as well as elaborate ornaments were found in the mounds, excitement and speculation mounted. Some farmers thought that the earthworks were a nuisance, for they occupied valuable agricultural land. They plowed them flat, scattering their contents. Other settlers were curious about the remarkable monuments, for Moravian missionaries had published brief descriptions of Ohio mounds in the eighteenth century. These and other travelers' tales did little more than describe the mounds as a phenomenon that existed in Ohio and elsewhere. In 1775 James Adair wrote in his *History of the American Indian* that "great mounds of earth, either of a circular or oblong type, having a strong breastwork at a distance around them, are frequently met with." The map makers were concerned about the reports of mounds, too. In 1785 John Fitch's map of the Northwest Territory marked Wisconsin as "country once settled by a people more expert in the art of war than the present inhabitants. Regular fortifications, and some of these incredibly large, are frequently to be found. Also many graves and towers like pyramids of earth."

It was not long before the intellectuals of eighteenth-century Philadelphia began to take a more than casual interest in the mounds. The pacification of the Ohio Indians had taken many years. Military garrisons had been stationed in the heart of mound country. Their officers had plenty of leisure to look around them and sent descriptions of the earthworks back east. General Samuel Parsons sent a particularly full report of a group of mounds at Marietta, Ohio, to Ezra Stiles, then president of Yale College. Stiles was a scholar of wide interests and lively imagination who thought that the mounds were the work of Indians of Canaanite origin. He consulted Benjamin Franklin, who replied that he had no explanation for the mounds. Conceivably, he wrote, de Soto's soldiers had built them.

Soon after the Indian wars the pace of settlement accelerated, especially in the Muskingum Valley. There the Ohio Company, floated by retired Brigadier General Rufus Putnam, had purchased huge tracts of land for about eighty cents an acre under circumstances that can only be described in retrospect as highly questionable. The Ohio Company's first operations began in 1787–88, when a settlement was laid out at Marietta, close by the complex of mounds that Parsons had described to Stiles. Marietta was planned with remarkable care, the earthworks being regarded as a valuable resource for the town. This extraordinarily enlightened attitude was conditioned partly by the size of the mounds, but also by Putnam himself, who took the trouble to draw up plans of the earthworks, which are still preserved at Marietta College. His accurate survey, with its precise dimensions, is a landmark of serious inquiry into America's past.

Mound of Great Works, Marietta, Ohio. *Peabody Museum, Harvard University*

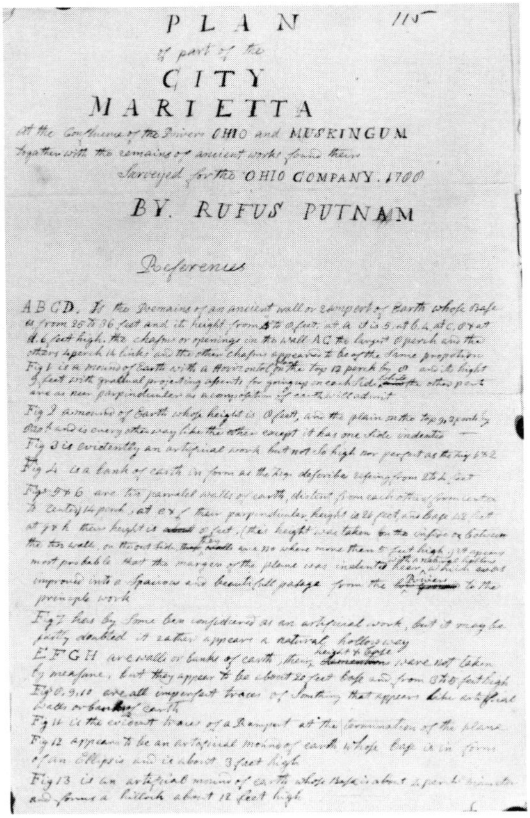

Rufus Putnam's plan of the
Marietta earthworks,
the first accurate survey
of a prehistoric site in
the Ohio Valley.
Marietta College

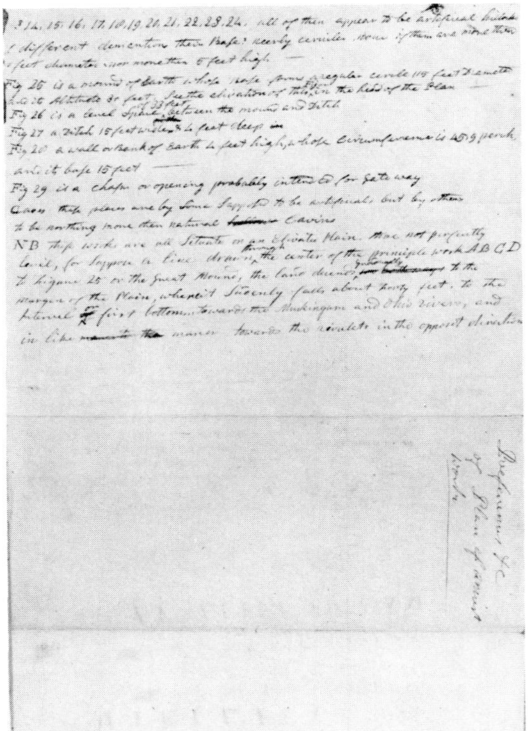

The center of Marietta was to be located at the junction of the Muskingum and Ohio rivers, where a complex of mounds, enclosures, and pyramids overlooked the water's edge. The Ohio Company set the enclosures aside as public squares to be planted with indigenous shade trees. The largest mound became the centerpiece of the town cemetery. Marietta's archaeological focal point has survived to this day, even if the boundaries of the enclosures and a pathway associated with them are now partly buried under the town. In the 1830s the citizens of Marietta raised money to fence off the earthworks and protect them from erosion caused by runoff from the denuded slopes eaten bare by cattle. But for these enlightened acts the Marietta mounds would have gone the way of thousands of others—leveled for cultivation, razed for the erection of cities, and looted for their alleged treasure.

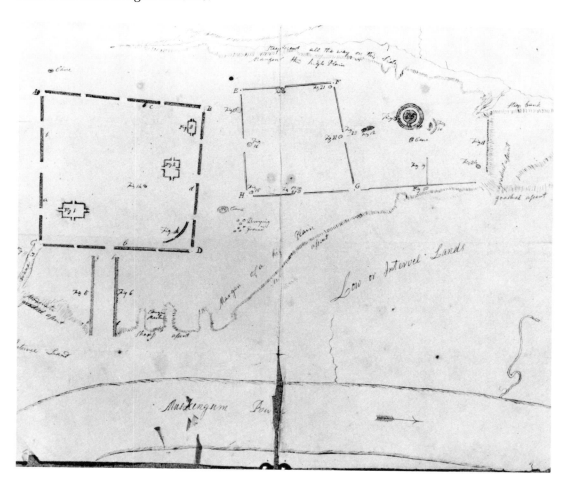

Putnam's agent in the Marietta land deals had
been the Reverend Manasseh Cutler, a Massachusetts priest of rather doubtful reputation. When
he arrived at Marietta the settlers were felling the
large trees that stood on the mounds. In a moment of
inspiration he counted the growth rings exposed in
the trunks of some of the felled trees, one of which
yielded a count of 463 rings. Assuming that a single
ring represented one year's growth, then the mound
upon which the tree grew had been built before A.D.
1300, perhaps earlier. Thus, speculated Cutler, the
mounds were the work of an industrious race that
had lived on the Ohio River long before the present
inhabitants had settled there. Cutler anticipated the
science of dendochronology, or tree ring chronology, by at least a century; the technique was later
developed in the Southwest and used on trees of
great antiquity.

The late eighteenth century was a period of
tremendous intellectual growth in American society,
especially in the comfortable cities of the East. A leisured world of polymathic scholarship revolved
around the coffeehouses and country estates of Virginia and Pennsylvania. A career in politics and in
affairs of state was combined both effectively and
humanistically with academic inquiry. Businessmen

indulged in a taste for part-time research into the fascinating and rapidly expanding world around them. It was in this spirit that Ezra Stiles had consulted Benjamin Franklin.

Thomas Jefferson retired from the pressures and frustrations of public office to his country estate at Monticello, where he indulged a passion for academic research. In a new country chronically short of educated and well-traveled scholars it was no coincidence that the best academic minds were deeply engaged in public affairs.

Thomas Jefferson had served an arduous term as governor of Virginia during the Revolutionary War. His administration was sharply criticized and investigated for its conduct during the worst months of the conflict when the British burned Richmond. In June 1781 he retired to the comfortable seclusion of his estate, disgusted with politics and exhausted by months of strenuous administration. Over a year before, the French government had sent him a questionnaire asking for a mass of information about the state of Virginia. Jefferson had had no time to complete his response while in office; now he was determined not only to answer the questions but also to write a more prolonged account of the territory he had observed and studied for so many years.

Surrounded by "his farm, his family and his books," Jefferson compiled a lengthy discourse that not only touched on philosophical matters but also treated of Indian life and lore, scientific data on all aspects of the natural history of Virginia, and native languages. *Notes on the State of Virginia* was the result, a classic work that discussed laws and money; products "animal, vegetable, and mineral"; and the "aborigines," the Indians of Virginia, ancient and modern. A major theme of this section was, of course, a description of the tribes of Virginia in his own time and their recent history, but it was inevitable that Jefferson would probe the question of their origins.

The European antiquarian literature abounded in accounts of picniclike excavations of burial mounds, described by one English author as a way of "exam-

Thomas Jefferson by Gilbert Stuart. *National Archives*

ining and pondering over the remains of past ages." Scientifically they were useless, little more than treasure hunts. These leisurely antiquarians contrived to play as their laborers worked and spent their digging time "in games of various descriptions—not exactly such as those which the builders of the mound celebrated when they laid the deceased on his funeral pile." But Jefferson conducted his excavations on a far more scholarly basis, motivated more by scientific curiosity than by a search for treasure, anticipating the objectives of many late nineteenth-century archaeologists by at least a century.

He began by hypothesizing that the mound he found near the Rivanna River was of Indian origin. It was, he said, a "repository of the dead," much smaller than the huge mounds of the Southeast and those of the newly opened western territories. There was nothing "as respectable as would be a common ditch for the draining of lands." The only signs of communal effort were a low mound of earth and loose stones. Such tumuli were commonplace, the subject of intense curiosity. Many had yielded human remains. Theories about them abounded. Some held they were the funeral pyres of people fallen in battle. Others believed they were the collective burials of generations of Indians piled together in a great heap from villages scattered for miles around. Still others thought of the mounds as village burial places, the only tangible remains of long-vanished settlements built on the "softest and most fertile meadow-fields on river-sides."

"There being one of these in my neighborhood," recalled Jefferson, "I wished to satisfy myself whether any and which of these opinions was just." Here, for the first time, was a deliberate archaeological excavation, undertaken to verify one of several hypotheses about Indian mounds.

The mound that Jefferson had selected lay on the banks of the Rivanna River near the site of an old Indian village. By Ohio standards the mound was of modest size, about forty feet across and about twelve feet high, "though now reduced by the plough to seven and a half, having been under cultivation about a dozen years.'' When first discovered the mound had been capped with sizable trees and was surrounded with a ditch five feet deep. The excavations began, not with a frontal assault, but with cautious trial trenches that "came to collections of human bones, at different depths, from six inches to three feet below the surface." The bones lay in the soil in complete confusion, "so as, on the whole, to give the idea of bones emptied promiscuously from a bag or basket." Jefferson counted the bones, finding mainly "sculls," jaws, and limb bones, not only of adults but also of infants. "The sculls were so tender," he added, in a manner familiar to any student of early archaeological writing, "that they generally fell to pieces on being touched."

These discoveries were so promising that Jefferson decided to excavate on a much larger scale. A perpendicular cut was made through the mound "so that I might examine its internal structure." The trench was dug down to the natural soil, "wide enough for a man to walk through and examine its sides." Unlike a treasure hunter's frantic burrowing, Jefferson's excavation was carefully planned to extract the maximum amount of information from the site. The objective was to examine the internal structure of the mound, not simply to collect artifacts. When the digging was completed, he carefully recorded the various layers he had uncovered.

At the original ground level was a layer of human bones overlaid with large stones fetched from nearby. These in turn were covered with a thick layer of earth. There were four horizons of bones at one end of the trench, three at the other, those nearest the surface being the least decayed. "No holes were discovered in any of them, as if made with bullets, arrows, or other weapons," recorded Jefferson, so he rejected the hypothesis that the bones were those of a slain host. He estimated that a thousand skeletons were to be found in the mound. "Appearances would certainly indicate that it had derived both origin and growth from the customary collection of bones and the deposition of them

The ancient works at Marietta, Ohio. Frontispiece to Squier and Davis's classic study of American mounds.

together; that the first collection had been deposited on the common surface of the earth, a few stones put over it, and then a covering of earth, that the second had been laid on this, had covered more or less of it in proportion to the number of bones, and was then also covered with earth; and so on.'' He went on to give his reasons for arguing this way, ending with the comment that ''on whatever occasion they may have been made, they are of considerable notoriety among the Indians.'' A party of them had made a long detour to visit the mounds thirty years before and had stood before it ''with expressions that were construed to be those of sorrow.''

Jefferson's archaeological endeavor is remembered as one of the earliest examples of scientific inquiry into human prehistory ever undertaken. It was undoubtedly one of the few attempts to take a careful look at an Indian mound in the eighteenth century, when hundreds upon hundreds of other tumuli were razed during forest clearance and plowing. New settlers in the Ohio Valley chose to build their townships on the fine locations chosen by the Indians for their complexes of mounds and temples; few colonists could be bothered to follow the example of Marietta. Within a few years the mounds at the heart of Cincinnati were flattened under urban

development, but fortunately not before Colonel Winthrop Sargent had dug into them in 1794. He described his finds in the *Transactions of the American Philosophical Society* five years later.

A few years after, some copper implements were found in the same mound. The discovery caused considerable interest and bestirred amateur antiquarians to dig at Cincinnati for more. But few who traveled through the newly settled areas of Ohio or penetrated farther west were as thorough as Jefferson or even vaguely scientific in their speculations about the mounds.

One problem was a simple dearth of reliable information. There were few experienced scientists in mound country who could send back the sorts of reports that the intellectuals and armchair antiquarians of the East craved. Speculation was rampant; Thomas Jefferson himself declared in a letter to a friend in 1787 that "it is too early to form theories on those antiquities, we must wait with patience till more facts are collected. I wish our philosophical societies would collect exact descriptions of the several monuments as yet known and insert them, naked, in their *Transactions*."

Jefferson's comment was based not only on his own investigations, but also on the remarkable travels of William Bartram, naturalist, explorer, and antiquarian. Bartram's achievements and discoveries were widely discussed in the academic circles in which Jefferson moved. Then, in 1791, his masterly *Travels through North and South Carolina, Georgia, East and West Florida* was published in Philadelphia. Soon to become a best seller, this remarkable work brought Bartram world acclaim as a naturalist and scholar.

Born in 1739 the son of a Quaker botanist, William Bartram came into contact with the leaders of the Philadelphia scientific community at an early age through his father's celebrated botanical garden. After an unsuccessful apprenticeship to a merchant and various trading ventures that proved disastrous because of his devotion to the study of wildlife, Bartram found a London patron named John

Cherokee
(1820) Mr Martin

A watercolor of a Cherokee
Indian painted in 1820 by
Baroness Hyde de Neuville, wife
of the French minister to the
United States. The hunter carries
a bow and some long arrows.
New-York Historical Society

Fothergill who supported him on a salary of fifty
pounds a year as a collector of plants and mollusks
in Florida. For four years, from 1773 to 1777,
William Bartram sent specimens to London. He
traveled through country that was still densely settled by Indian tribes. Then he returned to spend the
rest of his life in Philadelphia as an expert scientist
whom scholars from all over the world consulted
until his death in 1823.

Bartram was blessed with a vivid writing style that
made the sights and countryside that he visited
come alive. He was mainly concerned with natural
history, but he also observed the landscape and the
people; indeed, his work depended on good relationships with Indian chiefs. Soon he was busy
observing earthworks and other antiquities. He
found the Cherokee living in square buildings
constructed of logs, while "the council or town-
house is a large rotunda, capable of accommodating
several hundred people; it stands on the top of an
ancient artificial mount of earth, of about twenty feet
perpendicular. . . . But it may be proper to observe, that this mount on which the rotunda stands,
is of a much ancienter date than the building, and
perhaps was raised for another purpose. The Chero-
kees themselves are as ignorant as we are, by what
people or what purpose these artificial hills were
raised . . . but they have a tradition common with
the other nations of Indians, that they found them in
much the same condition as they now appear, when
their forefathers arrived from the West."

Bartram went on to add that the people whom the
Cherokee had themselves conquered had told their
new masters the same story. "Perhaps," he speculated, "they were designed and appropriated by the
people who constructed them, to some religious purpose, as great altars and temples similar to the high
places and sacred groves anciently amongst the
Canaanites and other groves of Palestine and Judea."

This biblical analogy was hardly surprising, for
the Scriptures were still one of the primary historical
sources of the day, the veracity of which was un-
questioned. There seemed nothing strange in going
back to the Bible for historical precedent when

100

something new or even mildly exotic came to light. William Bartram never dug into a mound. He contented himself with observing that "the pyramidal hills or artificial mounts, and high-ways or avenues . . . and obelisks or pillars of wood, are the only monuments of labour, ingenuity and magnificence, that I have seen worthy for notice, or remark." After speculating about the probable functions of the pyramids and plazas and making an attempt to distinguish between defensive earthworks and religious places, Bartram ended by deeming "it necessary to observe as my opinion, that none of them that I have seen discover the least signs of the arts, sciences, or architecture of the Europeans or other inhabitants of the old world; yet evidently betray every sign or mark of the most distant antiquity."

Archaeologists have tried to follow up on many of the allusions to mounds in Bartram's narrative. He had expressed strong admiration of Mount Royal near the Saint John's River in Florida where a mound he visited in 1765 "appeared wild and savage." A "noble Indian highway" led from the great mound three-quarters of a mile through a sunken defile to a pond. The surrounding forests created a magnificent sylvan setting for the mound. But when Bartram returned in 1774 everything was changed. The trees had been cleared away and the land planted with cotton and corn; after cultivation for several years it lay abandoned. "It appears, however, that the late proprietor had some taste, as he had preserved the mount, and this little adjoining grove inviolate."

A century later Clarence Moore, a famous mound excavator, dug into Mount Royal and found numerous burials and copper and stone artifacts within the tumulus. The mound itself was 16 feet high and over 550 feet in circumference. Bartram had contented himself with observing "quantities of fragments of Indian earthenware, bones of animals and other remains, particularly in the shelly heights and ridges all over the island." This was on an island in Lake George near Mount Royal. He also camped on the edge of an Indian cemetery and described Choctaw "bone houses," where corpses were left to

101

decompose before the bones were placed in "a curiously wrought chest or coffin." The coffins were then taken to a "place of the general interment," where they were set in order and then covered with a burial mound.

Bartram's torrent of words about the mounds contains little that was new, except for elegant description. He did, however, distinguish between the huge older mounds and the smaller structures used by the modern Indians. The large mounds would take "the united labor and attention of a whole nation, circumstances as they were, to have constructed one of them almost in an age."

Poor Bartram! Science has been unkind to him, for most of his published observations were too imprecise to be of much use to his colleagues in Europe or Philadelphia. But he achieved fame as a creative and evocative writer who described the southern countryside before the full impact of European settlement was felt and dozens of archaeological sites were razed. This pioneer of mound archaeology earned an epitaph from a loving nephew, who thought he recounted natural history "in all the fervour of a true lover of nature's works and with such innocent enthusiasm, that we cannot fail to love and venerate the author."

It was with such innocent enthusiasm that dozens of writers now wrote of the remarkable mounds that were to be seen everywhere in the western territories. Armchair writers speculated freely about the mounds in an atmosphere of puzzlement. They looked to Herodotus for parallels with ancient mounds in the Mediterranean world, convinced that the Indians could never have built earthworks on the scale of that at Grave Creek on the Ohio River or at Cahokia near the Mississippi. Perhaps Mexican Toltecs had built the mounds. Homer's warriors, several writers noted, buried their dead under great funeral tumuli. The Canaanites of biblical fame had worshipped their gods in high places. Had not the mound people come from the Old World, later being replaced by the Indians? After all, such savages could never have built the mounds. The more extravagant theories appealed to those with theological or racist axes to grind, for the vast mounds and earthworks added a touch of the archaeologically exotic to the forested environment of the New World.

A myth of a magnificent race of Mound Builders rapidly took hold in American scientific literature, a myth that overshadowed the careful observations of Thomas Jefferson and the accurate measurements of General Putnam at Marietta. It was built on the assumption that "proofs of skill and refinement" were to be found, to be explained on the "supposition that a superior race, or more probably a people of foreign and higher civilization, once occupied the soil." The very existence of this myth led to a quickened assault on the mounds themselves.

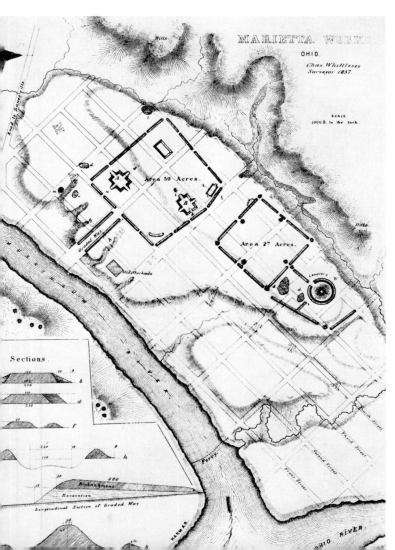

The Squier and Davis plan of the Marietta earthworks. Compare this with the original Putnam plan.

6 "Peoples of Ancient Strength and Respectability"

"Let us open the tombs of the ancient Americans. In these dark abodes, the first asylums of man on this globe, we may discover materials that will enable us to throw some light upon the ancient history of the Americans. If we are not sufficiently animated by the love of science, let us remember, that in the tombs of the Mexicans and Peruvians, the Spaniards have discovered treasures of gold, of silver, and of precious stones; and that even in the tombs in Florida, valuable pearls are said to have been found. I think, there can be little doubt that the opening of the North American tumuli will reward the labourers with valuable spoils." Benjamin Smith Barton wrote this in the *Transactions of the American Philosophical Society* in 1799. He had described the artifacts from a mound recently found at Cincinnati, where "one of the main streets of the town passes through the western part of the grave.''

This stirring cry to action was prompted by motives other than simply the hope of finding more mysterious artifacts in the mounds. Barton decried the lack of data, the dearth of information on the contents of the mounds. He regretted that he had been unable to prove that "highly civilized" nations had lived in America before Columbus, although he felt that there had been peoples "much farther advanced in civilization," peoples of "ancient strength and respectability."

There had been no rush to dig into the mounds, once it was clear that they lacked buried treasure or great caches of gold. The monuments of Egypt and the temples of Greece had attracted tourists for hundreds of years. Many visitors to classical lands had recognized the great commercial value of the fine sculptures of Athens, Egypt, and Rome and had sedulously collected them. But there were no such monuments in North America, no regular tourist attractions or flamboyant artistic traditions to assemble in one's cabinet of curiosities. It was only when antiquarian curiosity spread across the Atlantic and the settlers were confronted with large numbers of Ohio and Florida mounds that digging and destruction accelerated hand in hand with intense speculation about the peoples who had built them.

Descriptions of mounds became more commonplace in the pages of learned journals, many of them springing from the founding of new townships such as Athens, Cincinnati, Chillicothe, and other places in Ohio. The settlers simply chose as town sites the same places the Mound Builders had used for their settlements. As the townships developed and expanded, the mounds gave way to streets and houses. The process of destruction familiarized people with the contents of the earthworks, with the burials, stone tools, pottery, fine copper pieces, and other artifacts that were uncovered. Farmers plowed hundreds of earthworks into the landscape. The mounds interfered with the business of making a living in a pioneer land.

As the speculations about the mounds reached new heights, the Ten Lost Tribes of Israel emerged as the most popular attribution of ownership. Writers recalled the idolators of the kingdom of Israel as documented in II Kings, the religious splinter groups who "built their high places in all their cities." "And they set them up images and groves on every high hill," went on the chronicler. "And there they burnt incense in all the high places, as did the heathen." Divine punishment ensued, ending in Sargon of Babylon's conquest of the Israelites, who were forced to settle in Assyrian towns. At this point the ten dissident tribes vanish from history except in the minds of historical beholders. To those searching the Scriptures there was no reason why the mounds and earthworks of Ohio could not be "high places" identical with those erected by the Israelites.

Everyone assumed that the Indians living in mound country in modern times were themselves incapable of conceiving of or erecting the earthworks on their own. Even Vitus Bering's eighteenth-century discovery of the strait later named after him, which showed the proximity of North America and Asia, had not diminished speculation. The Indians might have come across from Asia, primitive and simple as they were. But this did not account for the Aztec or Inca—or the Mound Builders. As more and more earthworks were discovered and investigated, the fantasies mushroomed, mainly in the minds of eager clergymen with theological points to make and little else to occupy their inquiring intellects in a harsh and still untamed rural environment. Those who believed that the mounds were of Indian origin were in a definite minority.

The traditions of the Indians themselves had long interested missionaries working on the western frontier. People were fascinated by missionary John Heckewelder's chronicle of the Delaware. They had actually fought the Ohio mound dwellers during a migration eastward from their original homeland across the Mississippi. These "Talligew" were said to be "remarkably tall and stout, and there is a tradition that there were giants among them, people of a much larger size. . . . it is related that they had built to themselves regular fortifications or entrenchments, from whence they would sally out but were generally repulsed.''

Heckewelder himself had seen many of their ''intrenchments.'' He described fortifications by

A map of twelve miles of the Scioto Valley drawn by Squier and Davis that shows the great density of earthworks in this area of Ohio.

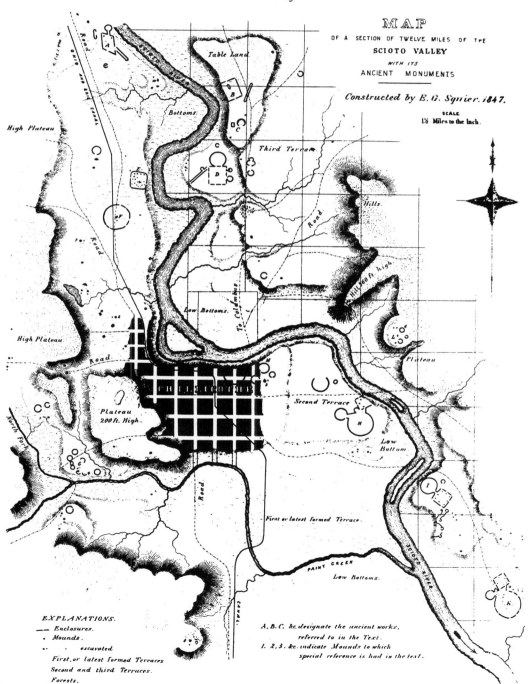

MAP
OF A SECTION OF TWELVE MILES OF THE
SCIOTO VALLEY
WITH ITS
ANCIENT MONUMENTS

Constructed by E. G. Squier. 1847.

SCALE
1½ Miles to the Inch.

EXPLANATIONS.
— — Enclosures.
• Mounds.
•• excavated
First, or latest formed Terraces
Second and third Terraces.
Forests.

A, B, C, &c. designate the ancient works, referred to in the Text.
1, 2, 3, &c. indicate Mounds to which special reference is had in the text.

Lake Erie near which were "a number of large flat mounds in which, an Indian guide said, were buried hundreds of these slain Tallegeui. . . ." Although Heckewelder's observations seemed to point clearly toward an Indian origin for the mounds, the myth makers seized on them with delight and wove their complicated networks of arrival dates, routes, and personalities around carefully selected portions of his narrative.

The new myths focused on the story of "stout and tall" people, ignoring the descriptions of Indian-occupied earthworks and the traditions of the Cherokee of Tennessee, who claimed that their direct ancestors had built Grave Creek mound and tumuli in the Ohio Valley. But even the Delaware and Cherokee did not claim that they had built all the earthworks. Many of them were constructed before the Cherokee arrived on the Ohio, a story William Bartram had verified some years before. There was a gentle touch of myth and fantasy in many of the Indian traditions. Their legends had been snowballing for generations. A few allusions to "tall people" or "white skinned warriors" could be used to perpetuate and magnify traditions out of proportion to the size and extent of the archaeological sites that they purported to explain.

These were rough and rowdy days at the frontiers of American settlement; it was a period of vicious and undeclared war with the Indians when land-hungry settlers simply killed, transported, or enslaved the indigenous tribes that stood in their way. The suppression of the Indians could be justified if it could be proved that they were not the original owners of the land they now occupied. And if they could not explain the vast earthworks, which were, in any case, beyond their limited technological abilities, then they were no more the owners of the land than the new settlers. Genocide and colonial initiative could be justified, even, perhaps, as a war of revenge. Scholarship was submerged in a morass of land grabbing, skirmishes with Indians, and back-breaking pioneer farming.

The few people who dwelled as scholars and antiquarians in the midst of the rough-and-ready settlers were almost invariably leaders of their communities. Many had been pioneer members of the American Philosophical Society, an august body whose early *Transactions* contained many essays on the mounds. Another group of antiquarians had successfully petitioned the Massachusetts legislature in 1812 for a charter to incorporate the American Antiquarian Society, the first meeting of which was held in Boston on November 19, 1812. A library was soon established, and collections for a museum were assembled. Research, especially on the Ohio mounds, became a major objective. The first volume of the society's proceedings, entitled *Archaeologia Americana*, came out in 1820. It contained the usual jumble of contributions typical of such *Transactions* in the early nineteenth century. The most important was a long essay by Caleb Atwater, "Description of the Antiquities Discovered in the State of Ohio and Other Western States." The editor of the *Transactions* felt it necessary to apologize to the society's readers for the "hurried productions of a professional man, constantly engaged in various branches of business." Atwater lived so far away from Boston—in Circleville, Ohio—that it had not been possible to send him the proof sheets of his essay. Thus certain "errors" had crept in "which have unavoidably occurred from reading letters not written in a manner the most legible."

Caleb Atwater (1778–1867), an infant when Thomas Jefferson was digging into his Virginia tumulus, lived most of his long life in the heart of mound country. In 1815 he had moved from the East to become postmaster of Circleville, Ohio, a township that had been built on the site of some Indian earthworks in 1805. A circular "fort" with earthen walls at least twenty feet high and a square enclosure occupied the site of the new township. By Atwater's time the works and ditches of these remarkable monuments were "disappearing before us daily, and will soon be gone." The postmaster started his archaeological career by studying these earthworks, the several gateways and defensive mounds of which had been razed to make way for modern buildings. "The present town of Circleville covers all round, and the western half of, the square fort," he reported. "These fortifications, where the town stands, will entirely disappear in a few years; and I have used the only means within my power, to perpetuate their memory, and the annexed drawing and this brief description." Atwater was right; nothing remains of the Circleville earthworks today.

From Circleville it was a logical step for this enthusiastic antiquarian to range widely over the Ohio Valley in search of other remarkable earthworks. He paused at Newark, Ohio, where an octagonal fort with eight openings and a forty-acre expanse inside its earth walls occupied his attention. (It is now part of the municipal golf course.) Some holes near the riverbank below the town excited Atwater's attention, holes that were the work of a gentleman who had dug "in and about these works, in quest of the precious metals; but he found nothing very precious."

While only fragments of the Newark earthworks have withstood the test of time, those at Marietta were in excellent shape in Atwater's day. "No despoiling hand has been laid upon them; and no blundering, hearty traveller has, to my knowledge, pretended to describe them. . . . Cutler, Putnam, and Harris are intelligent men," wrote Atwater approvingly, referring to the wisdom of those who had saved the tumuli from destruction. His descriptions of the mounds merely confirmed those of earlier observers. In one place the locals had dug down into a deep reservoir, normally full of water, that had silted up after clearance of the site. Twelve feet of decayed vegetation were removed before the bottom came to light. The filling yielded an interesting by-product of the excavation: "several hundred loads of excellent manure." Atwater picked up fragments of pottery, both in this hollow and outside the earthworks. "This ware is ornamented with lines, some of them quite curious and ingenious, on the outside. . . . it seems to have been burnt, and capable of holding liquids." Several pieces of copper had come

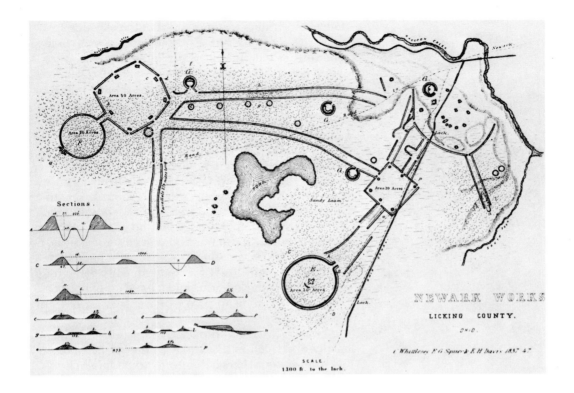

from the earthworks, too, while a "magazine of spear and arrow heads, sufficient to fill a peck measure," had been found at Waterford nearby when the roots of a pear tree were being removed from a meadow. The weapons were "laid in one body . . . as though they had been buried in a box." Clearly, there were plenty of antiquities to be found near the earthworks.

Atwater himself seems to have been more interested in monuments than the finds made in them, arguing that the builders of the Marietta ditches and mounds had had only wooden tools to assist them in their enormous task. Others were more interested in the contents of the earthworks. At Portsmouth, Ohio, a large earthwork with "high, perpendicular banks" had yielded "large quantities of iron, manufactured into pick axes, shovels, gun barrels etc.," buried by the French. Atwater noticed

Squier and Davis's plan of the Newark earthworks.

111

Crested wood-duck bowl,
ten inches by twelve inches,
carved from a single piece
of diorite. From Moundville,
Hale County, Alabama.
*Photograph courtesy of the
Museum of the American
Indian, Heye Foundation*

that "excavations made in quest of these hidden treasures, are to be seen on these walls, and in many other places near them." Signs of destruction were even more evident at Cincinnati. Daniel Drake, a member of the American Antiquarian Society, had seen four mounds there in 1815, the largest of which was still twenty-seven feet high in his day. In 1794 General Wayne had cut off about eight feet of it to level a site for a lookout post. The internal structure of the mound had been investigated in the same year, for the earthwork "has been penetrated almost to its center, and found to consist of loam. . . . the fruits of this examination were only a few scattered and decayed human bones, a branch of a deer's horn, and a piece of earthen ware containing muscle [sic] shells." Another, smaller mound nearby had been razed as the main street was graded, and "some fragments of human skeletons and a handful of copper beads which had been strung on a cord of lint" were found in the remains.

Atwater's investigations led him to classify the earthworks of Ohio into three groups: those belonging to Indians, others belonging "to people of European origin," and those "of that people who raised our ancient forts and tumuli." The "antiquities which . . . belong to the North American Indians are neither numerous nor very interesting," he wrote. "They consist of rude stone axes and knives, of pestles used in preparing maize for food, of arrowheads, and a few other articles." He was moved to comment on the degraded life of the Indian who takes "whatever the earth or water spontaneously produces, and is satisfied."

If Atwater's observations were advanced for his time, his interpretations were not. Like other writers of his day, he was convinced that the mounds were built by "people far more civilized than our Indians, but far less so than Europeans." By taking this position he excluded any thought that the higher civilizations of the Old World had built the mounds. But there was much that was special about the Mound Builders, including the ability to forge metals, something then considered to be beyond the abilities of modern Indians. Atwater himself had found some metal objects in a small mound at Circleville, "which the ruthless hand of man is destroying."

But his discoveries were eclipsed by those of his colleague Samuel Hildreth, who found "several curious articles" with a mound burial during June 1819. As a mound was being leveled a skeleton came to light "to whose memory this mound was erected. . . . lying immediately over, or on the forehead of the body, were found three large circular bosses, or ornaments for a sword belt, or a buckle; they are composed of copper, overlaid with a thick plate of silver." The burial lay under a mound ten feet high and thirty feet in diameter that was covered with large trees when Marietta was first founded. Hildreth recalled Manasseh Cutler's attempts to date the mounds with tree rings and observed that the "funeral obsequies had been celebrated by fire" and that many of the bones "crumbled to dust on exposure to the air."

The results of this excavation were so exciting that plans were made to open other mounds as well. Hildreth himself dug into several more tumuli in the Ohio Valley. Most of these contained skeletons "partially, if not entirely, consumed by fire, before the mounds were built."

Now that European agriculture was taking hold throughout the Ohio Valley, many more archaeological sites were being disturbed. Atwater was constantly hearing of new finds, like an alleged "half of a steel bow" found by a farmer near Marietta. A blacksmith "worked up this curious article, I suppose, with as little remorse as he would an old gunbarrel." Some of the "many curious articles of Antiquity" discovered by the farmers were positively mystical, like an ornament "composed of very pure gold," which was discovered near Chillicothe "lying in the palm of a skeleton's hand, in a small mound."

The worthy postmaster constantly bemoaned the ruin of mound after mound, the conversion of the fortifications in downtown Columbus into thousands of bricks, the destruction of tumuli full of "many human bones" and an "owl carved in stone, a

113

rude, but very exact representation." But there was
nothing that a lone antiquarian could do. Atwater
was indeed a solitary archaeologist in the wilderness. He sent his report to the American Antiquarian
Society with a dedicatory letter that revealed his
loneliness. "While traversing the country where
these ancient works are found," he wrote rather
pathetically, "tracing the outlines of the works; making diagram sketches of them, seated on the summit
of a lofty tumulus, which overlooked all the works
belonging to some once celebrated spot, gilded by
the rays of the setting sun—how anxiously have I
wished for the company of some one like the person
to whom these observations are addressed, so that he
might participate with me in the emotions which
filled my breast."

By the standards of his day Atwater was a pioneer
with a talent for accurate observation. His own conclusions about the Mound Builders never rivaled the
wilder excesses of those who embraced the Ten Lost
Tribes theory or combed the works of Herodotus for
accounts of ancient Mound Builders. He believed
that shepherds and farmers from India, China, and
the Crimea had built the mounds after a long journey
across the Bering Strait, which had taken place soon
after the Flood. The Mound Builders had moved on
to Mexico when they abandoned their earthworks.
Atwater compared the Ohio tumuli to the hundreds
of mounds on the banks of the Mississippi. These
were larger than the Ohio sites. "There was a population as numerous as that which once animated
the borders of the Nile, or of the Euphrates, or of
Mexico" along the river, he wrote. In an age when
most people believed in the absolute truth of the
Scriptures, Atwater was hardly out of line in his
explanations.

Those who sought to create a mythical, mound-
building civilization in the Ohio Valley took Atwater's observations and twisted them to their own
purposes. Samuel Mitchell of the University of New
York decided that vicious wars between the Tartars
and "ferocious and warlike European colonists, who
had already been intrenched and fortified in the
country between them," had raged in the Ohio

114

Valley. William Henry Harrison, whose presidency
was the briefest in U.S. history, thought that the
Mound Builders were a vanished race. The earthworks were symbols of a national religion which
brought into play "all that was pompous, gorgeous,
and imposing, that a semi-barbarous nation could
devise." The altars of those people often smoked
"with hetacombs of victims."

Less sober authors played on the public appetite
for sensation, with stirring epics of the last years of a
mighty empire destroyed and raped by barbarian
warriors. Tale after tale hit the presses, and all were
devoured by a public disposed to escapism.

One of the most popular of these works came from
the pen of Josiah Priest, a vivid writer who knew his
audience's interests well. *American Antiquities and
Discoveries in the West* appeared in 1833. Door-to-
door salesmen sold over twenty thousand copies in
two and a half years. Priest's mound dwellers were
interred in vast cemeteries, the casualties of great
revolutions and costly wars when "armies, equal to
those of Cyrus, of Alexander the Great, or of
Tamerlane the powerful, might have flourished their
trumpets, and marched to battle, over these extensive plains." The mound dwellers were "white
people of great intelligence and skill" who "perished amid the yells of their enemies," reduced
by siege and famine. This was splendid, heroic stuff
that appealed to the patriotic spirit of the times.
Hints of a glorious and faintly exotic past have always titillated the public fancy—and made money
for the titillators. The Mound Builders appealed in
the nineteenth century to the same interests and
emotions that the Ancient Astronauts and extrater-
restrial visitors arouse today.

Like the ancient Egyptians, the mound dwellers
attracted both poets and novelists. In 1839 Cornelius
Mathews's *Behemoth: A Legend of the Mound-
Builders,* an attempt to give America an epic past
fully as stirring as that of Homer's Greece, was
widely enjoyed. Mathews's mound dwellers were
threatened by a huge, mammothlike beast, Behemoth, who ravaged several settlements, defeated
whole armies, and broke through the strongest of

115

earthworks. Only when Bokulla, the heroic warrior of the hard-pressed mound dwellers, killed the huge animal by a cunning strategem did peace return to the great nation.

Poets, too, were moved to verse by the sight of the silent tumuli. The New England poet William Cullen Bryant visited mounds in Illinois in 1832, an experience that prompted him to write:

> Are they here—
> The dead of other days?—and did the dust
> of these fair solitudes once stir with life
> And burn with passion? Let the mighty mounds
> That overlook the river, or that rise
> In the dim forest crowded with old oaks
> Answer. A race, that long has passed away,
> Built them;—a disciplined and populous race
> Heaped, with long toil, the earth, while yet the Greek
> Was hewing the Pentelicus to forms
> of symmetry, and rearing on its rock
> The glittering Parthenon.

Bryant was obsessed with death, with the thousands of long-deceased warriors who lay beneath American soil. Others followed this artistic lead and cashed in on the lucrative "lost civilizations" market. The notion of an exotic American past seemed irresistible. By 1840 the great myth of the mound dwellers was at its height, not to be laid to academic rest until this century. Religion, casual and more serious archaeological observation, public attitudes, and the need for an escape from the real world had all conspired to perpetuate the myth in a world far more theologically minded and naïve than our own.

The myth of the mound dwellers left us one legacy that began in the outpourings of literature of Caleb Atwater's time. In about 1809 the Reverend Solomon Spaulding composed a long and incomplete story, allegedly a translation of twenty-eight parchments found in an "artificial case covered by large flat stones atop a mound near Conneaut, Ohio." The devout author of *Manuscript Found*, which did not appear in print until 1885, described how a group of Christian Romans were blown off course in the Atlantic and cast up in the New World. Their colony was forced to move westward into new territory, where they found the Mound Builders living in vast cities with highly civilized institutions. The remainder of Spaulding's manuscript was a description of this remarkable civilization; it ends with the convenient demise of the harmonious society in civil war.

Spaulding's work can at best be described as a poor literary effort. It circulated widely in manuscript form and might now have been long forgotten were it not for the alleged similarities between *Manuscript Found* and the Book of Mormon, compiled by Joseph Smith and Oliver Cowdery in 1830. Smith had written the Book of Mormon from a set of "golden plates" that had been lent to him by a messenger of God named Moroni. The Church of Jesus Christ of Latter-Day Saints originated in Smith's revelations and the epic teachings of the book.

According to the Book of Mormon, a group of settlers came to America during the confusion resulting from the destruction of the Tower of Babel. Their great American cities flourished until a terrible civil war reduced all their settlements to "heaps of earth upon the face of the land." A second migration of Israelites around 600 B.C. repeated the process, and a second fraternal war culminated in a last desperate battle. Then the colonists divided into two factions, one of which, the Lamanites, were evil, savage, and of reddish skin color as a result of divine wrath. The Lamanites eventually destroyed their richer neighbors' cities, but not before the prophet Mormon described the history of his nation on golden plates—the very ones found by Joseph Smith centuries later.

Mormons gave the Book of Mormon a spiritual status equivalent to that of the Scriptures, accepting the essential truth of the story of the mound dwellers perpetuated by the golden plates. Since its very beginnings the Mormon faith has been surrounded by controversy, not the least of it over the sources from which the Book was compiled. Was Joseph Smith merely a simple farmer whose obsession became a religious faith generated from reading about a popular myth of ancient mound dwellers? Was the Book of Mormon plagiarized from Solomon Spaulding's work and other such accounts? Or did the founder of the Mormon faith really receive divine revelation? Like all such controversies, the answer is a matter of personal belief and simple faith. Whatever one's views on the theological controversies, the existence of the victims of these great wars, "frequently amounting to tens of thousands," was verified by the hundreds of recorded instances of skeletons coming to light as mounds were excavated by treasure hunters or razed by the plow.

Caleb Atwater himself is remembered as an enthusiastic antiquarian and devoted public servant. Today his pioneer observations of mounds and earthworks are rarely studied, but they are important as a prophetic commentary on the destruction of the American past. His concerns were mirrored by a contemporary, the Reverend Doddridge of Brooke County, Virginia. Doddridge wrote to Atwater on May 27, 1819, answering the postmaster's queries about the Grave Creek mounds near Wheeling, then in Virginia. He wrote of the "Big Grave" that it was one of the "most august monuments of remote Antiquity any where to be found." The "lofty and venerable tumulus" had been opened on a small scale and found to contain "many thousands of human skeletons." Fortunately, Joseph Tomlinson, the owner of the site, had forbidden any further excavation. "I, for one," wrote Doddridge, "do him honor for his sacred regard for these works of Antiquity. I wish that the inhabitants of Chillicothe and Circleville had acted like Tomlinson. In that case, the mounds in these towns would have been left standing. They would have been religiously protected, as sacred relicks of a remote and unknown Antiquity."

Perhaps Atwater and Doddridge realized the futility of their hopes. Few people are interested in preserving archaeological sites of alien societies, especially if they contain no treasure or valuable statuary. Today it is estimated that fewer than 25 percent of the river valley sites in the Midwest have not been at least partially destroyed.

118

7 "The Taste of These Ancient People for Monumental Splendor"

The veil of obscurity that had covered the archaeological sites of Mexico and the rest of Mesoamerica for several centuries remained firmly in place during the decades when the myth of the Mound Builders was gaining hold in the American mind. Dense rain forest had again hidden the ruins of Palenque as Antonio del Río's abortive report lay ignored. Then in 1804 Charles IV of Spain commissioned the Frenchman Guillermo Dupaix to examine the prehispanic ruins of Mexico.

Dupaix traveled widely in Mesoamerica, accompanied by an artist who sketched Palenque and recorded carved stones and other artifacts found in villages and towns along the way. He made some casual excavations and found a few potsherds and human bones, which he threw away in disgust. At

119

Cholula, Mitla, and Palenque he marveled at the architectural and artistic achievements of the pre-Spanish inhabitants. He found Palenque overwhelming, especially the "erect and well proportioned" figures whose "attitudes display great freedom of limb, with a certain expression of dignity." But the journey to Palenque had been difficult and arduous. Dupaix was waylaid by Indians and drenched in floods, and he had marched for miles through practically impenetrable forest. Indians "of extraordinary strength and agility" carried his baggage. "Loaded with a weight of two hundred and fifty pounds, enough for the back of a mule, they proceeded on with unslackened pace, and climbed like deer the passes of the mountains."

Dupaix's reports were filed away in Mexico City in 1808 and ignored by the bureaucracy, although copies were published in Europe by the eccentric Lord Kingsborough in his vast *Antiquities of Mexico*—losing much in the translation. The account of the discoveries was read by a handful of European scholars interested in American antiquities and then quietly forgotten.

So were the discoveries of John Galindo, a political operator turned archaeologist who visited

Dupaix's artist drew this schematic rendition of the Palace and Tower at Palenque. It was later published in Lord Kingsborough's *Antiquities of Mexico*.

120

Palenque and Copan in 1831 and 1834. Galindo, Irish by birth, Guatemalan by naturalization, was ruthlessly ambitious. He arrived in Central America in 1827 and was employed as secretary to the British consul in Guatemala. Within a few years, after a successful political alliance with the liberal army of General Morazan, Galindo was appointed governor of the Peten, a post that enabled him to explore the interior and to visit Palenque.

Galindo was filled with a desire for academic glory, and he wrote reports describing Palenque's architecture. He noted resemblances between the human figures on the structures at Palenque and the modern Indians, proclaiming that ancient Maya civilization was the most advanced prehispanic culture in the Americas, a civilization that saved "ancient America from the reproach of barbarism." Three years later Galindo was appointed a member of a three-man commission set up to examine prehispanic ruins at first hand. This was his chance to visit Copan in Honduras, the magnificent Maya ceremonial center that had been abandoned only recently, when the Spaniards arrived. The great retaining wall along the river excited his imagination. Inside lay plazas and pyramids adorned with stelae, altars, and grotesque human figures. In a small room in the wall he dug into the floor and discovered that it was a burial chamber filled with pottery, human bones, a miniature jade head, and a host of other small objects. Galindo's report described the finds, but it languished in government files until long after his death. Two short descriptions of Copan appeared under his name in the *Literary Gazette* of London and in a letter to the American Antiquarian Society, but these accounts did not do justice to the site. Even a copy of his full report sent to the Geographical Society of Paris never appeared in print, despite its higher quality.

Galindo failed totally in his efforts to interest people in the ancient Maya. When he sent four stucco hieroglyphs from Palenque, along with a vase and some small heads from Yaxha, to the Royal Society of London, his covering letter and illustrations

A drawing of a stucco plaque from Palenque executed by the artist on the Dupaix expedition. The rendition was subsequently published in Lord Kingsborough's monumental *Antiquities of Mexico* (1831–48).

121

Jean Frédéric Waldeck.
From Julian Winsor (ed.),
*Narrative and Critical History
of America* (1889).

of his gifts were published without editorial comment or commendation. The trouble was that Galindo was an opportunist and publicist. His descriptions of Copan were overlain with extravagant theories about human history that hailed the Peten as the center of early civilization. His motives were grandiose and entirely nationalistic. He envisaged a vast and glorious past for the new, modern nations of Central America. Predictably, such extravagant claims received no scientific attention whatsoever, let alone popular acclaim.

The history of Mesoamerican archaeology is full of strange and appealing characters, not least among them Jean Frédéric Waldeck, artist, socialite, and archaeologist. His early life is shrouded in mystery, for he invented various biographies for himself claiming Paris, Prague, or Vienna as his birthplace. He assumed the title of count or duke and hinted at a varied career as an explorer and artist, having trained under the famous French artist Jacques Louis David. Waldeck always said that during the Napoleonic wars, he had served in Italy and Egypt. There he worked with Geoffrey Saint-Hilary and Edmé François Jomard, both members of Napoleon's celebrated team of savants who did so much to bring ancient Egypt to the attention of the outside world.

After the wars Waldeck traveled widely, making his living as an artist, illustrating Antonio del Río's report on Palenque for its London publisher in 1822. Three years later he was employed in an English-operated mine at Tlalpujahua in Mexico, a job that he held for less than a year. Waldeck was apparently more interested in local customs and sketching the scenery than in mining. It is from this point that details of Waldeck's life are on a firm basis; his adventures as an explorer and as a soldier of Napoleon may be a complete fabrication, tales embroidered in the telling by a man with a definite artistic temperament.

In 1826 Waldeck made his way from the mine settlement to Mexico City, which was destined to be his home for the next six years. There he set himself up as a free-lance artist, undertaking all kinds of com-

122

missions, from portraits to classical house decoration. Occasionally he taught a few students, living from commission to commission, pupil to pupil. He was supporting himself and a wife and child in London, but whenever he had any spare money he purchased prehispanic antiquities for his small collection. Once or twice he was reduced to selling duplicates from his collections so he could buy a meal, but this was very much a last resort, as he valued his collection above everything else.

Jean Frédéric Waldeck
being carried over the Chiapas.
A painting by the
artist, 1870.
*Robert Isaacson Collection,
New York*

Waldeck had now developed a passion for Mexican archaeology which he cultivated sedulously, maintaining regular contacts with other collectors, traveling to visit nearby ruins, and working with friends at the National Museum. There he set to work to draw artifacts and statuary in the national collections with gratifying results. The museum agreed to publish some of his work and produced a short leaflet of his drawings. Then the project ran out of money and Waldeck was back where he had started. But the artist's antiquarian contacts eventually bore fruit. He was able to obtain official support for a privately financed expedition to study Palenque and other ruins in Yucatan at first hand. It was an ambitious scheme, floated as a fund-raising project with a goal of $10,000 (Mexican) and a major book in mind. The Geographical Society of Paris had recently offered a $250 prize for the best study of Palenque. Waldeck obviously had his eye on this prestigious trophy.

Money for the Palenque project was slow to come in, but Waldeck was undeterred. He set off in March 1832 with only about a third of his financing in hand. The artist settled for a long stay in a small village near Palenque. Later he actually lived at the site, making a leisurely examination of its many structures. He cleared a road to the site and settled down to work under rather difficult circumstances. The government had led him to believe that he could employ Indian laborers without charge as an official emissary from Mexico City, but the locals soon disabused him. He not only had to pay wages, but he had to pay them in advance. The Indians did not turn up unless they felt like it, his domestic servants deserted him frequently, and the steady tropical downpour hampered work outdoors. Day after day Waldeck struggled with his art work, harassed by insects, rain, and the humidity of the rain forest that pressed in on Palenque from all sides. Despite these difficulties he drew over ninety pictures of the ruins and its artistic wonders.

Waldeck soon found that he was not the only visitor or archaeologist wanting to study or exploit the

124

site. He found that many of the stucco figures had been disfigured and many loose pieces of statuary carried away. Nothing portable remained. Decorated stones from Palenque adorned the walls of the locals' houses. Worse than that, there was even some illegal exporting in progress. Waldeck was horrified to find that the famous "Tablet of the Cross" was in pieces, part of it lying on the ground. A local entrepreneur was in the process of exporting this unique art piece to the United States. Waldeck complained furiously to government officials—and the tablet stayed at home.

Waldeck's laborious weeks at Palenque were lonely ones, relieved only by occasional visitors, notably a French doctor named Francis Corroy, who had some antiquarian tastes. Soon the two men quarreled, however, because Waldeck heard that his visitor planned a two-volume work on Palenque that threatened to compete with his own project. The Frenchman's book came to nothing, for Harper's, the New York publisher, rejected it on the grounds of expense. Furious, Waldeck denounced the Frenchman as a plagiarist and busied himself with the completion of his work at Palenque. Waldeck was fully aware that the stakes were high. Whoever

Waldeck published this view of his living quarters at the foot of the Temple of the Cross at Palenque in 1833.

would reveal the real glories and fascination of the prehispanic ruins of Mesoamerica to the wider public and the scientific world of Europe and North America would not only achieve overnight fame and scientific recognition, but would also make a fortune.

As Waldeck explored the pyramids and temples of Palenque, he fantasized about fame and fortune, about the success that would raise him from his grinding poverty. He cleaned up obscured stuccos, traced giant human figures at the Palace, and discovered fine carved heads which he claimed were those of elephants. The same heads were to be seen in the hieroglyphs and were soon the object of controversy. Some claimed them to be the heads of tapirs; later they were identified as the masks of rain gods. But Waldeck's claim that he had found elephants sat well with those who felt that Yucatan temples were built by migrants from over the sea. Waldeck's elephants have reasserted themselves whenever scholars or mystics have attempted to attribute the Yucatan sites to peoples from across the Atlantic and will, no doubt, remain a permanent part of the lunatic fringe of archaeology.

Waldeck himself spent many hours studying the fine masonry at Palenque, the delicate moldings, and two fine pyramids somewhat like the truncated versions so common in Mesoamerica. These, naturally, Waldeck claimed to be of Egyptian origin. But the sculptures were so exotic that he considered them to be of "a quite different character from all that had hitherto been known." The origins of Palenque puzzled him, with its amalgam of "elephants," pyramids, and other strange features. He concluded that the people who built Palenque were "formed by a mixture of various nations of the old continent; to all appearance the Chaldeans were the original stock, and the main body consisted of Hindoos."

Plagued by chronic money shortages, for his subscription sources dried up, Waldeck's spirits reached a low ebb. Cholera epidemics were reported in nearby villages. Boils covered his legs. His highly placed political friends in Mexico City were no

126

longer in power, and his only assets were a one-room hut at Palenque and his drawings of the ruins. In despair Waldeck left Palenque and pushed on toward Yucatan. Cholera epidemics and revolution in Tabasco held him up, in fear for his life. Meanwhile he bombarded Lord Kingsborough, a wealthy and eccentric Irish peer and Maya enthusiast, with proposals for research at Palenque and elsewhere. But no replies came. Waldeck was again forced to freelance as a portrait painter to make ends meet. From May to August 1834 he sat at Campeche in despair, turning out dozens of inferior portraits, waiting for a letter from Ireland. Then Kingsborough sent him enough funds to carry on with his travels, including a sum to pay for his son's school fees in Europe.

Once the rains had abated, Waldeck headed toward Uxmal, a ceremonial center little known in the outside world. There he spent many days drawing and recording the intricate details of the ornamentation on the pyramids and the Nunnery, an elaborate structure so named by early Spanish visitors. Later he made wild claims to the effect that he had spent forty days copying one intricate frieze of

Waldeck's version of a motif in the courtyard of the Nunnery at Uxmal. This illustration appears in his *Voyage pittoresque.*

127

This figure, alleged by Waldeck to be one of four at the entrance to the Temple on the Pyramid of the Dwarf at Uxmal, has eluded later investigators. Illustration from his *Voyage pittoresque.*

serpents in the Nunnery. Even more remarkable is a magnificent sketch Waldeck made of the facade of the Pyramid of the Dwarf, a drawing of four giant figures, clothed only above the waist. The giants had been discovered lying on the ground in fragments, explained the artist, but he had been able to piece one of them together for his sketch. No one has ever found even a trace of the figures, which Waldeck claimed to have reconstructed and buried to protect them from corrupt Mexican government officials.

Waldeck's concerns at the activities of government officials were apparently well justified. His prolonged stay at Uxmal had raised the suspicions of those in authority, and he was known to be friendly with well-placed members of the previous administration. Soon a "government order to seize my papers and sketches" was served on him by the *alcalde* (local mayor). Waldeck had just returned from a side trip to Chichen Itza and had made arrangements for the transcription of his notes and manuscripts. Fortunately, the originals had been dispatched to a British government official. The Mexican authorities made off with only the duplicates. The governor of Yucatan was rightly concerned lest Waldeck export artifacts from his investigations. A search of his possessions yielded nothing, and Waldeck was able to walk off with a fine jade idol safely in his keep. It was the only antiquity he had brought with him.

Quite clearly, Waldeck was now persona non grata in Mexico, and he decided to leave. An official newspaper story accused him of vandalizing Palenque and of discourteous behavior. His diaries show that the artist had a low opinion of Mexicans, their lifestyle, and government officials. Perhaps he opened his mouth too much; we do not know. But late in 1836 he left Mexico forever, went to London to collect his papers and his family, and then crossed to Paris, where he published *Voyage pittoresque et archéologique dans la Province d'Yucatan et aux Ruines d'Itzalane* two years later. This short book of only a hundred pages contains twenty-one of Waldeck's drawings, many of them of Mexican costumes.

The book was designed to cater to the popular market, and it tells us little of the Maya or their archaeological sites. Waldeck titillated rather than informed, aiming at the armchair traveler rather than the scholar. One has the suspicion that money rather than academic glory was the goal. His account of Uxmal is a good example of his rather "picturesque" style. "Prior to my expedition," he wrote, "the ruins of Uxmal had been visited only by the owners of the neighbouring farm, worthy people for whom a shattered city is not more than a quarry for building materials; but these ruins . . . are the remains of a powerful city, comparable in size with our greatest European capitals." This tantalizing introduction is deliberately pitched to excite a sense of discovery. Solon-like, the experienced author leads his readers to a unique and sensational discovery. Waldeck was trying the art of vicarious enjoyment. He continued: "The structures at Palenque are, with the exception of the palace, on a small scale; those at Uxmal are of colossal dimensions, and are all constructed of dressed stone. Four great principal buildings, separated by open spaces, enclose an area of 57,672 square feet. . . . The teocalli is set on a pyramid; its principal staircase has 100 steps. . . . Asian influence can easily be discerned in the architecture of these monuments. The symbol of an elephant occurs on the rounded corners of the buildings, the trunk uplifted on the East side, and lowered on the West. . . . It is chiefly in the ornaments that we can admire the patience of the craftsmen employed on these buildings, and perceive the taste of these ancient people for monumental splendor." He claimed that the Maya marked the doorways of their buildings to measure the passage of time. It was the Maya, he added, "who passed on to the Toltecs and Aztecs their civilization and part of their future."

Waldeck drew his readers' attention to the carefully assembled masonry at Uxmal, with even, tiny stones "shaped with enormous care, and the whole . . . assemblage as perfectly fitted as a joiner's." His finely executed plates, drawn with a fineness and accuracy of line that is ample tribute to his artistic skill, added to the impression of perfection. He

129

stressed the extraordinary achievements of the ancient Maya, castigating the Spaniards for fostering the belief that the Indians were savages. It was not the fault of the Indians, argued Waldeck. "If they do not know how to appreciate the splendor and beauty of the ruins which bestrew their country's soil," he wrote, "it is because they themselves sleep in the profoundest ignorance."

Like antiquarians in Mesopotamia and Egypt, Waldeck found the local inhabitants, whether Indian or Spanish, living in close association with vast and mysterious ruins which they regarded only as quarries for building stone. As time wore on, too, the contents were collected and smuggled out of Yucatan for sale, often with the connivance of government officials. In North America mysterious earthworks and mounds had attracted all sorts of wild speculations. Those who tilled Indian lands searched consciously, or unconsciously, for justification of their land grabbing and thinly disguised genocide. But the Spaniards had been in Mexico so long that much of the fabric of Maya life had vanished centuries before. Religious dogma and missionary objectives had long before provided ample reasons for seizing gold and taking over Indian land. Earlier societies were considered ancient, worthless, irrelevant, and pagan anyway.

Only a few Spanish intellectuals had more than a passing interest in the ruins of Yucatan. A tiny minority of European scholars were even peripherally interested in the prehistory of the Americas. The New World was still frontier country, far from the comfortable cultural centers of Europe. In any case, antiquarians were much more excited by archaeological discoveries nearer home. Napoleon's expedition to Egypt had resulted in enormous antiquarian endeavors. The magnificent twenty-three-volume *Description de l'Egypte* had laid out the glories of ancient Egypt for the public for the first time. The museum directors and private collectors of Europe were hot on the trail of Egyptian antiquities, eager to be a part of the frenzied action that had sent hundreds of tourists and collectors to the Nile

130

Valley. Long-lost Mesopotamian cities were the subject of new interest. Biblical archaeology excited
others, partly as a result of Egyptian discoveries.
America and its ruins seemed to be, and were,
another world.

Waldeck's book was not a commercial or scholarly
success. In fact, it laid a polite academic egg and was
ignored by the reviewers. The French government
refused to buy the remainder of Waldeck's drawings.
It was not until 1860, when Napoleon III was officially encouraging the study of Mexican antiquities, that Waldeck sold 188 of his remaining drawings to officialdom. By this time he was a very old
man, so the bureaucracy gave him a small annuity
instead of a lump sum. Waldeck was furious and decided to live as long as he could in revenge. In this
plan he succeeded admirably—by all accounts one
of the few schemes in his life that came to fruition.
The remainder of his long life was spent in a comfortable Paris world, where he lived simply in
Montmartre, keeping open house, and enjoying a
wide circle of friends. He became a minor geriatric
legend. For years he had been a corresponding
member of the Massachusetts Historical Society.
When Waldeck stopped writing, the society
dropped him from its rolls, assuming he was dead,
but hastily restored him in 1869 when they discovered he was still alive. Jean Frédéric enjoyed being a minor, if poverty-stricken, celebrity. "I have
passed the age when man dies," he is reported to
have remarked. "Now there is no reason that my life
should end. My archaeological studies make me
believe that I have reached a state of petrification
which can endure for centuries." And endure he did,
until 1875, when he died suddenly at the alleged age
of 109. Legend has it that he suffered a stroke in a
sidewalk café after turning to look at a beautiful girl.
Waldeck's second wife gave a more prosaic account
of his demise: it was the result of a fall after a party.

Jean Frédéric Waldeck was a skillful artist. A
passion for perfection led him to Maya architecture
in a way that took him far beyond the actual monuments into a world of fantasy and legend. It is as an

artist and a minor character that Waldeck is remembered, not as a discoverer of the Maya ruins.

Archaeology as a profession or a science did not exist in the 1830s. The archaeologist of the time was either a wealthy collector or an amateur scholar who combined his antiquarian interests with a career or a life of leisure. Public respect and attention was focused on the professional travelers and the explorer-journalists. Their vivid writings sold by the thousands, bought by armchair travelers with a taste for the exciting and the exotic. The prosaic life of the merchant and tradesman produced a longing for escape, for journeys into lands of hostile natives, wild beasts, and arduous safaris. Archaeological sites and exotic antiquities were very much a part of this scenario.

An obscure artist of marginal literary abilities had no chance to compete in this fast-moving world. The steamy Central American rain forest had not yet attracted a professional explorer who could write movingly and excitingly about the strange temples and obscure Indians in their midst. Waldeck and his predecessors had set in position a few stage props that had sparked off considerable academic speculation in Europe and New York. The moment for scientific exploration and precise artistic and literary description was clearly at hand.

Two scientific expeditions were mounted to unravel the mysteries of the strange temples in the rain forest. One, organized with semiofficial backing from the United States government, was to become famous through the writings and artistic efforts of Frederick Catherwood and John Lloyd Stephens. The other, a local effort organized in Honduras, was soon overshadowed by the publicity accorded the American explorers. But to two obscure travelers, Lieutenant John Caddy, Royal Artillery, and Patrick Walker, a civil servant, goes the credit for producing the first really scientific and elegant account of Palenque, one that was forgotten until its rediscovery a few years ago.

Caddy was an artist of no mean ability; his companion, the leader of the expedition, a rising young administrator. The plan for the expedition stemmed from good old-fashioned national rivalry. When Catherwood and Stephens arrived at Belize in 1839, on their way to visit Copan and other sites in the forests of the interior, they stayed with the British resident, Colonel Alexander MacDonald. By all accounts Mac-Donald was a firebrand who was not about to let the Americans steal British thunder. Rumors about mysterious ruins in the interior had circulated in Belize for years, but no one had bothered to check them out. As soon as Stephens and Catherwood were on their way, MacDonald ordered his two subordinates to travel to the rumored temples near Santo Domingo de Palenque. While the British could never hope to rival the elaborate preparations of the Americans, it was easy enough for them to visit Palenque without incurring vast expenses. The Americans were informed of the MacDonald plan but do not seem to have worried about it, although for a while Stephens feared that the presence of the British would result in his exclusion from the site.

An informal race developed between the Americans and the Caddy-Walker expedition in the eyes of the Belize press. After hasty preparations the small party of twenty-eight civilians, soldiers, and bearers set out for Palenque on November 13, 1839. They traveled by boat for the first stage of the journey, following well-established cattle and logging routes. After several days they transferred to muleback, acquiring troublesome beasts who "kicked our portmanteaus into the air several times with every mark of disrespect." The rainy season was in full swing as the party, tormented by mosquitoes, struggled forward through villainous swamps and dense forest. Caddy used his rifles freely to supply meat for the pot and even quietly bagged an emaciated cow he found drinking at a creek. The commandante of Peten, mounted on a fine horse and accompanied by a ragged bodyguard, greeted the group in some style near Flores. This proved to be a pleasant settlement where they paused to spend Christmas, attend dances, and buy provisions. Caddy reported that the Peteneros were "decidedly idle, to a degree that is nearly incredible." He remarked on the lack of roads, an impression reinforced by the first ten days of traveling after leaving Flores. Steep hills and forested valleys impeded progress. Mud, snakes, perennial rainfall, and dampness made life almost unbearable. At a brief stop at Tenosique on the Usumasinta River the local priest got up a dance and disgraced himself by swearing in broken English. It was not until January 28 that the explorers rode into Santo Domingo de Palenque. Taking over the small store as lodgings, Walker was fortunate enough to be able to engage as a guide a colorful Mexican army officer on half pay who had also worked for Waldeck. Don Juan subsequently guided Catherwood and Stephens as well, so he assisted all three major expeditions to Palenque in the early nineteenth century. Three days later Caddy and Walker finally reached Palenque, to find no sign of the Americans. They were the first to arrive.

For two weeks Caddy and Walker stayed among the ruins, Caddy sketching hard and compiling a simple description of the mysterious structures. They spread their tarpaulins in the Palace, in agony from the mosquitoes. Palenque was masked in dense forest and could be reached only by a much obstructed path. Conditions for scientific observation were appalling. "One requires to tread with some circumspection," wrote Walker in his official report, "else a false step may entail some disastrous consequences on the frail anatomy of his person."

"The ruins which have best withstood the ravages of time are situated on the summits of mounts of considerable height," Walker reported. He climbed several pyramids and found thick-walled temples elaborately decorated with "splendid exterior ornature." Caddy wrote a description of the principal structures and sketched a remarkably precise layout of the Palace which survives among his papers. He described the exotic figures on the temple walls and "large tablets of Hieroglyphics let into the walls." But both men were rather disappointed; local rumors and Catherwood and Stephens's stories in Belize had led them to expect elaborate temples as magnificent

134

as the enormous structures of classical Greece and Rome. But they were still deeply impressed, racking their brains for analogies in the Old World from which the strange temples and their adornments might derive. "Here had once existed a people, great, powerful, and perfected in art, the grand test of advancement in civilization," wrote Walker. He went on to conclude that the "rigidly constructed" buildings had the "despotic character" of Egyptian architecture and that Palenque was of "Egypto-Indian origin." The temples and pyramids were, the two men thought, used for habitations and burial places. As they gazed on the complicated jumble of buildings, temples, and pyramids, they conjured a vision of Palenque's inhabitants, "a people, great, powerful, and perfected in art, the grand test of advancement in civilization." Caddy attempted to document the Palace and details of the ruined structures with dozens of sketches. Unfortunately, only a few of these have survived.

Time was now running short. Walker was anxious to return to Belize via the Gulf coast. A journey around the coast of Yucatan would give Walker a chance to spy out the diplomatic territory at a time of considerable political unrest. So the carriers and the interpreter were dispatched back to Belize overland, while Caddy and Walker traveled light by a longer route. The carriers transported a small collection of antiquities from Palenque that came from abortive excavations in the floor of the Palace. After brief stops in Ciudad del Carmen, Campeche, and Merida the two travelers returned to Belize on April 6, 1840.

Walker immediately sat down to write an official report of the expedition. The result was a tedious, bureaucratic account of a long journey through little-known country that reads at times like a statistical report. Palenque was supposed to be the highlight of the expedition. In fact, Walker's report was sketchy and almost cursory, confined to some general observations and a few conclusions about the exotic origins of the ruins. Colonel MacDonald forwarded the report to London in the fall of 1840, accompanied by a small portfolio of Caddy's drawings. The

135

colonial secretary, Lord Russell, replied in February 1841 that he had read the report with interest and forwarded it to the Royal Geographical Society. "The drawings are very curious & interesting & I give Mr. Walker and Lt. Caddy great credit for the zeal & spirits of enterprise which they have evinced," he added. In the next sentence he cautioned the two men against irresponsible publication of their journey.

And there the matter lay. The Royal Geographical Society showed little apparent interest in Caddy's drawings. The Treasury engaged in a faintly indignant and sporadic correspondence about the unauthorized expenditure of government funds on the expedition. The correspondence ended with a minor bureaucrat complaining that the expedition, mounted for reasons of national prestige, "was not very wise, and the result is that we have been beaten by these new rivals in scientific research, who will now boast over our inferiority instead of having to boast only over our comparative inactivity. . . . In short the whole affair has been a blunder, though a very well meant one."

By this time, in any case, it was too late. Catherwood and Stephens had arrived at Palenque only four months after the two Englishmen. Stephens was not one to let the journalistic grass grow under his feet. His *Incidents of Travel in Central America*, describing Palenque and other ruins, appeared in New York in 1841 and received instant acclaim. No one was now interested in the report of two obscure English travelers, even if Caddy's drawings were of a quality that at times rivaled the artistry of Frederick Catherwood.

The Walker-Caddy expedition was soon forgotten; indeed, the British government quietly buried it. In 1842 the Society of Antiquaries was entertained with an exhibit of "a Series of interesting Drawings of ancient Sculpture, etc., from the Palace, Temple, or Pyramid at Palenque in Yucatan. . . . Having the appearance of great accuracy, and varying as they do from others published by Lord Kingsborough and Mons. Waldeck, they are entitled to particular atten-

136

tion to the English antiquary." The Minute Book of
the society says no more. John Caddy seems to have
given up his attempts to publish his drawings. They
were scattered and forgotten for almost a century.
Within a few short years Catherwood and Stephens
had achieved archaeological immortality. Their
British rivals and their disappointing report were
relegated to a footnote in the history of Maya archaeology. Caddy resumed his military career and
retired early to become a respected artist in Canada;
Walker drowned during a border dispute between
Nicaragua and Britain over the Mosquito Nation.
The inexorable current of events had overtaken the
Maya ruins, producing in John Lloyd Stephens and
Frederick Catherwood the catalysts that would bring
a great indigenous American civilization onto the
world stage.

8 "A Man of Good Sense and Sound Feeling"

John Lloyd Stephens was born in Shrewsbury, New Jersey, on November 28, 1805, the son of a wealthy New York merchant. He entered Columbia College at the age of thirteen, where during four impressionable years he received a traditional classical education tempered by an awareness of Goethe, Schiller, and other intellectuals, as well as the American and English poets of the day. Stephens emerged from Columbia as a humanist in outlook imbued with an endless curiosity about the world around him. It was this curiosity that was to be a major factor in his active and adventure-filled life.

Stephens decided to become a lawyer and enrolled in Tapping Reeves's Law School in Litchfield, Connecticut. It was a distinguished institution; over a fifty-year period beginning in 1782 Tapping Reeves and his successor, James Gould, graduated a succession of eminent lawyers, including three vice-presidents, two Supreme Court justices, and ten governors. John Stephens seems to have enjoyed his legal training, a thorough one based on, we are told by the school's catalog, "every ancient and modern opinion, whether overruled, doubted, or in any way qualified." In September 1824 he graduated and returned to New York, without, however, making any immediate move to be sworn in as a counselor at law in Albany, the first act of most Tapping Reeves graduates. Instead, he announced to his astonished family that he was going to take a long journey out west, as far as Illinois, where the Stephens family had a distant relative. The family seems to have had no strong objections. Stephens and his cousin John Hendrickson were soon on their way, armed with new boots and a brace of brass pistols each.

At the time when the two headed westward to Pittsburgh and beyond, excitement about the distant frontier was at fever pitch. Travelers' tales spoke of wide-open plains, small log cabins, buffalo, and Indian braves—the stuff of which the Wild West was made. And thousands of people were crowding west of the Alleghenies to settle on the distant frontier, to escape debts or family ties, or simply out of a sense of adventure. It was a world of covered wagons, family Bibles, and transient religious sects, of itinerant merchants and constant movement as the frontiers of civilization expanded to the Mississippi and beyond.

Young Stephens's wanderlust was deeply stirred by this new world, which was a far cry from the comfortable routine of the family business; John Stephens was never again the same. He reveled in the journey from dirty Pittsburgh to Cincinnati, where he and Hendrickson visited a female cousin before going by steamer to Louisville, right on the edge of the wild frontier. So far their travels had been comfortable enough, although they complained that traveling "takes the money out of your pocket very fast." The journey to Illinois was long and tedious; the last stage to their Uncle Caleb Ridge-

John Lloyd Stephens.
The frontispiece of
*Incidents of Travel in
Central America.*

139

way's place at Carmi took them through almost deserted country.

In November 1824 Carmi was only a tiny settlement where Stephens's uncle maintained a farm and ran a small school. John Stephens soon tired of his relatives. After only a few days his wanderlust took him to Saint Louis on the way to New Orleans. The cross-country journey to the Mississippi gave Stephens a taste of wilder travel, for the two men were forced to camp by the roadside in deserted country, lighting campfires with pistol flints. Stephens was so attracted to rough living that he was reluctant to return to New York and civilization. He could easily have joined a wagon train going farther west, given the chance. But his cousin was homesick, and Stephens had promised to see him back safely. The steamer trips from Saint Louis to New Orleans and home were uneventful and brought the travelers back to New York in February 1825. John Stephens returned with a fine set of reddish whiskers, a liking for cheroots, and an incurable taste for adventure.

An immediate problem was to make a living, so Stephens finally gained admittance to the New York Bar. He put out his shingle in Wall Street and became deeply involved in the family business. A convincing and articulate speaker, the young lawyer was soon actively campaigning for Andrew Jackson's 1828 presidential bid. Stephens felt a great sympathy for the rough and tumble of the political arena and enjoyed his growing reputation as an articulate and sometimes inflammatory public speaker. Electoral riots in which "respectable persons were beaten and trampled in the mud" kept the mayor of New York and a troop of horses busy— riots in which Stephens probably had a hand. Stephens himself was obliged to retire from the hectic mayoral campaign of 1834 when an infected throat induced by excessive public speaking laid him low. The infection persisted, and the concerned family doctor recommended a leisurely trip to Europe. Nothing loath, Stephens took a ship to France on the second of his remarkable journeys.

Never particularly enthusiastic about the law, John Stephens never practiced it again.

Europe after the Napoleonic wars had become a fashionable overseas vacation area for wealthy Americans. Paris was crowded with a sizable permanent American colony. Rome was a favorite mecca of the American abroad, too. Both cities were on Stephens's itinerary, and he passed rapidly through the major tourist experiences, visiting Paestum and even climbing Vesuvius. The invalid was reinvigorated by travel that took him from Naples to Greece and then on to Constantinople. Stephens seems to have traveled on impulse, wandering all over war-ravaged Greece, which was then slowly recovering from the trauma of civil war. He was in his element, traveling light and accompanied by only a mustachioed Greek servant. Everywhere Stephens went he saw evidence of the destruction of war, of struggles for political liberty that had excited the imaginations of Americans a decade before.

The experience of seeing Lord Byron's death place at Missolonghi, the disabled veterans of terrible campaigns, and island villages deserted after Turkish plundering produced deep emotions in Stephens. In April 1835 he arrived at Smyrna, where he wrote the first of a series of long letters home describing the journey there from Missolonghi, a voyage crammed with fast-moving description, emotional experiences, and fascinating people. Stephens had fallen under the epic spell of Homer and the *Iliad*, that major work which evokes so much about the past. His verbal portraits were full of acute observation, vivid word pictures of the terrors of war and of the "awful solitude, a stillness that struck a cold upon the heart," that he felt in the ruins of a war-ravaged village. The recipient of the letters—Charles Fenno Hoffman, editor of *American Monthly* magazine—was so entranced that he published the correspondence in three successive issues. They attracted wide attention and launched Stephens, unbeknownst to him, on a new career.

Meanwhile the wanderer had taken a steamship to Constantinople, then on to Odessa in Russia, where

A view of Petra from its amphitheater which appeared in Leon de Laborde's famous book on the lost city. This was one of the illustrations that excited Stephens.

he "was obliged to strip naked" for customs examination. This did not prevent him from smuggling a copy of Byron's banned *Childe Harold* into the tsar's kingdom—Byron had dubbed the tsar "an autocrat of waltzes and war." The two thousand miles of bouncing travel that ensued in an unsprung wagon, across Russia through Kiev to Moscow, did not seem to have deterred Stephens in the slightest. He commented on the downtrodden state of Russian serfs, admired the elegant six hundred churches of Moscow, and then drove in comfort to Saint Petersburg, where he celebrated July 4 with the American ambassador. The journey from Saint Petersburg to Poland, Austria, and Paris seems to have been relatively uneventful, if bumpy, broken only by illness in Poland, where Stephens suffered more from the doctors than from the illness itself.

It had been his intention to return home from Paris, but the boats were crowded with emigrants escaping the political turmoil of 1835 and the growing unrest under the Bourbons. It was at this point that another chance encounter changed Stephens's life. While browsing in a bookstall by the Seine, he came across a folio that brought his newfound interest in antiquity, nurtured on classical Greece, to a head. The folio, Leon de Laborde's *Voyage de l'Arabie Petrée,* had appeared in 1830 and contained lithographs of a mysterious city carved out of rock in far-off Arabia.

Petra had been rediscovered for the outside world by Johann Ludwig Burckhardt, Arabist, traveler, and eccentric, famous as the first European to write a description of Ramesses II's temple at Abu Simbel. Laborde and his companion, Maurice-Adolphe Linant, had visited Petra fifteen years later in great style, traveling with a large retinue to impress the Bedouin of the desert with their importance. Otherwise Petra was virtually unknown and completely isolated. Stephens, like many cultured Americans of his day, found ruins fascinating, especially those presented in the romantic style favored by Laborde and his ilk. Only a few weeks after seeing the Petra lithographs he was on his way to Alexandria, with the site as his ultimate objective.

But ancient Egypt came first. Stephens took a leisured boat ride up to the First Cataract accompanied by George Gliddon, American consul-general in Cairo and later a well-known lecturer on Egyptology. By this time American tourists in some numbers were venturing as far as the Nile. Stephens was on familiar territory, where he found the temples and

A *camera lucida* drawing of the Temple of Edfu on the Nile by Frederick Catherwood. This temple was built between 237 and 157 B.C.
British Museum Add. Mss. 29832

Watercolor of the Temple of Dendera near Coptos by Frederick Catherwood. This ranks among the finest of ancient Egyptian monuments and was built in the first century B.C. *British Museum Hay Add. Mss. 29814*

pyramids "beautiful, far more beautiful than I had expected." He also found time to have a Turkish bath: "I have been shampooed at Smyrna, Constantinople, and Cairo," he wrote, "but who thought I would have been carried to seventh heaven at the little town of Mingeh?"

By the time Stephens returned to Cairo, he was an experienced desert traveler, wearing Arab costume and going by the name Abdel Hasis. It was in this disguise, accompanied by a Greek named Paolo Nuozzo, that he now proposed to cross the desert to Petra. Nuozzo, whom Stephens described as "stout, square built, intelligent; a passionate admirer of ruins of the Nile; honest and faithful as the sun, and one of the greatest cowards that luminary ever shone upon," made his living as a guide. Everyone in Cairo tried to dissuade Stephens from his adventure, for there was a real chance that he would be murdered on the way. He promptly recruited an experienced camel driver and set off. After nearly dying of thirst and stopping at Mount Sinai, Stephens fell in with the sheikh of Petra, who conducted him to the ruins—for a price. It cost Stephens five hundred piasters to enter the ruined city through a narrow defile that gave little hint of the wonders that lay within. Stephens was entranced and wandered around Petra in a daze of exhilaration and excitement.

The temple facade inside the gorge displayed a dazzling symphony of white and red stone cut out of

144

the hillside. Stephens was a changed man. "The first view of that superb facade must produce an effect which would never pass away," he recalled. "Even [after I] returned to the pursuits and thought-engrossing incidents of a life in the busiest city in the world, often in situations as widely different as light and darkness, I see before me the facade of that temple." Stephens became an archaeologist overnight, entranced by rock-carved temples and amphitheaters that had vanished into historical oblivion in the seventh century A.D. A fascination with long-lost antiquity stayed with him for the rest of his life. The vivid memories of Petra remained with him all the way home as he paused in Jerusalem, Acre, Alexandria, London, and New York. He returned home debilitated by dysentery after two years of arduous traveling that had only whetted his appetite for further exploration and more archaeology.

John Lloyd Stephens found himself to be a well-known traveler upon his return, for his letters and reputation had preceded him. A stopover in London put him in touch with the literary world. There, new friends urged him to write a book. He was curious, too, about a panorama of Jerusalem displayed in a rotunda in Leicester Square. Soon he met its designer, Frederick Catherwood, an artist-architect with a fixa-

"The Wilderness of Sinai." From Leon de Laborde's *Arabie Petrée.*

"Ravine leading to Petra, and the Tomb with the Greek Inscription." Laborde's first view of the lost city.

tion on ancient civilizations. Catherwood was an Englishman, born in London and trained as an architect in the best classical tradition. He had spent many years wandering in Greece and the Near East, studying archaeological sites and drawing important ruins. The panorama of Jerusalem was an attempt to raise money after a long expedition to the Nile Valley, where Catherwood had worked alongside the celebrated antiquarian Robert Hay in one of the first attempts to make a systematic record of Egyptian temples and monuments. An enormously skilled but rather dour man, Catherwood was now in his late thirties. He had crammed several careers into a short lifetime, having worked as an architect, artist, archaeologist, even a railroad builder. He had advised the pasha of Egypt on mosque repairs in Cairo and taught architecture at the city's university. He had now returned to England with empty pockets, a huge portfolio of drawings, and a reputation as an expert archaeological draftsman. The panorama of Jerusalem had proved an immediate success and solved Catherwood's financial problems, but it was time for him to look around for a new adventure.

This quiet man with a passion for exploration and archaeology captivated Stephens. Both men shared an admiration for ancient civilization, adored ruins, and realized that their futures were bound up in the past. Despite the striking differences in their personalities, Catherwood and Stephens soon became close friends; their mutual liking for archaeological exploration cemented the friendship. Soon Catherwood drew his new friend's attention to two little-known publications that described mysterious ruins in Guatemala and the Yucatan. By chance the artist had come across Antonio del Río's *Description of the Ruins of an Ancient City, Discovered near Palenque.* The book had received little public attention, although a long and pompous essay by the Italian Paul Felix-Cabesa that accompanied the del Río report spoke freely of Phoenicians and Egyptians, hinting broadly at a link between the American ruins and the civilizations familiar to Catherwood and Stephens. These exotic ruins which were apparently almost

146

unknown to scholars in North America were an obvious and exciting site for the two adventurers to explore. They agreed that someday they would mount an expedition to Central America.

In the meantime Stephens had to make a living. He sailed for New York and plunged into politics with renewed energy and was soon making speeches as vigorously as ever. But a visit to Harper's publishing house in fall 1836 convinced Stephens that there was a market in America for the sort of travel book that sold by the thousands in Europe, describing precisely the sorts of experiences he had enjoyed. So he cloistered himself for months to write the book that his friends had pressured him to give the world as soon as possible.

A year later *Incidents of Travel in Arabia Petraea* by "An American" was the literary sensation of North America. The massive two-volume work of 180,000 words had taken Stephens about six months to write. *Incidents* is an impressive book that disguises Stephens's thorough research and impressive scholarship. The style is vivid and easy. It titillated, entertained, and instructed the reader; it was a narrative heightened by charming touches of humor. It was travel without a message or a commercial objective. The reviewers were ecstatic. Edgar Allan Poe said Stephens wrote "like a man of good sense and sound feeling" in a twelve-page article in the *New York Review* that attracted wide attention. "We hope it is not the last time we hear from him," enthused Poe. "He is a traveler with whom we shall like to take other journeys." Stephens had found a new career, one that freed him from the tiresome restrictions of law and allowed him to travel whenever he wished. The royalties from *Incidents* totaled well over $20,000—more than enough to make Stephens one of the few Americans of the day to support himself entirely by writing. Twenty-one thousand copies of the book were sold in the first two years. He promptly followed *Arabia Petraea* with another "Incidents" book, this time about Greece, Turkey, Russia, and Poland, which became a best seller in 1839.

Interior of a rock-cut temple at Petra. After Laborde.

Stephens soon became the best-known traveler in America. He mingled freely in literary circles and spent much time with Frederick Catherwood, who had established himself as an architect at No. 4 Wall Street. The Catherwood practice prospered, as did his new panorama of Jerusalem on Broadway at Price Street. The two men were frequently to be seen in Bartlett and Welford's bookstore, where the literary circle gathered for gossip and conversation. There they read Jean Frédéric Waldeck's *Voyage pittoresque*, admired his folio drawings, and studied everything they could find on the mysterious ruins of Yucatan.

Catherwood and Stephens discovered that there was very little information to go on beyond the vague and unsatisfactory accounts in the obscure reports of del Río, Dupaix, Waldeck, and a few others. Middle American Indians were, it was generally thought, a pretty sorry lot, certainly incapable of erecting temples or other monuments on the scale described by these authors. Spanish archives were unknown to English-speaking scholars; even when they were available, their scholarly readers discounted them. The eighteenth-century Scottish historian William Robertson dismissed the Mexicans and Peruvians in his *History of America* as not "entitled to rank with those nations which merit the name of civilized. . . . The Spanish account appear highly embellished," he added, the ruins "more fit to be the habitation of men just emerging from barbarity than the residence of a polished people." Even if one did admit that the temples existed, they were probably the work of the Ten Lost Tribes of Israel, of Jewish peoples. Indeed, the hooked noses of the Indians caused William Penn to imagine himself standing "in the Jewish quarter of London." The nine volumes of the newly published *Antiquities of Mexico* had just arrived in New York. They were the work of the eccentric Lord Kingsborough, who died in debtor's prison after having squandered his fortune on the gorgeous folios. Kingsborough had arranged for all the surviving Maya codices to be copied and reproduced with a narrative that claimed a Jewish origin for the Indians.

In a few months John Stephens had mastered all the available literature on the archaeology of Mesoamerica. Like other great travelers and popular writers, Stephens had a sense of history and of timing. He felt that interest in Mexican antiquities was rising fast and was aware of the pioneer research such as that being done by the historian W. H. Prescott of Boston who delved into Maya history using hitherto unknown Spanish archival sources. The time had come for a firsthand look at the ruins. Fortunately Stephens's income was now assured independently of the family business; so he came to an agreement with Frederick Catherwood, managed to secure a presidential appointment as American diplomatic minister in Central America, and plunged into elaborate preparations. On October 3, 1839, Catherwood and Stephens slipped away from New York; their destination was the small, isolated town of Belize in what is now the country of the same name.

A greater contrast to New York than Belize could scarcely be imagined. The settlement consisted of two streets of European-style houses on stilts that set them above the odorous mud and termites around the port. Six thousand people, mainly blacks, lived there. It was a town without a color bar, as Stephens found when he was seated at breakfast the first day between "two coloured gentlemen. . . . some of my countrymen would have hesitated about taking it, but I did not; both were well dressed, well educated, and polite." He "hardly knew whether to be shocked or amused at this condition of society." Belize itself was a British colony, a precarious foothold of little economic significance to the vast British Empire, but much coveted by Mexico and other Central American states. The important point was that it was a foothold on the American continent, a base for colonial expansion on the mainland and in the Caribbean.

Inland lay the dense rain forest country of the Yucatan, incredibly arduous to traverse, inhabited in places by hostile Indians, and in a state of political confusion. This was the country that Stephens proposed to penetrate in search of Maya ruins, terri-

149

tory that few except mahogany loggers bothered to enter. Belize itself left much to be desired in terms of creature comforts. Fortunately, the British resident, Colonel MacDonald, offered the two travelers accommodation in his official residence. MacDonald was a Napoleonic war veteran, "six foot tall, and one of the most military-looking men I have ever seen. . . . Rich in recollections of a long military life, personally acquainted with the public and private characters of the most distinguished military men of the age, his conversation was like reading a page of history," Stephens wrote. "He is one of a race that is fast passing away and with whom an American seldom meets," he added. Official hospitality was overwhelming, and the local agent of the steamship company held up a boat bound for Guatemala for an extra day so that Stephens could complete his business. A thirteen-gun salute sped the two men on their way, an official honor that both surprised and moved the novice diplomat, who "endeavored to behave as if I had been brought up to it."

The journey to Izabal in Guatemala was uneventful, except for the clattering steamboat, which, not for the first time, spoiled much of Stephens's enjoyment. "Steamboats," he wrote, "have destroyed some of the most pleasant illusions of my life. . . . to follow the track of Columbus accompanied by the clamor of the same panting monster, struck at the root of all the romance connected with his adventure." Izabal itself was a lovely place, with only one substantial structure, the warehouse of the steamship company. Stephens called on the commandant with his diplomatic passport, only to find that he could be given no guarantee that any of the three political factions warring in the interior would respect it. Undeterred, Catherwood and Stephens arranged to join a mule train that was leaving with the steamship's cargo the next day.

A caravan of a hundred mules left at seven in the morning. The Stephens party consisted of five mules; the two Europeans and their servant, Augustin, recruited in Belize; four Indian carriers; and several muleteers, whose leader carried a machete and wore a pair of murderous spurs. Augustin, a French Spaniard, turned out to be an invaluable asset, with his gift for inconspicuous scrounging and improvisation that only those who have been on their own in the wilds can appreciate fully. The party was forced to communicate in French, as this was the only language common among them. The road to the interior was far from being an impressive highway. At every step the mules sank up to their fetlocks in mud or stumbled into deep holes. Every yard was an effort, through dry stream beds or up precipitous and barely discernible paths on mountainous slopes. The caravan was soon in chaos and falls were frequent. Catherwood was once thrown so violently that he remarked to Stephens as he got up that "if he had known of this mountain, you might have come to Central America alone." Gunpowder, a "new condiment" that did not go down well even with an experienced traveler like Stephens, spoiled their stores.

Only twelve arduous miles were covered the first day. After a night's rest in a ranch house the travelers awoke to find that their muleteers had gone on ahead with the baggage and some had deserted. Fortunately, the worst terrain was behind them; they were now in the highlands. But they had little food, for their supplies were far ahead. The local people lived on tortillas and black beans, a diet that Stephens compared to that found in a penitentiary. Broad rivers and steep, pine-studded mountains relieved the desolate plains. Stephens and his party stayed for a while at the "house of a don" by the Motagua River, whose accommodations for himself, his family, and his guests consisted of a communal room with three beds. The Americans slung their hammocks among the beds, "submitting with resignation," as Stephens put it, to whatever beset them. But the family was entirely at ease and treated them like part of the furniture. The next day they caught up with their possessions, enjoying clean clothes for the first time in days.

The small town of Gualan, a settlement with one principal street, a plaza, and about ten thousand in-

Frederick Catherwood's
drawing of stela S at Copan.
From *Incidents of Travel*.

habitants, was in fiesta. A two-day delay to purchase
mules gave the Americans time to enjoy the festival
commemorated with earnest prayers, drinking, and
"what in English would be called flirtations." Inquiries about the site of Copan evoked little reaction
from the local priest. The mules materialized; soon
the great heights of the Verapaz Mountains were surmounted; and the town of Zacapa lay in front of
them. A comfortable lodging was available at the
residence of Don Mariano Durante, who kept open
house for visitors. The owner was away, but Catherwood and Stephens made themselves at home, invit-
ing a later arrival—who turned out to be the owner—
to dinner. Zacapa was alive with rumors of political
intrigue. A parade of twelve hundred "ferocious
and banditi-like" soldiers paraded in the plaza, a
military scene that prompted Stephens to debate the
follies of war. The sixty-year-old Napoleonic veteran
in charge of the motley detachment was far from enthusiastic about Stephens's passport. He questioned
Augustin closely and gave the party clearance but
with ill grace, afraid that Stephens was on his way to
cause trouble in neighboring countries. But the next
morning Stephens and Catherwood rode out for
Copan, without incident, leaving their hostess with a
gold ring that bore the motto "Souvenir d'amitié."
"Her husband could not understand French," remarked the amorous Stephens, who had admired the
lady from afar. "Nor, unfortunately," he added,
"could she."

The route to Copan now lay through a region
ravaged by civil war. The group passed a ruined
church, evidence that the new government was
pursuing a policy of diminishing ecclesiastical
power. By four o'clock they had reached the village
of Jocotan, the site of another gigantic church. They
had hoped to find out something about Copan in the
village but the muleteer refused to stop. After a violent parley the travelers agreed to continue, although
they were weary. Two hours later they reached
another huge ruined church, the seventh of the day,
an edifice with "colossal grandeur and costliness."
In a nearby deserted village a dilapidated shed provided shelter for the night.

152

Stephens was just undressing when the door burst open and a ragged group of soldiers, Indians, and the local mayor rushed in armed to the teeth. A young officer with "a glazed hat and sword and a knowing and wicked expression" was in charge of the group. He examined Stephens's passport and declared it was not valid. Furious arguments ensued, Stephens in exasperation offering to return home rather than go on to Copan. The officer would not agree even to this and refused to budge. So Stephens buttoned his coat with the document inside it and told the officer to take it away from him by force. He responded, with "a gleam of satisfaction crossing his villainous face," that he would. "During all this time," added Stephens, "the band of cowardly ruffians stood with their hands on their swords and machetes, and two assassin-looking scoundrels sat on a bench with muskets against their shoulders, muzzles pointed within three feet of my breast." The Americans were more indignant than afraid, Augustin urging Stephens in French to disperse the ugly crew with a single shot. Fortunately, an older officer arrived just before violence broke out and asked to see the passport. Stephens refused to hand it over but read the contents aloud. Eventually he managed to prevail on the mayor to send a letter from him to the general who had issued the passport in the first place.

A note—in Italian—was hastily scribbled and sealed with the imposing imprint of an American half dollar in lieu of a diplomatic seal. Twelve men were posted at the door, men whom Stephens described as the sort of people "who would have been turned out of any decent state prison lest they contaminate the other boarders." A peep at the guard did nothing to reassure the travelers. "They were sitting under the shed directly before the door, and smoking cigars around a fire, their arms in reach. Their whole stack of wearing apparel was not worth a pair of old boots, and with their rags, arms, and their dark faces reddened by the firelight, their appearance was ferocious; if we had attempted to escape, they would have been glad, doubtless, of the excuse for murder."

Stela and stone idol
at Copan.

A bottle of wine was some consolation as Stephens and Catherwood hung their hammocks for the night. Suddenly the door opened again and everyone burst in, arms at the ready. To Stephens's astonishment they were given permission to proceed to Copan. All was now in order, but Stephens worried about the reception that might await them farther in the interior. After much discussion and a cup of chocolate, the party decided to press on.

Two days later, the village of Copan, "half a dozen miserable huts thatched with corn," came into sight. The travelers' arrival caused a great sensation. They were directed to the hacienda of Don Gregorio, a fifty-year-old landowner who obviously wanted nothing to do with the visitors because of possible political repercussions. Hospitality was grudgingly forthcoming, but Stephens himself was ignored, much to his annoyance. He was forced to sleep in a crowded space where there was room only to sling a hammock so that "my body described an inverted parabola, with my heels as high as my head. It was vexatious and ridiculous." The next day a young guide arrived, produced by one of Gregorio's sons. He led them across Gregorio's fields into thick forest, where he cleared a way through the dense undergrowth. Stephens remembered that "soon we came to the bank of a river, and saw opposite a stone wall, with ferns growing out of the top. Perhaps a hundred feet high, it ran north and south along the river, in some places fallen but in others entire; it had more the character of a structure than any we had ever seen ascribed to the aborigines of America. This was part of the wall of Copan, an ancient city on whose history, books throw but little light." Catherwood and Stephens had reached a goal of which they had dreamed for weeks, a magnificent archaeological site that was to make their names household words throughout America and the world.

9 "A Mourning Witness to the World's Mutations"

Before Catherwood and Stephens's visit no qualified archaeologist, let alone an explorer who had spent any amount of time among the ruins of Egypt or the Near East, had been to Copan. Nor had an accomplished writer set out to describe the temples and plazas that made up this and other Mesoamerican ruins. The vague descriptions of earlier visitors gave Stephens little to work with, beyond a feeling that a foreign race had built Copan. Catherwood, however, had already pointed out that the art Waldeck had copied was quite unlike any known Near Eastern styles. Stephens had read about, and seen, the mysterious mounds of the North American Midwest, the work of unknown peoples who had been, Stephens thought, the subject of "wild and wandering ideas." Both Catherwood and

Copan. "The city was desolate. No remnant of this race hangs round the ruins, with traditions handed down from father to son and from generation to generation."

Stephens arrived at Copan with "the hope rather than the expectation of finding wonders."

"As we gazed on the wall of the city on the opposite side of the river," wrote Stephens, "this account of the city's conquest which the Spanish historians had given us, seemed to us most meager and unsatisfactory." Copan seemed to be a much larger and more important place than the Spaniards had described. After riding a little way upstream the explorers were able to ford the river and gaze at the wall from close range. It was made of well-laid cut stone in an excellent state of preservation. A set of steps led to a terrace that was completely mantled in vegetation which José, the guide, hacked away with his machete. Catherwood and Stephens stumbled across the terrace at the foot of a pyramid and came on a square stone column elaborately sculpted in bold relief. "On the front side was carved the figure of a man (evidently a portrait) curiously and richly

dressed, whose face was solemn, stern, and well fitted to excite terror." Large hieroglyphics adorned the other faces of the stela, now known as stela B.

This discovery electrified Catherwood and Stephens. They were certain they had not only found a hitherto undiscovered people, but a completely new art style as well, a style that proved "like the newly discovered historical records [of Prescott] that the people who once occupied the American continents were not savages." Fascinated, they stumbled after their guide as he cut his way through the undergrowth. Catherwood clasped his sketch pad, occasionally pausing to note a particularly fine sculpture. Altogether they came on at least fourteen more stelae, several of them displaced by giant creepers.

The brooding trees and underbrush seemed to preserve a solemn stillness over the site. "The only sounds that disturbed the quiet of this buried city were the noises of monkeys moving along the tops of the trees and the cracking of dry branches broken by their weight. They moved over our heads in long and swift processions, forty or fifty at a time. . . . It was the first time that we had seen these mockeries of humanity and, amid these strange monuments, they seemed like wandering spirits of the departed race guarding the ruins of their former habitations."

Rarely has the first discovery of an archaeological site received such polished literary treatment. And Copan raised Stephens's pen to higher planes. His note pad was much in evidence as José guided the travelers to the middle of a plaza "with steps on all the sides almost as perfect as those of the Roman amphitheatres." The plaza was a kaleidoscope of sculptures, steps, and dense vegetation that powerfully affected the explorers. They sat in wonder and speculated about the builders of Copan. The local people knew nothing of the history of the ruins. "There were no associations connected with this place," wrote Stephens. "But architecture, sculpture, and painting, all arts which embellish life, had flourished in this overgrown forest; orators, warriors, and statesmen, beauty, ambition, and glory

157

The hut at Copan.

had lived and passed away, and none knew that such things had been, or could tell of their past existence."

Then he went on, in a famous piece of writing: "The City was desolate. No remnant of this race hangs round the ruins, with traditions handed down from father to son and from generation to generation. It lay before us like a shattered bark in the midst of the ocean, her masts gone, her name effaced, her crew perished, and none to tell whence she came. . . . the place where we were sitting, was it a citadel from which an unknown people had sounded the trumpet of war? Or a temple for the worship of the God of peace? Or did the inhabitants worship idols made with their own hands and offer sacrifices on the stones before them? All was mystery, dark, impenetrable mystery, and every circumstance increased it. . . . an immense forest shrouds the ruins, hiding them from sight, heightening the impression and moral effect, and giving an intensity and almost wildness to the interest.''

Their experiences moved the two travelers deeply, and it was late in the day before they returned to the icy atmosphere of Don Gregorio's hacienda. There they found that stories of Catherwood's abilities as a medical man had followed them; the artist had cured a muleteer's boy of a fever. The don's family unbent a little at this news, but the Americans resolved to set up camp among the ruins anyway. At this point the owner turned up, waving a title deed to the site, which Stephens inspected gravely. Don José María turned out to be an "ignorant and inoffensive" farmer who was "tall and well dressed (that is to say, his cotton shirt and pantaloons were clean)." He put the Americans in touch with a poor white who lived with his sick wife in a small hut near the ruins. The very presence of the Americans scared the wife back to health, while their host turned out to be an educated man who begged his visitors for books. The two archaeologists reveled in the friendly atmosphere, smoking their host's fine, locally grown tobacco as Stephens contemplated his new discovery. His initial plan was to buy Copan and remove it, stone by stone, to New York. This scheme was quickly aborted when rapids were discovered downstream which ruled out water transportation. No one in his right mind would try to carry Copan over the mountains. So Stephens resolved to take at least one column home for exhibition in New York.

Catherwood was now faced with a challenging and exacting task: that of recording a hitherto unknown artistic tradition on paper, one that had no precedents in classical art. The physical difficulties were formidable. It was the height of the rainy season and the forest enveloped everything. The designs were very complicated and hard to distinguish in anything but very strong light. With great

159

Stela B

Stela D

Frederick Catherwood's intricate drawings of stelae
at Copan, which have seldom been bettered by
photographers.

Stela I   Stela P

difficulty the Indians with the party cleared the trees and brush away from a stela and Catherwood set to work, up to his ankles in mud, plagued with mosquitoes, and irritated by the sheer complexity of the reliefs.

Stephens wandered off with two mestizos to investigate further. Everything was a mystery. "We could not see ten yards before us, and never knew what we should stumble on next. At one time we stopped to cut away branches and vines, which concealed the face of a monument, and dig around and bring to light a fragment, a sculptured corner of which protruded from the earth. I leaned over with breathless anxiety while the Indians worked, and an eye, an ear, a foot, or a hand was disentombed; and when the machete rang against the chiseled stone, I pushed the Indian away and cleared out the loose earth with my hands."

Over fifty art pieces came to light in two hours of exploration. Stephens soon abandoned the idea of shipping antiquities back to New York; the logistical problems were simply too severe.

Meanwhile Catherwood was having his problems. Forced to work in gloves with damp paper, the complexities of the hieroglyphics defeated him time and time again. The task of recording Copan seemed to be beyond him. But soon he found ideal light conditions and made better progress, standing on a piece of oiled canvas. Stephens cleared the next stela for him, turning over in his mind a strategy for buying Copan outright from Don José María.

The presence of the Americans had caused a sensation in the village, both for political reasons and because of their wealth. Stephens found Don María hesitant to sell, for he was a subtenant of the surly Don Gregorio, behind in his rent, and terrified of political fallout from a sale. The humble don evidently thought the Americans had taken leave of their senses. At the same time he was eager to get rid of the unproductive land. Indeed, it turned out he did not even own it but was holding it under lease from someone else. Don María vacillated for several days, until John Stephens tried a master stroke of

162

crafty diplomacy. "For a finale, I opened my trunk and put on a diplomatic coat with a profusion of large eagle buttons. I put on a Panama hat, soaked with rain and spotted with mud, a checked shirt, white pantaloons, yellow up to the knees, and was about as *outré* as the negro king who received a company of British officers on the coast of Africa in a cocked hat and military coat, without any inexpressables." The display, especially Stephens's bright buttons, overwhelmed Don María; he felt the illustrious señor should certainly buy the ruins. "The reader is perhaps curious to know how old cities sell in Central America. Like other articles of trade, they are regulated by the quality in the market and the demand; but, not being staple articles like cotton and indigo, they were held at fancy prices, and at that time were dull of sale. I paid fifty dollars for Copan . . . for which Don José María thought me only a fool; if I had offered more, he would probably have considered me something worse." It was November 17, 1839, a historic day in American archaeology.

Having concluded the bargain of the century, the two men returned to the serious business of surveying the site. A compass and a veteran tape used by Catherwood in Egypt were the only tools. It took three days to complete the task, achieved by cutting straight lines through the jungle. From these efforts Catherwood conjured a rough plan of Copan that was the authoritative source for over a half a century. For thirteen more days Stephens wandered through the courts and temples of Copan while Catherwood strove to reduce the intricate art to a manageable conception on paper. Stephens's lyrical account of the three main courts, pyramids, and temples of Copan is a classic of archaeological reporting. He found that Copan extended over two miles, a vast complex of savage sculpture and astonishing portraiture overgrown with trees, with steps rising up ranges of terraces and pyramids. But the description is devoid of interest without Catherwood's astonishing visual record of the stelae and the great head of the Lord of the Harvest, Yum Kaax, which

Plan of Copan prepared by
Catherwood and Stephens.

Stephens found above the eastern courtyard. So
great was the travelers' passion for accuracy that
Catherwood corrected the lithographs several times
at proof stage. They remain among the finest and
most vivid records of Copan.

Finding that Catherwood had at least a month's
work ahead of him, Stephens resolved to press on
with his diplomatic mission. By now Catherwood
had acquired a separate passport for himself and
could safely be left alone with his drawings. So
Stephens left Copan for Guatemala City, accompanied only by Augustin and a muleteer. The arduous journey was relatively uneventful, but the
British vice-consul's house was barred and shuttered
when Stephens knocked on the door; apparently the
military had mutinied and was threatening to sack
the city. The American was hastily admitted when

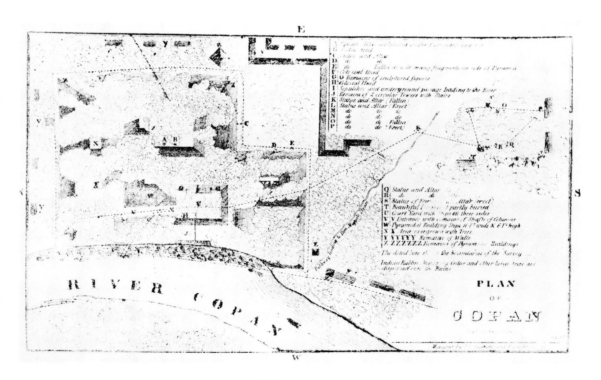

he showed his credentials. It was the first time in two months that Stephens had enjoyed the luxury of clean sheets and a comfortable bed. He was glad to ignore the revolt and admire the pure air and fine layout of Guatemala City, with its spacious houses "with large doors and windows protected by balconies." The next day he moved into the house of the American chargé d'affaires, a charming residence with a handsome courtyard. His first act was to forward the legation's archives to New York, a task with which he had been charged as a priority. There appeared to be no government in the city, and his fellow diplomats were as puzzled as he. The populace as a whole lived in trepidation as faction after faction threatened to take over the city by force. The churches were crowded with apprehensive worshippers praying for peace and security. Only a semblance of government was maintained. Stephens attended a meeting of the constituent assembly, where thirty deputies, mainly priests with black caps and gowns, sat in solemn session. The scene took Stephens back to "the dark ages and seemed a meeting of inquisitors," incompetent ones at that.

Diplomatic initiatives were obviously fruitless, so Stephens spent his time visiting the Pacific coast at Izapa, discreetly courting a beautiful young widow, and pondering upon the state of the country. He was presented to Rafael Carrera, at that time barely twenty-three years old, and predicted that the young man would "have a long career before him." Carrera fulfilled Stephens's prophecy and stayed in power until his death in 1865. At the time of Stephens's visit he did not represent the central government; that was nominally in the hands of the liberal politician Francisco Morazan, who was rumored to be in San Salvador. Stephens felt that he was wasting his diplomatic time in Guatemala, especially now that Catherwood had joined him after a harrowing time at Copan, where he had been robbed by his servant and forced to rely on Don Gregorio's hospitality for a while. But the precious drawings, soon to achieve archaeological immortality, were intact. John Stephens's accreditation was to Central

The Great Square of
Antigua, Guatemala.
From *Incidents of Travel
in Central America.*

America as a whole, so on January 5, 1840, he "rose
to set out in search of a government," a move that
caused some consternation in fearful Guatemala
City. Government officials were unwilling to give
him the necessary authorization to leave until
Stephens insisted on his diplomatic rights and left
with grudging permission. Then began a remarkable
journey that took the itinerant diplomat down to the
Pacific coast, and from there by French vessel to San
Salvador, where he interviewed the vice-president of
the central government. This gentleman was without
a substantive government with which to rule, and it
was clear that normal diplomatic activity was out of
the question. Stephens promptly slipped off to the
coast of Costa Rica and rode north into Nicaragua,
to inspect a possible route for a canal across the
isthmus. In Granada he met John Baily, a young
British officer on half pay, who had just completed a
survey of a canal route through Nicaragua. Baily
gave his visitor exhaustive information on depths

166

and altitudes that enabled Stephens to write a detailed and thoroughly practical proposal for an isthmus canal that would cost seven million dollars. His arguments were persuasive and elegant as only Stephens could make them. "This work has been well characterized as the mightiest event in favor of the peaceful intercourse of nations which the physical circumstances of the globe present to the enterprise of man," he wrote. His mind was still on archaeology, too, for he added: "To men of leisure and fortune, jaded with rambling over the ruins of the Old World, a new country will be opened. After a journey on the Nile, a day in Petra, and a bath in the Euphrates, English and American travellers will be bitten by mosquitoes on the lake of Nicaragua."

Stephens now retraced his steps to San Salvador, visiting Managua and Leon on the way. The last vicious manifestations of civil war seriously disrupted the return journey to Guatemala City, where Carrera was now in firm command, and Stephens was lucky to escape with his life. Literally the moment he rode into the city after an incredibly rough journey of over twelve hundred miles, Frederick Catherwood arrived from Antigua after a second visit to Copan as well as to other ruins. "In our joy at meeting we tumbled into each other's arms," wrote Stephens. "In the very first moment we resolved not to separate again while in that distracted country."

There was certainly no point in continuing any diplomatic work. Although Carrera and his men were favorably disposed toward Stephens, there seemed little prospect of any stable government for a while. So Stephens decided to return home, stopping at Palenque on the way. Catherwood's work at Copan was completed, too, and an attempt to purchase another complex of ruins at Quirigua nearby had failed. Both men wanted to see Palenque and its spectacular temples, even if it was a thousand miles away through rough country. The rainy season was approaching and there was little time to lose. No one in Guatemala City had ever made the journey, reliable servants were unobtainable, and many preparations were needed. Everyone advised the two

167

Americans to abandon the idea, for the Indians were in revolt and atrocities were rumored. But the travelers were adamant. They were given every facility, passport, and blessing, even that of Carrera, who fortunately had the impression that Stephens was an eminent personage in North America.

The small party followed a road to Mexico that took them through well-cultivated highland country. They paused at the ruins of Utatlan near Santa Cruz de Quiche, where Catherwood found little to sketch. During their second day at the site the archaeologists were accosted by a strange, laughing figure, who stumbled up to them perspiring freely under a red umbrella. He turned out to be the local priest, a high-spirited and cultured Andalusian who arranged to be sent in the Dominican service to Central America in hope of finding peace and quiet—vain hope, he admitted laughingly, for he had ended up in the middle of a revolution.

The happy priest and his cigars captivated Catherwood and Stephens. They spent the night at his convent, conversing about politics, history, and Indian life. His room was a morass of papers and books, skulls, cheese, manuscripts, and clothes. There was barely room to sit down.

When they could stop laughing, Catherwood and Stephens discovered that the priest was a mine of information about the local countryside. The padre had visited some of the ruins. He spoke of a group of Indians living on the other side of the Cordillera who had never been conquered by the Spaniards. Four days farther along on the road to Mexico, he asserted, was a "living city, which was large and populous, and occupied by Indians in precisely the same state as before the discovery of America." He himself had climbed ten thousand feet up in the Cordillera and looked down over an immense plain that extended as far as Yucatan and the Gulf of Mexico. There he saw, far away, a large city "with turrets white and glittering in the sun." Apparently, the Indians who lived in the city were Maya speakers. They permitted no stranger to visit their city and return alive. Even the cocks were kept under

guard to prevent their crowing aloud. The night
hours passed quickly as the aged priest pointed out
the craggy summit of the sierras from which he had
seen the "white turrets." One look at that city would
obviously solve many of the conundrums surrounding the mysterious ruins of Central America. But
regretfully the two weary travelers abandoned any
attempts to solve this exciting mystery, considering
it a venture that should be undertaken by two
younger men with much more time to prepare for the
expedition. No one has ever found the padre's city.

Now the way to Mexico lay through incredibly
rough terrain, where the mules stumbled and the
cold was piercing. Magnificent views were scant
consolation for an exhausting day's ride. At Huehuetenango, the last town before Mexico, the

The Plaza at Quezaltenango,
Guatemala. Illustration
from *Incidents of Travel
in Central America.*

party were forced to rest their mules, were taken to see the site of a recent discovery of some mastodon bones, and visited the Zacalan ruins nearby. The collapsed and overgrown pyramids were owned by a mestizo who gladly gave Stephens permission to excavate one of the burial mounds, on the condition that he be given all the treasure inside it. The burial mound was found to be lined with a rough layer of stones and lime, a vault that contained some human bone fragments, and "two vases," the one "graceful in design, the surface polished, and the workmanship very good." Unfortunately there was no time to dig further.

By this time Catherwood and Stephens were virtually indistinguishable from the locals. They wore large brimmed hats, Latin costume, and *armas de agua*—embroidered and undressed goatskins that hung down from their saddlebows to protect their legs from the rain. It was at this point, too, that Stephens acquired another American for the party: Henry Pawling, like Stephens a New Yorker. He had spent a number of years traveling as a circus publicity man in Mexico and had then become a plantation manager. Disgusted with political conditions, he had loaded everything on his mule and ridden to meet the two travelers hoping to join them. Fortunately Stephens's party was depleted and in urgent need of a fluent Spanish speaker, so Pawling was promptly engaged as expedition manager.

Within a few days the party reached Comitan in Mexican territory, where Stephens presented his diplomatic passport to the authorities. A chance encounter with an American in Comitan yielded the information that Palenque was closed to all foreigners, without exception. Only recently three Belgian scientists had been refused permission to visit the ruins and Stephens's application might suffer the same fate. But fortune was on the American's side. The effect of his courtly manners, honed by long experience in Guatemala, produced magical results with the *prefecto* of Comitan. So did the diplomatic credentials from Washington. A blanket clearance was forthcoming, although Palenque itself was not specifically included. Stephens was greatly relieved. "I recommend all who wish to travel to get an appointment from Washington," he later wrote.

But the passport was only one of the difficulties that lay ahead. Yucatan was in a state of revolution and civil strife was commonplace. The route to Palenque was said to be far rougher than the arduous path they had already traversed. Catherwood and Stephens decided to take the risk, arguing that there would be few soldiers to guard remote Palenque in a time of revolution. On May 1, 1840, the small party moved out of Comitan, bound for Ocosingo, where they would join the route taken by Dupaix to Palenque in 1807. From there it was only eight days' journey to Palenque over a road that Dupaix had called "fatiguing." And he had taken forty Indian carriers with him.

The rains had now broken with a vengeance, the Indians on the way were said to be hostile, and the terrain was appallingly steep. Stephens calculated that it would take five days for the journey, through country that he described as being "as wild as before the Spanish conquest and without a habitation." The paths were so choked with undergrowth that the party was constantly obliged to cut a way through with machetes. Mules could pass, but their riders had to bend double to avoid the branches of trees. Mosquitoes made sleeping impossible. The rains poured down incessantly. Carriers came and went, anonymous people without remarkable personalities, who were a far cry from the memorable Greek, Arab, or Bedouin guides that both men had enjoyed in the Near East. Their reception at the small village of Santo Domingo de Palenque, eight miles from the ruins, was officially cordial, although Stephens described the village as the most "dead-and-alive place" he had ever seen. It transpired that the *prefecto* was expecting them, having been advised of Stephens's plans by a Belize acquaintance who had spent two weeks at Palenque not long before. To Stephens's relief, there was no problem about a visit to the site. Early the next morning the two archaeologists set out along an ill-defined In-

Palace and Tower at Palenque. From *Incidents of Travel in Central America.*

dian path, ankle deep in mud and enveloped in rain forest. Three hours later the Indian guides cried out that a "*palacio*" lay ahead, a stucco-decorated temple that was entwined with foliage, that in "style and effect was unique, extraordinary, and mournfully beautiful." Palenque was finally before them.

The Americans took up quarters in the Palace, turned loose their supply of turkeys and chickens in the overgrown courtyard, and erected simple beds of poles inside the building. On the walls around them were to be discerned the names of other visitors, among them Stephens's acquaintance from Belize and one William Bearham, an Irishman who had been murdered some time before while lying in his hammock at a camp near Palenque. The new quarters were inadequate to shelter them from the afternoon downpour that arrived in the middle of dinner. It was so damp that they were unable to light a candle, so Stephens amused himself by catching some fireflies. "Four of them together threw a brilliant light for several yards around, and, by the light of a single one, we read distinctly the finely

printed pages of an American newspaper. . . . It seemed stranger than any incident of my journey to be reading by the light of beetles in the ruined palace of Palenque the sayings and doings of great men at home."

After a miserable night Catherwood and Stephens set out to survey the ruins. Fortunately Waldeck's guide was still available, for even a hundred feet away the structures were invisible in the dense undergrowth. They were visiting Palenque under the very worst conditions. Heavy rain fell every day; they had no axes, only machetes. All the local Indians were busy planting their fields and only a few workmen were available. And the mosquitoes made the nights almost unbearable.

But the magnificent ruins made the effort of recording them worthwhile. Pawling and Stephens

The Palace complex at Palenque.
Peabody Museum, Harvard University

173

supervised the clearing of vegetation and the erection of crude scaffolding for Catherwood. Their first task was to examine and record the Palace in which they lived, a complex of thick-walled rooms grouped around several courtyards, a structure 300 feet long, 240 feet wide, and 30 feet high. The walls were decorated with "spirited figures in bas-relief" and hieroglyphs. The most conspicuous figure stood "in an upright position and in profile, exhibiting an extraordinary facial angle at about forty-five degrees," a classic sign of skull flattening. Catherwood found the art easier to copy than that at Copan, for it was executed in low relief, with bolder treatment.

The site plan that emerged from the party's work is astonishingly accurate, and it was accompanied by a series of fine copies of the grotesque figures that adorned the structure. Stephens wandered through the Palace and the tower that surmounted it in a thorough search for small objects. He was unable to excavate anywhere because of a shortage of laborers, so he contented himself with admiring the "grim

Stucco bas-relief figure from the
Palace at Palenque (Catherwood).

and mysterious figures" that stared him in the face wherever he walked. It is impossible for the modern traveler to realize the powerful effect that this mysterious ruin must have had on Catherwood and Stephens, experienced archaeologists that they were. The humid atmosphere, the all-embracing rain forest, and the savage figures peering out at them from the undergrowth must have been quite overwhelming in a way that the neatly cleared ruins of today make hard to imagine.

The discomforts of working at Palenque were extraordinary. Mosquitoes and ticks were now joined by chiggers, which infested Stephens's feet. Pawling removed the insects with a knife, but the infected parts swelled up so badly that Stephens was forced to retire to Santo Domingo to recuperate. Within a few days the swelling went down, and Stephens was able to get around again. His infection coincided with a visit from three priests, a great event in the village. Stephens dined with the visitors, prelates with a taste for cards and music. The next day he guided them to the ruins, where Catherwood's appearance shocked Stephens. "He was wan and gaunt; he was lame, like me, from the bites of insects, his face was swollen with his left arm hung with rheumatism as if paralyzed." The Palace was soaked and all their leather possessions were green and mildewed.

By the end of May the situation was intolerable. As soon as Catherwood had finished his work the party pulled out thankfully, like "rats leaving a sinking ship," as Stephens put it. One cannot fail to be impressed by Catherwood's extraordinary artistic achievements under these terrible conditions. His drawings are vivid and accurate, dramatic and sensitive, bringing the ruins of Palenque to life in their dense setting of sprawling vegetation. Stephens's lengthy descriptions of the structures are an equally memorable tribute to the two explorers' tenacity and single-minded dedication to archaeology. For the first time Palenque and Copan had come under the critical scrutiny of two travelers who had witnessed the achievements of ancient civilizations in Arabia

176

and up the Nile. They were able to make sober and well-considered comparative observations, which both emphasized the indigenous qualities of the Maya artistic traditions and brought out the occasional analogy with Egypt and other places.

The temples on top of the pyramids at Palenque

The Temple of Inscriptions at Palenque.
Peabody Museum, Harvard University

177

were heavily overgrown. Several showed signs of breached walls, doubtless broken down by del Río's Indians. There were also signs that many decorated slabs had been removed. One sculptured stone lay at the foot of a pyramid, abandoned when the Mexican government issued an order forbidding further removal of stones from Palenque. Some of these tablets elicited Stephens's highest admiration. One bore figures with a "symmetry of proportion perhaps equal to many that are carved on the walls of the ruined temples in Egypt." Another statue partially buried in the soil was rolled over with crude levers. "We were at once struck with its expression of serene repose and its strong resemblance to Egyptian statues," wrote Stephens, "though in size it does not compare with the gigantic remains of Egypt."

This discovery made Stephens realize why early investigators had compared Egyptian art with that of the Maya and concluded that the American ruins were of Egyptian origin. But when he looked at the whole range of Maya art, he found that it was far more exotic and that there was "no resemblance in these remains to those of the Egyptians; and, failing here, we look elsewhere in vain. The works of these people, as revealed by the ruins, are different from the works of any known people; they are of a new order, and entirely and absolutely anomalous; they stand alone." He went on: "We have a conclusion far more interesting and wonderful than that of connecting the builders of these cities with the Egyptians or any other people. It is the spectacle of a people . . . originating and growing up here, without models or masters, having a distinct, separate, indigenous existence; like the plants and fruits of the soil, indigenous." John Lloyd Stephens had set the stage for the study of Maya ruins as a cultural phenomenon in their own right.

Catherwood was now exhausted. The equipment was completely ruined by rust and mold. The artist's health was not improved by a dunking in a stream when his mule stumbled and fell. He was put to bed to recover, while Stephens made preparations for the journey to the coast and attempted to buy Palenque,

178

as he had purchased Copan. There was one major problem: under Mexican law, the six thousand acres of land upon which the ruins stood could not be purchased by a stranger unless he was married to a Mexican woman. Stephens considered the proposition, for the "ruined city of Palenque was a vast piece of property." The price of fifteen hundred American dollars was easily agreed with the *prefecto,* as the government wanted to encourage colonization and the sale of land. Stephens looked over the ladies of Santo Domingo de Palenque: "The oldest young lady was not more than fourteen, and the prettiest woman, who already had contributed most to our happiness (she made our cigars), was already married." Nearby was the house of two sisters, one a widow, the other a single, good-looking sister. Both were about forty; Stephens was thirty-four. But he hesitated. With either of them would come their attractive small house, two fine tablets from Palenque in the house, and the dream of the ruins themselves. The only trouble was that both the ladies were equally interesting and attractive.

So Stephens contented himself with making an offer through the American consul at Ciudad del Carmen, who was married to a local woman. Pawling was to bring back money from Laguna and to consummate the sale with the *prefecto.* Everyone at Santo Domingo was eager for the sale to go through. They wanted Stephens to take parts of the ruins to New York and, of course, to unearth the treasure that obviously lay in the depths of Palenque. Catherwood gave Pawling detailed instructions on how to make plaster casts so that he could execute accurate copies of major inscriptions. Both Catherwood and Stephens were acutely aware of the potential commercial and scientific impact on the American public of accurate drawings and artifacts. In the final analysis Stephens's travels were a carefully planned commercial venture.

Catherwood and Stephens left Palenque with indelible memories. "In the romance of the world's history nothing ever impressed me more forcibly," wrote Stephens, "than the spectacle of this once

"Casa no. 1 at Palenque."
A sketch that gives a
vivid impression
of the clinging vegetation.

great and lovely city, overturned, desolate, and lost;
discovered by accident, overgrown with trees for
miles around it, it did not have even a name to distinguish it. Apart from everything else, it was a
mourning witness to the world's mutations.''

10 "The Memory of Their Fathers and Their Ancient Condition"

Bidding farewell to his faithful mule, Stephens now led his weary party to the Tabasco-Campeche plain. At the hamlet of Palizada on the Rio Usumaciuta they picked up a logging schooner with a cargo of dyewoods bound for Ciudad del Carmen on Laguna de Terminos. The skipper was inefficient; the schooner, in the last stages of decay. Huge alligators stared at the travelers as they floated downstream. The rain poured down and strong headwinds delayed their passage. A sudden storm nearly swamped the crazy vessel within sight of Carmen while the Americans were frantically trying to lower the jammed mainsail.

Carmen itself seemed a veritable metropolis after the villages of the interior. The harbor was active with shipping. There was even a hotel and a

181

barbershop. Charles Russell, the American consul, greeted the visitors warmly and entertained them royally. The day after Stephens arrived he broached the subject of Palenque. Russell immediately agreed to back the offer for the ruins. By fortunate coincidence a few barrels of plaster of Paris were on hand, and within a few days Pawling was on his way back to Palenque with the materials and correspondence necessary to buy the site and make plaster casts—a fruitless venture that had later repercussions.

Meanwhile Catherwood and Stephens set off by coastal brig, this time in search of Uxmal, another famous "ancient city" some fifty miles from Merida, the long-established capital of Yucatan built with the stones of Indian temples. A delightful voyage with twelve fellow passengers—large turtles—brought the two adventurers to Sisal, the port for Merida. The captain's wife patched their clothes, so that they would make a good impression on the owner of Uxmal, Don Simon Peon, whom Stephens had met many months before in New York. Unfortunately Peon was away at Uxmal, but his family was hospitable, supplying provisions for the journey and more contacts in the city. It was fiesta time, but Stephens found the processions disappointing after the flamboyant festivals in Guatemala. There was even time for a call on the bishop of Merida and a visit to the theater, where Stephens ignored the performance, finding "better employment . . . in conversation with ladies who would have graced any circle."

But at six thirty the next morning Catherwood and Stephens were on the road to Uxmal, traveling from hacienda to hacienda in very hot weather. These huge estates were positively baronial, run by feudal lords and staffed by hundreds of Indians. At one point Indian porters carried the American visitors along the road in a litter; the steward of an estate called for bearers, a makeshift litter of poles was quickly lashed together, and the two men were smoothly transported over the rough terrain, the only sound being the regular padding of the Indians' feet on the ground. "There was something mon-

strously aristocratic in being borne on the shoulders of tenants," wrote Stephens. So comfortable was the journey that he dozed off, waking only when the party arrived at their destination, another huge ranch house.

The next day Catherwood and Stephens rode to Uxmal itself, in agony from uncomfortable saddles and the extreme heat. There they thankfully settled into another of Don Peon's haciendas, sleeping through the heat of the day. Stephens walked to the ruins in the afternoon. Emerging suddenly from the woods, he came upon "a large open field strewed with mounds of ruins, and vast buildings or terraces,

The Hacienda of Xcanchakan.
From *Incidents of Travel in Central America.*

183

The Nunnery and the
House of the Dwarf
at Uxmal. A sketch by
Frederick Catherwood.

and pyramidical structures . . . richly ornamented, without a bush to obstruct the view, in picturesque effect almost equal to the ruins of Thebes."

Bursting with excitement, he returned to the ailing
Catherwood, who had stayed in bed, and promised
him wonderful discoveries on the next day. Catherwood was as electrified as his companion, but a hard
day's work sent him back to his hammock with
another violent fever attack. It was obvious that he
should leave the country as soon as possible or his
health would be broken forever. Fortunately, the
artist's one day at Uxmal had been a productive one.
If the two men were to catch the next ship to Havana,
Stephens had time enough only for another very
brief visit to the site. He wandered through the pyramids and plazas, amazed at the effect of the structures when devoid of vegetation. Stephens was now
on ground trodden by Diego de Landa, admiring the
same pyramids and temples ornamented with
"strange and incomprehensible" designs, grotesque
in their depictions of animals, humans, and plants.
The most elaborate building, now known as the
Governor's Palace, stood on three ranges of terraces,

184

with an ornately decorated facade 320 feet long. The finely plastered interior walls were in virtually perfect condition. Stephens tried to remove a wooden beam carved with hieroglyphs, but the pressure of time prevented him from carrying it away. Don Simon Peon promised to send the unique beam along after him, but it never arrived. Stephens found no stelae or stuccoed figures, but elaborate exterior decorations were commonplace and of a complexity and magnitude that would require an incredible expenditure of time to copy. Stephens left determined to return, captivated by the overall effect of Uxmal. At a distance the fallen-down structures "seemed untouched by time and defying ruin." The setting sun threw "from the buildings a prodigious breadth of shadow, darkening the terraces on which they stood, and presenting a scene strange enough for a week of enchantment."

The journey to the coast was quickly accomplished, Catherwood, barely able to stand, being carried in a litter. On June 24, 1840, the explorers departed for Havana on the Spanish bark *Alexandre*, hopeful of a smooth and uneventful voyage home. The passage nearly ended in disaster, for strong currents and persistent calms carried them off course. Three weeks later they were completely lost, the incompetent captain was in despair, and food supplies were running dangerously low. Just when the situation seemed most desperate an American vessel was sighted to leeward. Catherwood and Stephens rowed over in the jolly boat, which almost sank, and in a few minutes arranged passage to New York. On July 31, 1840, the two arrived home after an absence of "ten months less three days."

Stephens's immediate priority was to produce the eagerly awaited book on his travels. Within a few days of his return the Harper brothers were on his doorstep asking for a manuscript. Stephens agreed, but made it a condition of the agreement that the publishers market the book at a price within reach of most educated readers, rather than of just the few who could afford the like of Lord Kingsborough's massive tomes at four hundred dollars a set. Within

185

nine months Stephens had written three hundred thousand words of narrative and Catherwood had worked up over eighty illustrations from his sepia and wash drawings. On June 25, 1841, *Incidents of Travel in Central America, Chiapas and Yucatan* was published to rapturous acclaim from reviewers and scholars alike. Over twenty thousand copies were sold at the high price of five dollars a copy, a startling tribute to what was to become one of America's classic travelogues. *Knickerbocker Magazine* went as far as to state that "Stephens' volumes will take their stand at once among the foremost achievements of American literature." English reviews were similarly eulogistic. The only people who were upset were those who believed that Egyptians or other exotic peoples had settled in the Americas and built their temples in Mexico.

Incidents is truly a great book, written in an easy narrative style with no pretensions to academic eminence or profound philosophical discourse. Stephens himself comes through as a gregarious and humorous man, who relished his experiences and could laugh at discomfort. But the archaeological sections of the book are the most vivid and memorable. Stephens approached Copan, Palenque, and Uxmal with the eyes of one who was thoroughly familiar with the people living in Guatemala, Honduras, and Mexico centuries after these ancient sites were abandoned. He recognized that all three cities were built by people with common artistic traditions and culture that rivaled the artistic skills of the Egyptians and other Old World civilizations in their achievements. But the American ruins were of indigenous origin. Stephens reached this conclusion after lengthy perusal of the available literature. He rejected the extravagant conclusions of Waldeck, which were based on inadequate field observations and exaggerated notions of world history. Instead, with the aid of Catherwood's drawings, Stephens was able to write a closely reasoned description of the sites. After reviewing the literature and some current theories about the sites based on the work of earlier explorers, he described some of the damage done to the ruins.

186

Then he summarized: "We are not warranted in going back to any ancient nation of the Old World for the builders of these cities: that they are not the work of people who have passed away and whose history is lost, but that there are strong reasons to believe them the creations of the same races who inhabited the country at the time of the Spanish conquest, or of some not very distant progenitors." Not until the explorers had seen Uxmal did they realize that the sites were of Indian inspiration and manufacture. Stephens drew attention to the huge archives of early Spanish records and chronicles that remained untranslated—surely rich sources of information on the Mexican ruins. It was no coincidence that he referred to these sources, for one of his most frequent correspondents since his return had been the historian W. H. Prescott.

"House of the Magician: Uxmal." One of Catherwood's most famous watercolors, illustrated in his *Views of Ancient Monuments.* "We are not warranted in going back to any ancient nation of the Old World for the builders of these cities: that they are not the work of people who have passed away and whose history is lost, but that there are strong reasons to believe them the creations of the same races who inhabited the country at the time of the Spanish conquest, or of some not very distant progenitors."

William Prescott was a New Englander. He was destined for a career in the law, but an accident at Harvard blinded him in one eye. Having private means of support, he felt at a loss for something to do. Finally he turned to history, and to Mexican history in particular. Deprived of most of his eyesight, Prescott relied heavily on his many correspondents for copies of hitherto untapped archival material from Madrid, Mexico City, and Paris. Thousands of these documents provided the source material for his monumental *Conquest of Mexico,* which was finally published in 1843. The *Conquest* was a breathtaking work that wove the history of the Spanish conquest of Mexico against a background of the Aztec kingdom and its mercurial rise from obscurity. Prescott blended a host of different sources into a narrative history of astonishing depth and vividness. He speculated about the ruins that Stephens and Catherwood had visited: "What thoughts must crowd on the mind of the traveller . . . as he treads over the ashes of the generations who reared these colossal fabrics, which take us . . . into the very depths of time. . . . What has become of the races who built them? Did they remain on the soil and become incorporated with the fierce Aztecs who succeeded them? Or did they pass on to the South, and find a wider field for the expansion of their civilization, as shown by the higher character of the architectural remains in the distant regions of Central America and Yucatan?"

Incidents of Travel appeared two years before the *Conquest,* just in time for Prescott to digest its contents as he wrote his masterpiece. "I cannot well express to you the great satisfaction and delight I have received from your volumes," he wrote to the author. At every turn he sent copies of the Stephens travelogue to historian colleagues in Europe and Mexico. Prescott himself was delighted that Stephens, "no antiquarian, fortunately," had contented himself with describing the ruins rather than speculating about them. He also added, prophetically, in a letter to Stephens, "I have no doubt that your volumes will be the means of stimulating researches in this interesting country."

188

Stephens immediately began planning another expedition to complete the work at Uxmal cut short by Catherwood's illness. He advertised for a naturalist to join the party. A notice in the *Boston Courier* yielded Dr. Samuel Cabot, a young physician and amateur ornithologist, a friend of Prescott, who was only twenty-six years old. Cabot was later destined to become a distinguished surgeon and liberal, but at this point he was hungry for adventure and new experiences. Stephens, after initial misgivings, took to the young man. They soon became fast friends.

On October 9, 1841, only fifteen months after Stephens had returned to New York, the three men sailed for Yucatan almost unnoticed. They were enthusiastically welcomed back in Merida, where Catherwood had a chance to try out the new and revolutionary daguerreotype apparatus that the three had purchased in New York. The photographic experiments with the leading families of Merida caused a sensation. The governor of Yucatan promised every assistance in the expedition, although the tense political situation made travel in the interior by foreigners unwise.

It was in this atmosphere of goodwill that the party reached Uxmal without incident. From November 15 to January 1, 1842, the three men

The Nunnery at Uxmal.
*Peabody Museum,
Harvard University*

Inside a temple at Uxmal.
An illustration from
Stephens's *Incidents of Travel
in Yucatan*.

stayed among the ruins, mapping, surveying, and
drawing perhaps the most magnificent of all Maya
ceremonial centers. In looking at Uxmal, Stephens
was now addressing two fundamental questions: the
date of its construction and the identity of its
builders. Uxmal consists of a complex of stone buildings set on terraces and mounds. The Governor's
Palace is the largest structure, a huge building
adorned with a finely cut mosaic of sculptured

190

stones. Only bats and mosquitoes lived inside the Palace when the Americans arrived, so they camped in its vast interior. Their first task was to survey the ruins, a task made doubly hard by the brush cover that masked several of the buildings and by Cabot's habit of dropping a tape to follow a bird that struck his fancy.

Meanwhile Catherwood started to make a detailed record of the Nunnery, not only with pen, ink, and daguerreotype, but in sufficient detail to enable him also to build a complete replica if necessary—something that would certainly be a sensation in New York. The Nunnery was a strange building with massive walls and tiny rooms with the roof tapered to a V, the unusual shape adopted by architects ignorant of the use of the true arch. Stephens and Cabot cleared off other buildings, ranged over the countryside in search of new ruins, and raided an Indian cemetery to acquire skulls for Dr. Samuel Morton of Philadelphia, who had just published *Crania Americana*, a pioneer study of American Indian osteology.

The unhealthy climate of Uxmal soon had its effect. Clouds of mosquitoes brought down Stephens, and soon afterward Cabot, with vicious attacks of malaria. Fortunately a local Franciscan friar, Fray Estanislao Carrillo, arrived at Uxmal when Stephens's fever was at its height and took him to a convent to recuperate. It was not long before Catherwood was alone at Uxmal, drawing after drawing flowing from his talented pencil. Then, on New Year's Day, 1842, he was carried from Uxmal delirious with malaria, unable to work any longer. He joined the other two in the restful cloisters of the monastery of Tiacil but took a long time to regain his strength.

Around Uxmal were numerous lesser ruins, such as those at Kabah, joined to Uxmal at the height of its power by a well-maintained road. Stephens found this site on his own, delighted that he was the first to see it. Kabah lay near the Indian village of Nohcacab, whose people had never seen Americans before and were inclined to be hostile. It transpired that they

Sapote wood beam with carvings found by Stephens at Kabah in Yucatan.

191

resented Stephens's tactless habit of raiding modern Indian cemeteries for skulls. Since the local Indians were the only labor force available to clear Kabah from the forest, the situation was a tricky one. It was left to Albino, a blacksmith and former soldier whom Stephens had hired for the expedition, to handle the problem by some quick talking. Albino's military career had been cut short abruptly by a saber cut on the buttock at the siege of Campeche, "which rather intimated," wrote Stephens, with a hint of malicious delight, "that he was moving in an opposite direction when the sabre overtook him."

Kabah yielded many surprises, including wooden lintel beams carved with hieroglyphs. A series of stone door jambs had been adorned with a kneeling figure dominated by a warrior priest. Stephens was so taken with these slabs that he had them removed, packed in grass and straw, and transported to the coast. Teams of Indians took them to Merida, and from there the stones were shipped to New York. The original plan had been to use them for a proposed Museum of American Antiquities, but they arrived too late for the first exhibition. So Stephens gave them to a friend with an estate on the Hudson River. (They now reside in the American Museum of Natural History.)

From Kabah the expedition traveled light, discovering as many as a dozen new ruin sites in a month, during an arduous ride across Yucatan toward Campeche. Cabot and Catherwood suffered badly from fever and quarreled over ownership of a knife. They visited the Wells of Bolonchen, a huge, deep cave in limestone rock in which there were wells that provided unlimited supplies of water for eight months a year, then were dry for four. Torch-bearing Indians took the travelers down one of the perennial wells. A huge ladder, wide enough for twenty people to pass abreast, led 210 feet down a naturally lit shaft to the place where the Indians obtained water. Another, deeper branch was reached by a series of steep wooden ladders that had to be descended backward. The ladders were slippery, and the seventh and lowest was about 450 feet below

The great ladder at
Bolonchen, Yucatan. A painting by
Frederick Catherwood.
Henry Schnackenburg collection

the ground. A pool of water at the bottom provided
Stephens and Cabot with a welcome bath before the
Indians hauled them out.

The Americans' route now took them north-
eastward toward the ruins of Chichen Itza, sixty
miles from the sea near the town of Valladolid.
Chichen Itza was already famous for its great truncated pyramid that rose high above the Yucatan

193

The Castillo at Chichen Itza
in Stephens's time.

plain, and for its huge ball court. Stephens was determined to find out more about the site and to make an accurate plan. The road to the Chichen Itza hacienda passed through the ruins "casting prodigious shadows over the plain." As nightfall was upon them they rode on to camp, walking out to the site early the next morning.

It was during eighteen days at Chichen Itza that Catherwood drew his finest drawings of Maya archi-

tecture, working with a sure touch and an amazing mastery of detail. His fine depictions of shadow and sunlight chasing over the complicated trelliswork of hieroglyphs rival the best photographs.

The whole site was dominated by the great Castillo, the Temple of Kukulcan that stands like a hill seventy-five feet above the plain. Four great stairs led to its summit. A massive temple over forty feet square with lavishly carved door jambs and wooden lintels stood on the flattened top of the mound. Two great serpents' heads with open mouths and protruding tongues lay at the foot of the stairs on the north side. It was a steep climb to the top. The Americans spent a whole day in the temple, at intervals stepping outside to admire the view and a curious field of small, square columns that stood in tiered "rows of three, four, and five abreast, many rows continuing in the same direction, when they changed and pursued another." Few were more than three feet high. Stephens set Indians to work clearing the area and finally counted at least 380 deeply buried pillars. He was at a loss to explain their significance, suggesting that they had supported "a raised walk of cement." The mystery was not solved until a century later when a Carnegie Institute expedition reconstructed the area and restored the Temple of the Warriors to its former glory as a magnificent structure with a covered colonnade "carved and brightly painted with life-size figures of armed warriors."

The Great Ball Court of Chichen Itza, which Stephens named the Gymnasium or Tennis Court, lay to the northwest of the Castillo. It was a structure with two huge, parallel stone walls, 274 feet long, 30 feet thick, and 120 feet apart. Two temples with ornamented columns stood at either end of the walls between the two, forming a huge, closed I pattern Two massive stone rings decorated with "sculptured entwined serpents" were set into the center of each wall. Stephens remembered similar walls at Uxmal, used "for the celebration of some public games." He also recalled the Spanish historian Herrera's description of the Aztec game of *tlachti*, played with a rubber ball. "The King took much Delight in seeing

The Ball Court at
Chichen Itza.
"The King took much delight
in seeing sport at Ball."
Peabody Museum,
Harvard University

sport at Ball," he wrote; ". . . the balls, . . . tho'
hard and heavy to the hand, did bound and fly as
well as our footballs." After describing the players,
he wrote of the ball court, "On the side walls they
fixed certain stones, like those of a mill, with a hole
quite through the middle, just as big as the ball." A
successful strike through the ring won the game.

To Stephens the ball courts were yet another sign
of the close link between the modern Indians of Yucatan and the magnificent buildings and artistic de-
lights of Chichen Itza, Uxmal, and other sites. Catherwood recorded the sculptured and painted
figures on the ball court temples, the feathered warriors with spears in hand dancing across the walls in
stylized rows. Some of the painted scenes in one of
the temples still preserved their vivid tones of green,
yellow, red, blue, and brown. A canoe and scenes of
warfare and domestic life were to be seen on these
walls, much of the painting, alas, deteriorated beyond recovery.

196

Chichen Itza, a highly important religious center to the Toltec and the Maya, enjoyed a long period of prosperity from the ninth century A.D., although the site was occupied as early as 300 B.C. Stephens recognized resemblances to the culture and architecture of most of his other archaeological sites, especially to Copan, Palenque, and Uxmal. This basic unity of Maya culture impressed him deeply, armed as he now was with an unrivaled knowledge of the ruins of Yucatan and Guatemala. He had lived in close proximity with the Maya themselves and observed their hooked noses and facial geography which so closely resembled that of the people depicted in temple sculptures. The friendship of priests with antiquarian leanings and of local scholars gave him access not only to Prescott's sources, but also to some lesser-known but critical early Spanish works. These included an early account of Uxmal that described Indian sacrifices in its temples as late as 1673, an Indian map of Mani drawn a century earlier that showed Uxmal as a Maya temple, and a Spanish translation of the *Books of Chilam Balam* that told of the founding of Uxmal by Maya rulers. For the first time an archaeologist had gained access to the oral traditions of the Maya,

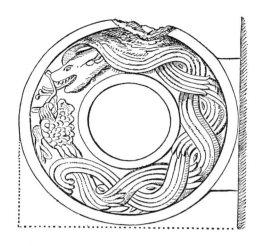

Catherwood's sketch of a stone ring from the Ball Court at Chichen Itza.

The "Group of the Thousand Columns" at Chichen Itza, as originally uncovered by Stephens. From *Incidents of Travel in Yucatan.*

Catherwood's sketch of the Monjas at Chichen Itza.

to historical material that had been neglected outside Yucatan for centuries.

The "best Maya scholar in Yucatan," a delightfully self-effacing gentleman named Don Pío Perez, lent Stephens a copy of a manuscript he had compiled on Maya chronology. Perez had written *Cronologia Antigua Yucateca* while he served as a local administrator at Ticul, a job that gave him access to many old Maya documents. He soon retired from active service in disgust over political intrigues. It was then that he set down the details of the Maya calendar with its 365-day years, the 5 "days with no name," 18 months of 20 days each, and cycles of 52 years. The long chronologies set up by the Maya measured not only current time but also the dates of events in the past and the procession of lunar and solar eclipses. The calendar was so perfected that each day of each year was represented by its own combination of hieroglyphs. It was partly recorded by Fray Diego de Landa, who noted some of the critical elements that enabled Stephens's successors to decipher the Maya script. And Stephens himself, in bringing Perez's work to the attention of a wider audience by translating some of his manuscript and publishing it, contributed to the unraveling of one of archaeology's most fascinating mysteries.

Stephens, Catherwood, and Cabot left Chichen Itza for the last time on March 29, 1842, bound for Valladolid and the coast. But before returning to New York, they were determined to visit Cozumel and Tulum, places that the first Spanish explorers had visited. On Cozumel Juan de Grijalva had sighted "a white house in the form of a tower" in

Gateway at Labna.
The party is shooting birds.
From *Incidents of Travel in Yucatan.*

199

1518. Later, Bernal Díaz had described a temple with "hideous idols" on the island, idols that Cortés had ordered replaced by a crucifix. Cozumel was deserted when the Americans reached it, Grijalva's tower being only a small Maya temple on a mound that could be seen from the sea. This was fortunate, for the island had been depopulated and was completely overgrown, making archaeological survey nearly impossible. From Cozumel they crossed to Tulum on the mainland, where a fine Maya temple "rises on the bank of a high, broken precipitous cliff, commanding a magnificent ocean view and a picturesque line of coast." Tulum was uncomfortable, for the local mosquitoes, resenting anyone disturbing the "abode of silence and desolation" that was Tulum, made sleep impossible. "A savage notice to quit was continually buzzing in our ears," wrote Stephens, "and all that we cared for was to get away."

This arduous coastal voyage, by local *canoa* in stormy and unsettled weather, was the closing stage of the expedition. The *canoa* was thirty-five feet long and had two masts. The sails provided the only shade, the motion was vile, with seasickness a persistent problem. Yet this fragile craft carried the three men not only to Tulum, but also back along the coast to Dzilan, the port for Izamal, where Diego de Landa had built his church and convent on a Maya mound. Izamal was in festival and of interest to the travelers only because of its antiquities. They lingered but a short time before going on to Merida, Havana, and New York, where they landed on June 17, 1842. Within nine months *Incidents of Travel in Yucatan* was in the bookstores, another two-volume work that again caused a public sensation and received rapturous critical acclaim. Prescott wrote from Boston that "there is but one opinion of the work here and all agree. It is better than its brother."

In the final chapters Stephens set down his thinking about the ruins of Yucatan. They were the works "of the same races who inhabited the country at the time of the Spanish Conquest, or of some not very distant progenitors." The archaeological evi-

The only known self-portrait of Frederick Catherwood
busy at work surveying the ruins of Tulum.
From his *Views of Ancient Monuments* (1844).

"The Well at Zabache, Yucatan." A watercolor by Frederick Catherwood, illustrated in his *Views of Ancient Monuments* (1844).

dence was overwhelming, but the lack of oral traditions was surprising. Or was it? For this Stephens blamed the king of Spain and the Catholic Church, for "the pages of the historian are dyed with blood; and sailing on the crimson stream, appears the leading, stern, and steady policy of the Spaniards, surer and more fatal than the sword, to subvert all the institutions of the natives and to break up and ultimately destroy all the rites, customs and associations that might keep alive the memory of their fathers and their ancient condition."

He ended with the statement that "in identifying [the ruins] as the works of the Indians, the cloud which hung over their origin is not removed. . . . They rise like skeletons from the grave, wrapped in their burial shrouds; claiming no affinity with the works of any known people. . . . I leave them with all their mystery around them." It was now up to others to carry on from where Stephens had left off.

Catherwood and Stephens designed a grand exhibition of their drawings and sculptures, and of the carved wooden lintels from Uxmal and elsewhere which they had brought back with them. The antiquities were displayed near Catherwood's panorama of Thebes, so that everyone could appreciate the dramatic differences between the two civilizations. Unfortunately, the attempt to make plaster casts at Palenque had failed when the local people heard of the sensations Stephens's work caused in New York and they demanded extortionate prices for permission to remove the casts. So the plan to reproduce the sculpture of Palenque was abandoned. Then on July 31, 1842, tragedy struck. A major fire destroyed Catherwood's rotunda and many of his drawings. The loss was irreparable, but both he and Stephens were philosophic and started to plan an ambitious folio work on *American Antiquities* to be financed by public subscription. This project fell through, although the artist himself published *Views of Ancient Monuments in Central America, Chiapas and Yucatan* in London two years later. The set of twenty-five lithographs, with a sober text by Catherwood, was dedicated to Stephens.

202

The south facade of the courtyard of the Nunnery at Uxmal.
From Catherwood's *Views of Ancient Monuments*.

This was the end of archaeological adventures for both men. After a period of prosperous architectural practice, Catherwood went to British Guiana to take part in an abortive railroad-building project. Meanwhile Stephens became embroiled once again in politics, in steamship navigation, and in the Panama Railroad project. In April 1849 the Panama Railroad Company was incorporated with Stephens as field manager. The survey and construction work lasted until 1855; Frederick Catherwood joined Stephens on site late in 1849. But both carried the malaria germ in their bloodstreams, and the humid climate of the isthmus brought out the fever immediately. Catherwood became so ill with blackwater fever in 1850 that he was sent away to California. Stephens lasted until February 1852, when he collapsed and was carried aboard a New York–bound steam packet. Nine months later he died quietly in his house in Greenwich Village, his death accelerated by the terrible rigors of tropical exploration in the days before preventive drugs. Catherwood died in 1854, going down in the S.S. *Arctic* in the mid-Atlantic, one of the nearly three hundred passengers who perished in that tragedy.

It was forty years before any more scientific work was done on the sites the two men had recorded with pen and pencil. Even today archaeologists use and take delight in the unrivaled and vivid descriptions of their discoveries. Never again would the ancient Maya return to their former oblivion.

PART THREE

The Beginnings of Archaeology

"My dear Spencer, I should define tragedy as a theory killed by a fact."

THOMAS HUXLEY

11 "Elevations and Embankments of Earth and Stone"

John Lloyd Stephens made a lasting impression on American archaeology by bringing the Maya and their artistic and architectural achievements into American intellectual consciousness. No longer could reasonable people deny the remarkable cultural accomplishments of the native Americans. Stephens did not, of course, stop speculation about the Ten Lost Tribes of Israel or other extinct peoples. Those who chose to believe that the Egyptians had built Palenque or that the Phoenicians had settled in Yucatan would never accept any other explanation for the past. Not even Catherwood's delicate representations or Stephens's elegant prose could change their minds.

The new consciousness about the American past came into being very slowly, at a time when major changes were afoot. More and more people were moving westward to the Mississippi and beyond. Many farmers in Ohio trekked farther west to avoid creditors and foreclosures. They settled in new land and exposed thousands of new Indian mounds. Rumors of buried treasure abounded, and every mortgaged property had its legendary crock of gold. The imaginary treasure was always there to plague one's dreams when debts became unbearable or the harsh labor of plowing and harvesting seemed a burdensome nightmare. The myth had strong roots in New England and Vermont, where thousands of poor farmers fervently believed that their rocky acres were rich in caches of hidden treasure deposited by long-departed ancient peoples. "We could name, if we pleased, at least five hundred respectable men who do in the simplicity and sincerity of their hearts believe that immense treasures lie concealed upon our Green Mountains, many of whom have been for a number of years industriously and perseveringly engaged in digging it up," wrote an anonymous correspondent in a Vermont weekly in the early nineteenth century.

As these people moved westward they took with them a battery of folklore about long-lost treasure, spells and incantations to find it, and all the paraphernalia of the amateur diviner and prospector to aid in the search. The treasure hunters made a beeline for the Indian mounds on their new homesteads. Unlike the rocky soil of Vermont, these earthworks yielded unexpected treasures: stone objects, copper artifacts, and skeletons. It was an incurious farmer indeed who did not dig at least superficially into an Indian mound on his property, especially with rumors of spectacular finds filtering in from neighboring towns. There was always a chance of finding buried Indian treasure or, conceivably, abandoned Spanish gold. Literally thousands of mounds were dissected in a vain search for the conquistadores' riches and, later, for Indian artifacts to be sold to curio dealers on the east coast. Indian mounds were either sources of wealth or impediments to agriculture and colonization. In either case

208

they were doomed at least to gradual extinction.

Then there were those who sought to profit from the treasure-hunting mania. In 1830–31 a "vagabond fortune-teller" named Walters set himself up in the Palmyra area of New York as a skilled treasure hunter. For a while the local farmers actually paid him the enormous sum of three dollars a day to hunt for buried treasure on their properties. He brought with him the usual apparatus of the digger: "crystals, stuffed toads, and mineral rods." Walters also claimed to have discovered an ancient Indian record of places where treasure was to be found. His technique was to read aloud in a "strange and exotic tongue" before telling his followers where to dig.

Nocturnal excavations and mysterious incantations were commonplace. The hocus-pocus sur-

Pottery effigy jar, five inches by eight inches, representing a panther or a cat from Pecan Point, Mississippi County, Arkansas. Photograph courtesy of the Museum of the American Indian, Heye Foundation

rounding treasure hunting was every bit as complicated as the rituals of the Arabs who sought buried
wealth in the depths of the Egyptian pyramids. The
Mormon leader Joseph Smith was among the many
who made a sketchy living as a money digger in the
1820s. His experiences with mound exploration may
have prompted him to write the Book of Mormon, a
work that began with his discovery of some mysterious "gold plates" on a hilltop in 1827. The Indian mounds of North America were regarded with
such curiosity that almost everyone was at one time
or another an amateur antiquarian. And the damage
to the mounds was catastrophic.

In the first half of the nineteenth century interest
in archaeology as a whole, in the Mound Builders in
particular, and in Indians generally was at a new
high. New York booksellers sold many copies of the
latest archaeological books from Europe. Sir Charles
Lyell's famous *Principles of Geology*, a lengthy treatment of the new stratigraphic field geology, was
widely read in the 1830s. Stephens's works appeared
in the 1840s, and in the following decade Charles
Darwin published *The Origin of Species*, his tour de
force on evolution and natural selection. The major
intellectual questions of European biologists and archaeologists were debated in North America as
freely as in the Old World; these debates had a
marked impact on the ways in which people looked
at the archaeology of North America.

In the 1840s the myth of the Mound Builders was
still firmly entrenched in the popular mind. In the
early 1830s the frontier of white settlement was near
the edge of the Great Plains on the Missouri River.
As the Indians of the Midwest were dispossessed of
their lands, the farmers cleared new homesteads and
settled most of the country in which mounds were to
be found. Thousands were destroyed in new agricultural endeavors; others were looted by amateur
antiquarians both out of curiosity and for profit. One
notorious collector was Dr. Montroville Dickenson, a
physician and amateur archaeologist who claimed
that he had excavated over a thousand Indian sites,
from which he had collected over forty thousand ar-

tifacts. Dickenson was a showman, too. He traveled the length and breadth of the United States displaying his finds for eight years from 1837 to 1844. Part of his show was a huge painted panorama, designed to be unrolled in small halls. As his audience gasped in amazement, the vast panorama slowly unfolded to show scenes of de Soto's burial in 1542, the effects of the great tornado of 1844, and views of the great earthworks of the Mississippi Valley.

Dickenson commissioned the artist John Egan to paint a scene depicting one of his excavations in an Indian mound. The painting shows the stratified levels of the mound, the skeletons lying in place, and the workmen clearing the lowest horizons. Several important mound groups were shown in the gigantic panorama, which was entitled *Monumental Grandeur of the Mississippi Valley*. The sites shown included Marietta and Circleville, as well as places in Louisiana and Arkansas. Dickenson accompanied

A detail from *Monumental Grandeur of the Mississippi Valley* showing Dr. Dickenson excavating a mound. Painted by the Irish-American artist John J. Egan (1810–82) in 1850. The layers of the mound and burials are clearly shown.
The St. Louis Art Museum

The Grave Creek Mound in Squier and Davis's time. A charming pastoral scene masks the excavations into this large monument.

the panorama with "scientific lectures on American Aerchiology" and claimed that the painting displayed "all the Aboriginal Monuments of a large extent of country once roamed by the Red Man." Thousands visited the popular show at twenty-five cents apiece. Eventually Dickenson donated his huge collection of antiquities to the Academy of Natural Sciences in Philadelphia.

Dickenson was one of the more ambitious collectors, but there were hundreds of other enthusiastic excavators who dug for fun or for profit. Others were more interested in the scientific information that could be obtained from the mounds. The Grave

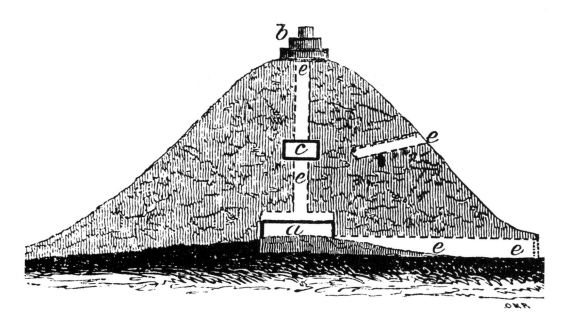

Creek mound, so carefully preserved by its owner,
Abelard B. Tomlinson, in 1819, was finally excavated by the same gentleman in March 1838. He sank
a huge shaft from the summit of the mound to its
base at a cost, we are told, of $2,500, a colossal sum
in those days. Seventy-seven feet below the surface
he unearthed a log-built burial chamber covered
with stones. A richly decorated skeleton inside the
chamber bore copper ornaments, shell beads, and
many mica plates. Even deeper, at 111 feet, a burial
vault came to light, dug before the mound was
erected, which was lined with timber and contained
two more skeletons. Other burials were later
unearthed nearby.

Tomlinson's finds caused widespread interest,
especially since he claimed to have found an
inscribed sandstone tablet bearing symbols of an unknown alphabet. The furor over the Mormon gold
plates was at its height at the time, so the new find
caused a sensation. It was examined by most authorities of the day, among them prominent French
and Danish scholars, and was championed by Henry

Squier and Davis's cross section
of the Grave Creek Mound,
showing the trenches sunk
through the earthwork and the
position of the burial chambers (a
and c). This type of tunneling is
both dangerous and destructive
archaeologically.

Rowe Schoolcraft, a geologist turned amateur ethnologist. He had become an expert on Indian customs and had written authoritatively about indigenous folklore. After serving for a time as superintendent of Indian affairs in Michigan, he devoted the rest of his life to the study of the archaeology of the mounds. He compiled a monumental and singularly badly organized six-volume work entitled *Historical and Statistical Information Respecting the History, Condition, and Prospects of the Indian Tribes of the United States,* which appeared in the early 1850s. It was published under quasi-governmental auspices, but few people have ever bothered to read this burdensome work. It is remarkable only for its conclusion that "there is little to sustain a belief that these ancient works are due to the tribes of more fixed and exalted traits of civilization, far less to a people of an expatriated type of civilization, of either an ASIATIC or EUROPEAN origin, as several popular writers very vaguely, and with little severity of investigation, imagined." He ascribed the mounds to the Indians, describing them as "the antiquities of barbarism, not of civilization." In these conclusions Schoolcraft was far ahead of his time, for few people were prepared to believe the American mounds were the work of the Indians rather than Israelites, Egyptians, or Phoenicians. The trouble was that no one had bothered to make a survey of the mounds on any comprehensive scale since the days of Caleb Atwater.

Atwater's work had been concentrated almost entirely in Ohio. Except for a cautious glance at the earthworks of the Mississippi, he had ventured little outside his home territory. The American Ethnological Society began a search for someone who would carry on where Atwater left off and produce a study of the mounds on a wider and more inclusive scale. They found their men in Ohio: a journalist and a physician who were destined to spend several years working on the archaeological sites of the Mississippi Valley.

Ephraim George Squier was born in Bethlehem, New York, in 1821. His early life was spent as a journalist in Albany and Hartford, but he became editor of the *Scioto Gazette* in 1844 and settled in Chillicothe, Ohio, the heart of mound country. Two years later he was elected clerk of the Ohio House of Representatives. But neither post prevented him from indulging in his favorite hobby of mound excavation. His companion was E. H. Davis, a local doctor, who seems to have been very much the junior partner in the enterprise. Between 1845 and 1847, supported by the American Ethnological Society, the two men excavated over two hundred mounds, surveyed many earthworks and enclosures, and assembled a large collection of artifacts, sufficient to prepare a massive corpus of information on the Mound Builders.

Squier's objective was, as he said, "to abandon all preconceived notions and to provide well authenticated facts" to replace speculation. His preliminary accounts of his researches, illustrated with thorough surveys of the mounds, were so exciting that the American Ethnological Society resolved that his promised monograph, said to be over three hundred pages long, should be published in full. The society descended on the newly formed Smithsonian Institution, which had just opened its doors in Washington in 1846 as a result of a curious bequest. James Smithson, a wealthy but highly eccentric Englishman, died in 1829. He had never shown any interest in the United States nor had he even visited it, but his will stipulated that if his nephew died childless, his estate should go to the United States to found an institution in Washington "for the increase and diffusion of knowledge among men." In 1835 the nephew did indeed die without issue, and over five hundred thousand dollars were suddenly available to found the Smithsonian Institution, an organization that was destined to play a vital role in the future of American archaeology.

It took eleven years to set up the Smithsonian, for political controversy surrounded Smithson's legacy. But eventually the physicist John Henry became the institution's first secretary. His immediate problem was to embark on a program of scientific publication

215

Ephraim George Squier. Copy of an engraving or mezzotint by P. M. Whelpley from a photograph by Mad. Whernert. Taken while Squier was chargé d'affaires in Central America after completion of his mound researches.
Smithsonian Institution National Anthropological Archives

under the Smithsonian's auspices. He planned a series of monographs entitled *Smithsonian Contributions to Knowledge*. The America Ethnological Society soon got word of his plans and arrived on Henry's doorstep brandishing a copy of the Squier and Davis manuscript, *Ancient Monuments of the Mississippi Valley*. Finally submitted to Henry in May 1847, it appeared the following year, a handsome production that remained the definitive work on mounds for many decades. It was the first of many Smithsonian contributions on the subject.

"The ancient monuments of the Western United States consist, for the most part, of elevations and embankments of earth and stone, erected with great labor and manifest design," begins this magnificent work. "In connection with these," it continues, "more or less intimate, are found various minor relics of art, consisting of ornaments and implements of many kinds, some of them composed of metal, but most of stone." After describing the general distribution of the mounds, Squier and Davis then classified their sites into two broad groupings: "CONSTRUCTIONS OF EARTH OR STONE, comprising *Enclosures, Mounds,* etc.," and "MINOR VESTIGES OF ART, including the *Implements, Ornaments, Sculptures,* etc.," of the ancient peoples. They divided the sites still further into "ENCLOSURES bounded by embankments, circumvallations, or walls; and simple tumuli or MOUNDS. . . . These grand classes resolve themselves into other subordinate divisions: ENCLOSURES FOR DEFENCE, SACRED AND MISCELLANEOUS ENCLOSURES: MOUNDS OF SACRIFICE, TEMPLE MOUNDS, MOUNDS OF SEPULTURE, etc."

Within these categories the two authors compiled an inventory of most of the major and minor archaeological sites of their research area. Based at Chillicothe, they wandered over the countryside, describing the earthworks and making detailed and elegantly drawn plans of the major sites. Their plans are a delight to behold, carefully related to general topographical maps. Even today visitors to some of the mounds receive a copy of a Squier and

Davis plan to guide them from feature to feature.

While most of the massive report is pure description, Squier, who did most of the writing, looked at the sites in a more general way as well. He was careful to distinguish between the sacred earthworks built on lower ground, which were placed in such a way that it was difficult to build defensive ramparts around the square, and the rectangular enclosures that Atwater and others had called forts. "Works of Defence," on the other hand, "usually occupy strong natural positions." They were placed on relatively inaccessible cliffs or on narrow peninsulas at the junctions of rivers or at the bends of meanders. The forts were often guarded by "double overlapping walls," embankments, sometimes with a mound in the interior of the earthworks "designed perhaps for a look-out, and corresponding to the barbican in the system of defence of the Britons."

As well as describing the earthworks, the two archaeologists worried about chronology.

The Fort Hill site, a huge complex of earthworks some thirty miles from Chillicothe, was a "natural stronghold with few equals," impregnable "to any mode of attack practised by a rude, or semi-civilized people." A large chestnut growing on the earthworks possessed "at least two hundred annual rings . . . to the fort . . . This would give nearly *six hundred years* as the age of the tree." Squier allowed four hundred years for the building and occupation of the earthworks, making a total "antiquity of at least *one thousand years*." "But," he added, "when we notice, all around us, the crumbled trunks of trees half hidden in the accumulating soil, we are induced to fix upon an antiquity still more remote."

Squier and Davis excavated nearly two hundred mounds, observing that their conspicuous stratification had not been "described with proper accuracy; and has consequently proved an impediment to the recognition of the artificial origin of the mounds." They noticed that the layers always coincided with the curvature of the mound. Many mounds contained skeletons, sometimes accompanied by "rude implements of bone and stone, and coarse

Edwin Hamilton Davis. From a photographic copy of a daguerreotype taken about 1855. *Smithsonian Institution National Anthropological Archives*

217

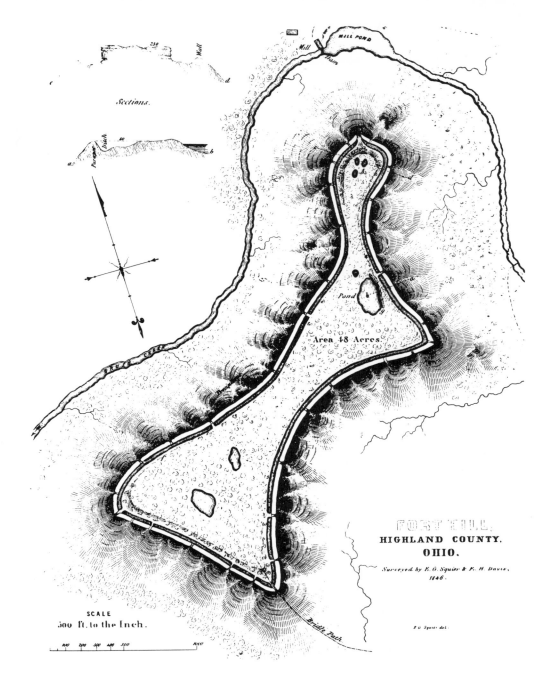

The Fort Hill earthworks as surveyed by Squier and Davis.

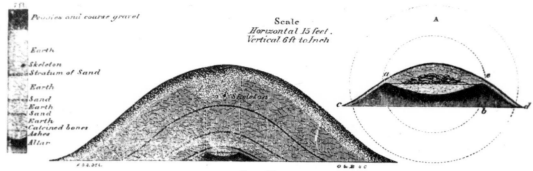

vessels of pottery, such as we know to have been in use among the Indians at the period of the earliest European intercourse." They described all kinds of burial mounds, the Grave Creek timber sepulcher dug in 1838, the many later burials in the mounds and "sacrificial altars" buried deeply. They conjectured that the "bodies of chieftains and priests" were deposited in the mounds. "The graves of the great mass of the ancient people who thronged our valleys," on the other hand, "were not thus signalized. We scarcely know where to turn to find them. Every day the plough uncovers crumbling remains; but they elicit no remarks—are passed by and forgotten." They reported extensive cemeteries in imminent danger of destruction that no one had investigated.

A hundred pages of the report were devoted to the artifacts from the mounds that "constitute a cabinet, as valuable in its extent, as it is interesting in the great variety and singular character of the illustrations which it furnishes of the condition of the minor arts." On page after page was a catalog of pottery (described by Squier as an art "hoary in its antiquity"), bone, ivory, shell, and stone artifacts. The hammers, copper axes, and adzes were correctly identified as emanating from an ore source near Lake Superior. The ore was transported over long distances, a trade well documented by more recent research. Carved pipes and other ornaments were described as a "higher grade of art," and the finely executed animal figures were considered to be "im-

Cross section of a mound from the Scioto Valley excavated by Squier and Davis. The mound was seven feet high, with a diameter of fifty-five feet. The text of their report describes the layers, one of the early attempts to summarize the stratigraphic layers of an American mound.

219

Artifacts from the Ohio mounds illustrated by
Squier and Davis in their classic report.

Stone effigy pipes.

measurably beyond anything which the North American Indians are known to produce, even at this day, with all the suggestions of European art and the advantages afforded by steel instruments."

The great monograph ended with six pages of conclusions. Squier wrote of the mound peoples in general terms, arguing that more data would be needed before anyone could settle the questions of age, identity, and migration routes of the Mound Builders, peoples "whose very existence is left to the sole and silent attestation of the rude but often imposing monuments which throng the valleys of the West." But earlier in the book the Chillicothe journalist brings to bear some of the commonplace prejudices of the day, which seem out of place amid such sober and accurate reporting. Looking at the defensive works he had surveyed, Squier was moved to observe that the builders had possessed a knowledge of defensive warfare "much superior to that known to have been possessed by the hunter tribes of North America previous to the discovery by Columbus, or indeed subsequent to that event. Their number and magnitude must also impress the inquirer with enlarged notions of the power of the people commanding the means for their construction." In other words, the Indians certainly could not have built the earthworks and mounds. Whoever the builders were, they erected a *system of defenses* extending from New York State to the Wabash River. "The pressure of hostilities was from the north-east. . . . from that direction came the hostile savage hordes, before whose incessant attacks the less war-like mound-builders gradually receded, or beneath whose exterminating cruelty those who occupied this frontier entirely disappeared, leaving these monuments alone to attest to their existence." This was splendid, epic stuff, oddly out of place in a monograph of sober archaeological reporting. The unspoken conclusion was that usurper Indians had ousted the earlier occupants of western America. Thus, by easy logic, one could conclude that the Indians were no more entitled to the farmland of Ohio than the colonists. They were a nuisance, being, to quote

222

Squier, "hunters averse to labor, and not known to have constructed any works approaching in skillfulness of design or in magnitude these under notice."

Despite its prejudiced attitudes, the Squier and Davis monograph stands as a notable archaeological landmark. With its lengthy catalogs and fine surveys

The Great Serpent Effigy Mound, Adams County, Ohio. After Squier and Davis.

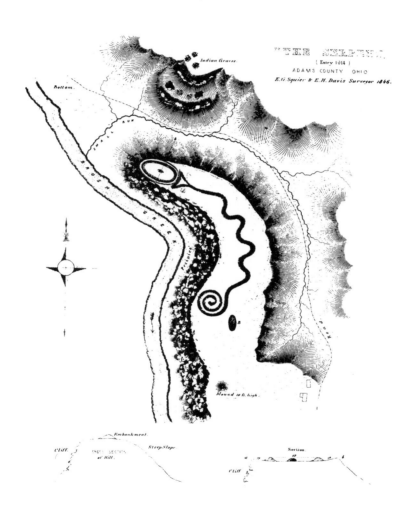

223

of sites and artifacts it placed an enormous quantity of archaeological material on record for the first time. Squier and Davis recorded hundreds of mounds found as far afield as Wisconsin and Michigan as well as in Ohio. The famous effigy mounds of Wisconsin that had first been reported by Richard Taylor in 1838 were the subject of a special chapter. These were remarkable monuments shaped like animals and human figures. A few plans of these new forms of earthwork were published in the monograph with an apologetic note by the authors who remarked that the few observations that had been made were those of men "of inquiring minds, in the scanty intervals of professional business." In this as in many other instances the Squier and Davis monograph both literally and metaphorically broke new archaeological ground and placed the serious study of Indian mounds on a new academic level.

The *Ancient Monuments of the Mississippi Valley* received immediate recognition as a classic work, appearing as it did only a few years after the great excitement generated by the historical work of William Prescott and the archaeological researches of Catherwood and Stephens. Ephraim Squier himself was active in the presidential campaign of Zachary Taylor in 1848, as a reward for which he was appointed American chargé d'affaires in Central America. This political gift suited Squier, for he could look for the origins of the mound peoples in Central America. Before he left for his new post, the journalist turned diplomat found time to write a shorter companion volume on the *Aboriginal Monuments of the State of New York,* which appeared in 1849, and attempted to sell his important collection of documented artifacts from the mounds to the New-York Historical Society, which refused to pay his asking price. The collection lay neglected in the cellars of the society until 1864, when they were finally bought by William Blackmore, a London antiquarian, who wanted to donate the collection to an American institution. Unfortunately neither the Smithsonian nor any other American museum would take the gift. So Blackmore took this vital assemblage to England,

and it ultimately ended up in the British Museum.

There was now a more serious and systematic approach to the archaeology of the mound dwellers, prompted by the work of enthusiastic amateurs, by the efforts of the American Antiquarian Society, and also through the publications of the Smithsonian Institution. An intellectual ferment about the past was in the air. Both serious archaeological research and wild speculation intensified as more and more people studied the mounds. One celebrated author was William Pidgeon, whose *Traditions of De-coo-dah and Antiquarian Researches* was published in 1852 and achieved best-seller status in 1858. Pidgeon claimed to be a trader with a long experience of Indians in the West. His fantasies were quite incredible. "It yet remains for America to awake her story from sleep, to string the lyre and nerve the pen," he began, "to tell the tale of her antiquities, as seen in the relics of nations, coeval, perhaps, with the oldest works of man. . . . This curious subject, although it is obscured beneath the gloom of ages, of which but little record remains, has nevertheless written that record in the dust, or in the form of mighty mounds, aboriginal fortifications, and complicated tumuli. . . ." After remarking how much interest there was in Old World ruins, he deplored the neglect of the "equally ancient relics of this broad country."

Then Pidgeon plunged into his stirring narrative, claiming that Adam himself built the first mound in America, and that all sorts of later visitors, including Alexander the Great, supposedly followed the practice. Egyptians, African immigrants, and Phoenicians had settled in North America, he said, leaving behind abundant traces of their presence. But Pidgeon's great preoccupation was the fate of the Mound Builders and their replacement by Indians. He bemoaned the disappearance of forty-two Indian tribes that had become extinct. "Philanthropic statesmen may fold their arms," he wrote, "and tell us they are moving them west; but forty-two tribes bear mournful testimony to the fact, that we are moving them to eternity." Presumably the fate of their mound-building predecessors was even more tragic.

Pidgeon himself seems to have led an itinerant life that took him from Virginia to Ohio, and apparently as far north as Prairie du Chien, where he met an old Indian named De-coo-dah, "a man of undoubted veracity, revered and respected by those that knew him." Having dug, he claimed, hundreds of mounds, Pidgeon spent two winters with De-coo-dah on an island near Prairie du Chien in the early 1840s. There he learned everything that De-coo-dah had to impart about the history of the Indians. Apparently the Mound Builders had used their mounds as hieroglyphic signs for passing on their great traditions. There had been a "plurality of nations" before wandering hordes of Indians overwhelmed the Mound Builders in a final orgy of violence and slaughter. For some reason Pidgeon was regarded as *the* trustworthy confidant for all that De-coo-dah had to tell. But De-coo-dah soon died. So Pidgeon promptly wrote down all his secrets for the entertainment and enlightenment of the world at large in a narrative that author Robert Silverberg has described as a "symbology of the mounds that for all its incoherence has about it the fascination of lunacy, like some monstrous bridge constructed of toothpicks."

Traditions of De-coo-dah was offered to the Smithsonian Institution, which rejected it out of hand. For the next twenty years the book made a fortune for William Pidgeon in the hands of a commercial publisher, even being quoted as a primary source by some gullible historians who should have known better. It was not until 1884 that a surveyor named Lewis bothered to check out Pidgeon's findings in the field. He stated that "the Elk nation and its last prophet De-coo-dah are modern myths" and debunked the whole elaborate work. But its impact on the general public was equivalent to that of Ancient Astronauts and all the mumbo jumbo of pseudoscience that has surrounded the work of Erich von Daniken in the 1970s. Although archaeologists delicately ignored Pidgeon, the public loved his vivid and all-embracing solutions to a historical problem of great contemporary interest.

226

The archaeologists of the time paid far more attention to a much shorter work, an essay by the librarian of the American Antiquarian Society, Samuel Haven. In 1856 the Smithsonian Institution published a carefully reasoned essay under his name, *The Archaeology of the United States, or Sketches Historical and Bibliographical, of the Progress of Information and Opinion Respecting Vestiges of Antiquity in the United States.* Haven was born in 1806 and became librarian of the American Antiquarian Society in 1837, a post he held until his death in 1881. He soon acquired an encyclopedic knowledge of American archaeology from the literature that passed through his hands.

The Archaeology of the United States is a lucid and concise essay on an elegant but economic scale. "After the discovery of America, the minds of the learned and ingenious were much exercised to account for its habitation by men and animals," he began. Early historians and the antiquarians who followed them had developed all sorts of ingenious speculations to account for the Indians. Haven carefully described each of the various hypotheses with a cool skepticism that cut through the rubbish obscuring the real issues. From the speculations he moved on to the "Progress of Investigation in the United States," a survey of current researches that threw clearer light on the origins of the Indians. He summarized the early linguistic work of Albert Gallatin, who had published a classification of Indian languages in 1836, described the physical anthropology of ancient and modern Indian skeletons, and concluded that the crania of these people were of "Mongolian" affinities. The archaeological researches of Squier and Davis, Schoolcraft, and others received careful attention, as Haven noted the general similarities between the artifacts and mounds observed by the early Spaniards and the earthworks attributed to the Mound Builders.

Then Haven marshalled all his scientific evidence line by line, an impressive mass of data by the standards of the day with America still little known. "We desire to stop where evidence ceases," he ended,

A portrait of De-coo-dah. Engraving from William Pidgeon's *Traditions of De-coo-dah* (1858). "De-coo-dah was of low stature, unusually broad across the shoulders and breast, his complexion somewhat darker than the Winnebago, with a large mouth and a short chin, his limbs were well proportioned, and he possessed undaunted courage." Pidgeon wrote that *De-coo-dah* meant "mocking bird." One wonders if he was laughing at his readers.

227

Samuel Haven.

"and offer no speculations as to the direction from which the authors of the vestiges of antiquity in the United States entered the country, or from whence their arts were derived." Stating that the native Americans were of great antiquity, he pointed out that "all their characteristic affinities are found in the early conditions of Asiatic races; and a channel of communication is pointed out through which they might have poured into this country." A conservative and well-balanced observer such as Haven was bound to hold great weight in the academic community. His essay formed a basis for the new science of archaeology to progress along fresh and aggressive lines, in the hands of professional archaeologists and institutions whose primary activities revolved, at least in part, around the study of the American Indian, past and present.

The Smithsonian Institution had already been active in archaeology for twenty years when another organization vital to the study of Indian archaeology and ethnology came into being. George Peabody was the archetype of the successful early nineteenth-century businessman. He rose from poverty to enormous wealth in a few decades, his business becoming one of the most respected in London and North America. Kings visited his offices and attended his receptions. Thousands benefited from his enormous philanthropic enterprise that included slum clearance in London and the Peabody Foundation for Education in the American South. This remarkable and much revered philanthropist became interested in the study of the American Indian through a nephew who spent October 1865 digging a mound near Newark, Ohio. Othniel Marsh had already been asked by his famous uncle to look for likely ideas for gifts to Harvard and other universities. Marsh thought of a museum of archaeology to be established at Harvard and suggested the idea to George Peabody. The following summer the details of a gift were worked out with Harvard University for the establishment of the Peabody Museum of Archaeology and Ethnology

228

and the endowment of a professorship of American archaeology and ethnology.

Peabody's letter of gift was dated October 6, 1866. After delineating the various details and conditions, Peabody wrote a memorable and prophetic paragraph: "Aside from the provisions of the instrument of gift, I leave in your hands the details and management of the trust; only suggesting, that, in view of the gradual obliteration or destruction of the works and remains of the ancient races of this continent, the labor of exploration and collection be commenced at as early a day as practicable. . . ." Peabody's directive was soon acted upon. Within a few years the Peabody Museum had acquired noteworthy collections of prehistoric artifacts from Europe, almost the first of their kind to reach America, and started a program of field research which, for over a century, has aided in the reconstruction rather than the destruction of the prehistory of the Americas.

Soapstone pipe in the form of a frog, four inches long across the base. From a site in Illinois.
Photograph courtesy of the Museum of the American Indian, Heye Foundation

229

12 "From the Known to the Unknown, Step by Step"

The great controversy over the origin of the Mound Builders was no abstract debate. It was a reflection of the feelings of a new nation engaged in vigorous expansion and colonization as well as thinly disguised genocide. As the frontiers of the United States moved steadily westward, so did official explorations of the unknown territories beyond the Great Plains. Not that this was territory newly settled by Europeans. Although Coronado's disastrous expedition was not followed by new attempts at colonization for nearly half a century, Catholic missionaries and Spanish explorers had traveled widely in the Southwest by the eighteenth century.

Spaniards had settled New Mexico in 1598, after an abortive colonization attempt eight years before, when Castaña de Sosa had besieged the pueblo of

Pecos. The Indians fled and de Sosa explored its plazas and rooms, with the multistoried houses "connected by wooden corridors or balconies which ran from house to house throughout the village." Oñate, accompanied by a small group of energetic Franciscans, quickly subjugated the pueblos. Churches and missions were erected. All seemed peaceful, although the Indians were increasingly resentful of the new religion and the oppressive rule of the Spaniards. These resentments boiled over in the Pueblo Revolt of 1680, which resulted in the slaughter of over four hundred Spanish colonists and a resurgence of the old religious ways under Popé, an Indian medicine man from San Juan. Even Santa Fe was evacuated as the Spaniards fled. Revolt succeeded revolt; as one district was pacified another would rise in rebellion. It took a decade for the colonists to reestablish their dominion over the pueblos. Only a combination of military force and diplomatic acumen ultimately saved the day for them.

The Pueblo Revolt was one of the few times that many of the various southwestern tribes were united against a common enemy. Spanish domination and oppression forced Christianity upon the Indians and put an end to intertribal fighting. The guns of the colonists enforced a restless and resentful peace. But, despite their traditional divisiveness, the pueblos wanted one thing above all: to be able to live in their chosen way, each pueblo isolated with its individual life-style, a dream built up by century after century of delicate adaptation to a harsh environment with simple but effective food-getting strategies. Even after the revolt failed there was further, sporadic violence, but mainly of an intertribal nature. The pueblos gradually lost some of their identity, even if many of their attitudes still remained, and the unchanging round of harvest and planting continued without interruption.

In the early eighteenth century one typical pueblo, Pecos, was in a state of slow decline, bothered by the Comanche who had moved to the southwestern Great Plains to become the scourge of eastern New

Richard Kern's sketch of
the pueblo of Jemez, 1849.

Mexico. Successive military campaigns left the
Pecos people and other pueblos decimated. In 1798
an epidemic of smallpox wiped out all but 180 inhabitants of Pecos. Forty years later the last Indians
abandoned that pueblo forever, settling at Jemez
eighty miles away. By this time many pueblos were
in ruins, their beams and timbers salvaged by the
Mexicans for firewood. Even the beams of the great
Spanish church at Pecos were removed and used as
corral posts in about 1860. One of the plazas became
a prison for Texans captured during the Mexican
War of 1841. The American force on its way to capture Santa Fe passed through Pecos five years later.

Its commander, Lieutenant Emory, described the ruined pueblo—indeed, illustrated it—in his report. But by this time a new era in the discovery and exploitation of the pueblos of the Southwest had begun.

The American settlement of the West accelerated dramatically with the completion of the transcontinental railroad in 1869. But while the frontiers of the United States were expanded ever westward, the main preoccupation of the national government was what one historian has called "a grand national reconnaissance of the entire trans-Mississippi country." The Corps of Topographical Engineers sent out dozens of expeditions. The engineers were instructed to pay as much attention to details of Indian life, plants, animals, and geology as they did to surveying. In this way a vast inventory of geographic and scientific information was accumulated in the Smithsonian Institution and other repositories, data potentially of great use to people moving to the West. The best scientists in America advised the Topographical Bureau. Universities and academies, including the Smithsonian, sent out trained field workers who collected scientific materials that were classified and described back home. The West was a vast natural laboratory to be explored at the same time as the California Gold Rush and other mineral strikes brought American civilization to the Rockies and the west coast. From these expeditions and studies, as well as from travel literature and adventure stories, even from novels and children's books, came the popular images of the West, and, indeed, of its Indians and archaeology, that have been with us ever since.

The Seven Cities of Cibola had remained outside American archaeological perspectives since Coronado's day. Accounts of their existence were buried in Spanish colonial archives and were read only by inquiring historians after the appearance of Prescott's magisterial volumes. The Spanish colonists of later centuries had no interest in deserted Indian towns and likewise ignored the pueblos as historical phenomena. But the military explorers of the 1840s

233

Pecos in 1846, showing the ruined church and monastery. A drawing made during the Emory expedition by an artist of the American Army of Occupation.

and 1850s were concerned with all aspects of the Far West. William Emory and John Abert carried out lengthy reconnaissances in the Southwest during the period of the Mexican War. They visited the ruins of Pecos and the Casa Grande of Arizona. Abert was later detached from the Army of the West, and he searched diligently for the Seven Lost Cities of Cibola. He believed he had found them in the pueblos of the Puerco Valley, especially in the pueblo of Acoma, built high on its own mesa, which seemed to coincide with a pueblo mentioned by Coronado's party.

Both the expeditions in which Abert was involved were hurried visitations sandwiched between other duties. But in 1849 Colonel John Washington led a punitive foray into Navaho country, taking with him Lieutenant James Henry Simpson and the Kern brothers, one of whom—Richard—was a celebrated

234

artist. They marched up the Chama River and discovered Chaco Canyon, where Simpson and Richard Kern spent much time mapping, excavating, and collecting in the ten major pueblos they found there. Kern's drawings provided the first accurate record of a pueblo, with a plan and tentative reconstruction of Hungo Pavie pueblo that showed this large structure to be a huge, stepped apartment block with blank walls to the outside, facing a court on its inner sides. His reconstruction has been shown to be essentially correct, as have his artistic efforts in the Canyon de Chelly, where the expedition spent time mapping the spectacular archaeological wonders of this Navaho stronghold.

James Henry Simpson's lengthy report was the first precise description of these archaeological sites, including the celebrated Casa Blanca of the Canyon de Chelly as well as Pueblo Bonito and Inscription Rock near Zuñi. Simpson's important researches were followed two years later by Lorenzo Sitgreaves's expedition down the Zuñi and Colorado

Richard Kern's hypothetical reconstruction of Hungo Pavie pueblo in Chaco Canyon.

rivers. Accompanied by Richard Kern, Sitgreaves investigated the Wupatki ruins of Arizona and wrote a magnificent description of Zuñi that is a classic. In 1859 Captain John Macomb sighted the cliff dwellings of Mesa Verde, although his discovery was overshadowed by the later and much better-known descriptions by the celebrated photographer W. H. Jackson.

All these gentlemen's reports were faithfully published by Congress, and many were reprinted for wider public distribution. Military expeditions continued through the 1850s, to Pecos again and as far as Gran Quivira and elsewhere. But these were not archaeological explorations alone. The surveyors were as much concerned with Indian life as they were with geology or antiquities. Living Indians, some of them primitive and warlike, were as much part of the marvels of the West as the spectacular scenery. Whatever practical solutions of the "Indian problem" the soldiers recommended—and these

Richard Kern's drawing of the Pueblo of Zuñi as it appeared in 1849.

236

ranged from economic aid to extermination—their information was of military value and of some anthropological use. The Indians and their ancient dwellings were an insignificant part of the great West, dominated as it was by the prodigious natural wonders of the Grand Canyon, the shimmering desert, Yellowstone, and Yosemite. As historian William Goetzmann points out, "Immensity—sublime, endless, empty immensity with here and there an Indian or a buffalo as allegorical nature god" was the artistic style of the time, a personification of the romantic and unknown West.

Civilian operations gradually replaced the military surveys of the 1850s. These were conducted through such agencies as the United States Geological Survey of the Territories, an agency of the Interior Department, formed in 1869. The survey was a catalyst for many important geological and surveying expeditions led by notable scientists, of whom one of the most remarkable was Ferdinand Vandiveer Hayden. Born in Massachusetts in 1829, Hayden became attracted to geology while at Oberlin College. He spent his early professional career on geological trips with the paleontologist Fielding Bradford Meek. Hayden spent much of his time in the area between Yellowstone and the Missouri River, acquiring a national reputation for stratigraphic geology that led to further invitations to go into the field. By the time of the Civil War Hayden was one of the leaders of the new scientific geology of the West. In 1867, once things had settled down after the war, Hayden was invited to carry out a geological survey of Nebraska on federal money, a task he completed so satisfactorily that he was invited to expand his survey to the Rocky Mountains.

Two years later Hayden was head of the United States Geological Survey of the Territories, in charge of a large party that included Cyrus Thomas, later to be a celebrated mound digger. This particular survey ranged widely over minerals, fossils, and geological strata; the report was so popular that all eight thousand copies were gone in three weeks. Hayden had

W. H. Holmes with a donkey.
Portrait by an unknown
photographer, possibly
W. H. Jackson.
*Smithsonian Institution
National Anthropological
Archives*

now set the pattern for his future surveys: reconnaissance of huge tracts of land which combined academic geology with prospecting for minerals, remarking on the scenery, and pointing out each potentially lucrative industrial resource or tourist attraction.

It was in 1870 that Hayden hired Sanford Gifford, a noted landscape painter, and William Henry Jackson, the greatest of all western photographers, to assist him in portraying the complex reality of the West and its geological phenomena, and, of course, to generate propaganda for new appropriations. Jackson was by now a very well-known photographer, with a flourishing studio in Omaha, Nebraska. He had won immortality with his photographs of the Union Pacific Railroad, often taken from the cowcatcher of the locomotive.

A five-hundred-page report came from the season's activities, a miscellany of information on numerous topics related to the development of the West. Less and less concerned with geology, Hayden wrote diary-journals of his survey's travels, returning year after year to the West with an ever larger party of topographers, artists, photographers, and geologists. While the quality of his surveys was uneven, Hayden, with the help of Jackson and others, did more than anyone to raise national consciousness of the potential of the West. Jackson captured Yellowstone in a series of immortal pictures. Both Hayden and his colleague were among those who lobbied for the establishment of Yellowstone National Park, which took place in 1872. That year the Hayden expedition numbered over sixty-one people, including an ornithologist, as well as W. H. Holmes, an artist and topographer who would soon be famous as an archaeologist. The peak of Hayden's career and reputation probably came in 1873 and 1874, when the discoveries of his party were the subject of wide public attention. In 1873 the Mount of the Holy Cross in Colorado was featured as one of the wonders of the West, immortalized by Jackson's photographs of a "great shining cross there before me, tilted against the mountainside." This was regarded at the time as a piece of religious symbolism of the greatest significance.

In the following year Jackson and his photographic party headed south from Denver into the San Juan country with the general intention of photographing the silver-mining areas there. On August 27, 1874, Jackson camped at the head of the Rio Grande opposite Cunningham Pass. There he fell in with a party of miners driving mules. In camp that night the miners suggested that he visit the cliff ruins near their claim on the La Plata River. The place was called Mesa Verde, and it was only a short way off Jackson's route, they added. The next day Jackson was introduced to Captain John Moss, an old western hand and itinerant miner who was boss of the claim. Moss was cordiality personified and agreed to lead Jackson into Mesa Verde. It

Cave dwellings and towers on the Rio Don Juan. This lithograph from the Hayden Report for 1876 helped launch W. H. Holmes on his long career as an archaeological illustrator.

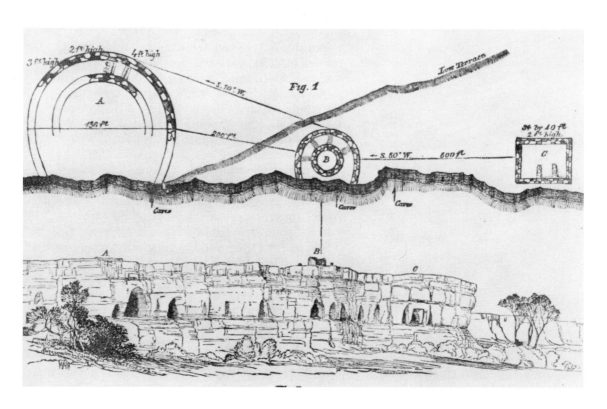

also transpired that he was a candidate for a local political office in an election for which the residence requirements were "on the sketchy side." "It was an easy matter for my photographic party, including the boys, to help vote him into office," wrote Jackson many years later. Moss then closed the polls and the party set off for Mesa Verde, a day and a half's ride away.

Late on September 9 the men arrived within rifle shot of the ruins, deep in Mancos Canyon with Mesa Verde eight hundred feet above them. Preliminary indications were rather disappointing, for there were few signs of ancient human occupation to be seen, and Jackson was discouraged. But after supper, as it was beginning to get dark, Moss pointed out a spot where an abandoned house could just be seen on a bench of sandstone several hundred feet above. The party began to climb up the cliff in the gathering twilight. Halfway up, everyone except Jackson and a newspaperman named Ernest Ingersoll gave up for the night. But the two were determined to press on and climbed via a tree and some convenient crevices. With some difficulty they emerged on the bench, where they found "a marvel and a puzzle." Perched on a ledge like a bird's nest was a house twelve to fourteen feet high "divided into two stories, and each floor into two rooms."

The next morning Jackson hauled his heavy camera equipment up the precipice and photographed this inaccessible dwelling. Ingersoll later wrote that it was "a two-story house made of finely cut sandstone, each block about 14 by 6 inches, accurately fitted and set in mortar. . . . There were three rooms on the ground floor, each one 6 by 9 feet, with partition walls of faced stone." Traces of a wooden floor could still be seen; all the walls were "nicely plastered and painted with what now looks a dull brick-red color." The house commanded extensive views of the valley for many miles.

Farther down the valley Jackson found other ruins, abandoned houses, and a few curious stone towers, which he felt were perhaps watch places. The party

Cliff Ruin, Mancos Canyon, Colorado, 1875.
Photograph by W. H. Jackson.
National Archives

A cliff dwelling found in Mancos Canyon by the Jackson party during the Hayden survey. This is one of the first photographs taken by Jackson in the Mesa Verde area.
Smithsonian Institution National Anthropological Archives

scrambled out onto the most precarious ledges to record and photograph structures perched under narrow cliff overhangs high above the valley. Then they rode out of the valley and into Utah without investigating any of the side canyons. Had they done so they would have discovered the Cliff Palace ruin, the most famous of all Mesa Verde landmarks, only finally stumbled upon by some cowboys in 1888.

As it was, the Mesa Verde discoveries caused a great deal of interest. Hayden suddenly became interested in archaeology, sending Jackson and William Holmes back not only to Mesa Verde, but also on a lengthy survey of all the southwestern ruins from the San Juan to Canyon de Chelly, into Chaco Canyon and to Pueblo Pintado, as well as elsewhere. The two men found nothing that had not already been reported by military surveyors or earlier explorers, but they produced a detailed and dramatic report that included not only photographs

and sketches, but also descriptions of artifacts, pottery drawings, and much information that put knowledge of the pueblos on a new footing.

So great was the interest in the pueblos that Jackson was commissioned to make a series of models of the major ruins for the Philadelphia Centennial of 1876, models that were later distributed to leading educational institutions throughout North America. The Mesa Verde discoveries were Hayden's last major public relations venture, for he ran afoul of John Wesley Powell's Indian surveys in the West and was forced to devote his efforts to geology alone after 1877. He died in Philadelphia nine years later, having contributed an enormous volume of new information on the West to the national consciousness. Jackson lived on to the ripe old age of ninety-nine, his photographs of the early West gaining him an even more lasting reputation than Hayden.

The great surveys of the 1860s and 1870s became an annual phenomenon, with expedition leaders vying with each other for congressional appropriations, pitting party against party in the field. There was much petty bickering and rivalry, quarreling in part engendered by the large number of expeditions and the increasing popular familiarity with the wonders of the Far West. The old frontier was rapidly passing into history as a new breed of scientists came to the West, scholars who specialized in one particular subject who were more interested in working for loftier academic goals than in titillating the popular imagination. The old romantic view of the West was to be slowly replaced with a more prosaic, scientifically based approach to the newly colonized territories that combined academic information with more pragmatic considerations. The West was now familiar ground. But its archaeology, geology, and Indians were not.

In April 1883 the Apache were on the warpath in Arizona. Movement by individuals and small parties was much restricted. In the midst of the disturbances Fort Apache, Arizona, was astonished by the arrival of a solitary mule rider, armed only with a blanket

243

An early and hypothetical
reconstruction of Pueblo
Bonito, after
William Jackson, 1870s.

roll and dressed in a "Scottish outfit." "Some crazy
bug hunter," commented the duty clerk in disgust,
as Adolph Francis Alphonse Bandelier dismounted
from his yellow mule and displayed an official letter
from the War Department that extended him the
courtesy of army facilities for his study of the
"ruined cities of the Pre-Columbian peoples who
centuries ago inhabited so much of the Southwest."

Adolph Bandelier is first encountered wandering
alone through the remote Indian territories of the
desert. Born in Berne, Switzerland, in 1840, Bandelier was actually raised in a small town in Illinois,
where he married a local banker's daughter. During
his youth Bandelier became disenchanted with the
banking world and what he called the "money-
changing" business. At the same time he somehow
acquired a profound knowledge of the history of the
Spanish conquest of the New World and became a
mine of information on New Spain's indigenous in-

244

habitants. It was not long before he came in touch with Lewis Henry Morgan, a wealthy Rochester attorney who was also an experienced anthropologist and avid student of Herbert Spencer's notions of human social evolution. Morgan had studied the Iroquois over a period of many years, developing a theory of human progress that he published in 1877 under the title *Ancient Society*. He proposed a universal scheme of human progress from a period of "lower savagery" up to an ultimate, seventh, stage, "the state of civilization." Humankind, he argued, had developed quite rationally and independently in different parts of the world through these several stages.

Ancient Society gained Morgan worldwide fame and exercised a profound influence on Marx's materialist philosophies and the work of Frederick Engels. To Bandelier, isolated among his books and dreams in a small Illinois town, Morgan soon became a folk hero and an influential patron. The two enthusiasts corresponded at length, and the younger man soon determined to test Morgan's theories in the field. Laboring for hours in the evenings after long days administering a coal mine, Bandelier had steeped himself in the Spanish records of Mexico and the Southwest to an extent duplicated by few other Americans. Fortunately he was an adept linguist, speaking French, English, German, and Spanish on a day-by-day basis. This meant he could make extensive use of the original sources little consulted by his contemporaries. By the time he left for New Mexico Bandelier had already published several monographs on Mexican culture for the Peabody Museum.

By 1880 life in Highland, Illinois, had become unbearable for Bandelier, who pleaded with Morgan for an opportunity to get out on field work. Lewis Morgan himself had just completed a long thesis on American archaeology, ethnology, and research priorities for the newly founded Archaeological Institute of America. His report stressed the need for studies of the social organization of the Indians of the Southwest and "the architectural

Adolph Bandelier, ca. 1882–84.
Photograph by
C. L. Maechtlen.
Museum of New Mexico

245

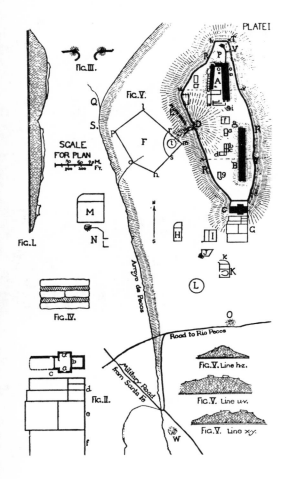

Bandelier's plan of Pecos, published in his 1881 report on the site.

character of the structures now occupied by them." The institute responded by asking Morgan for the name of a suitable applicant.

Thus it was that Adolph Bandelier found himself traveling to Santa Fe armed with a $1,200 yearly allowance from the institute. "I believe this is the poorest outfit ever extended," he wrote, "but the most valuable expeditions have cost the least money." By August 1880 Bandelier was on his way to New Mexico, the institute praising "his energy and zeal, his capacity of adapting himself to circumstances, his readiness to endure the hardships incident to the performance of his task," as well as his unusual training.

Only a few miles from Santa Fe lay Pecos, which Bandelier made his first stop, blissfully happy in his new free and penniless life. "I am dirty, ragged, and sunburnt, but of good cheer. My life's work has at last begun," he wrote. For days he worked at Pecos, describing and surveying the ruins. Others had worked there before him, but none so thoroughly. Bandelier stepped outside the ruins and summarized both the traditional and documentary history of the site. Sitting in the shade on hot evenings, he obtained vital historical information from the local people and old residents of the valley. There were still a few former inhabitants of the pueblo around, for Pecos had remained in use until the early nineteenth century. It had boasted a population of two thousand souls two hundred years before. But by the time the traveler and amateur naturalist Josiah Gregg visited the site in the 1830s, the last few families had abandoned Pecos forever. It was typical of Bandelier that he mastered the essentials of the local language in only ten days. His report, published by the institute a year later, was notable for its thoroughness, although it received little academic attention. It was to be years before archaeological excavations at Pecos proved the accuracy of many of his observations and estimates.

By September 1880 Bandelier had taken up residence in the Keresan pueblo of Santo Domingo, a visit that ended abruptly when he quarreled with the local authorities and the Indians refused to feed him. So he moved to Cochiti, where he lived for three months, "very happy, living, eating, sleeping, talking with the Indians. . . ." The Catholic clergy of New Mexico were his constant companions, for the association with the Church made Bandelier's travels and researches easier. In 1881 he converted to Catholicism, a move that may well have been partly an expedient, for a trip to Mexico and his subsequent conversion opened many doors that were closed to Protestant scholars.

From 1882 to 1892 Bandelier continued to work in New Mexico and Arizona, supporting himself with funds earned in a number of ways—by writing a Catholic history, writing articles, and serving for a time as historian of the celebrated Hemenway Expedition to the Southwest. He even wrote a novel, *The Delight Makers*, set in prehistoric times. His motives were partly financial, for Bandelier was living from hand to mouth. But he professed another motive in the foreword: "By clothing sober facts in the garb of romance I have hoped to make the 'Truth about the Pueblo Indians' more accessible and perhaps more acceptable to the public in general. . . . The descriptions of the country and its nature *are real*. The descriptions of the manners and customs, of creed and rites, are from *actual observations* by myself and other ethnologists."

The Delight Makers was no great commercial success, although it was reprinted twice during the First World War. It is a typical Victorian novel, full of intricate detail and complex plots, but written with a vivid insight into Indian life that reveals Bandelier's extraordinary knowledge of the pueblo peoples and perhaps the satisfaction that Bandelier himself gained from his long sojourn in Arizona and New Mexico.

Year after year he wandered through the Southwest mounted on a burro, compiling monumental records in his notebooks. The wealth of information they contained was published for the first time only in the 1960s and 1970s. Bandelier's contributions were enormous. Above all, he studied

247

Frank H. Cushing.
From his own book.

the Indians of the Southwest in the context of their past, as recorded in documentary and traditional, oral history, and from the archaeological standpoint as well. He was one of the first archaeologists to interpret the past on the basis of modern ethnographic data, to work, as he put it, "from the known to the unknown, step by step." Church records, traditional histories, and the architecture of ruins were all grist to the archaeological mill. They were the foundations of a method of studying the Indian past that proved to be one of the fundamental principles upon which today's study of American archaeology is based. Bandelier regarded archaeology as a means of extending anthropology and recorded history into the more distant past. It was not the objects themselves but the history and information they supplied that were important. Lewis Morgan had given him a conceptual framework with which to work: that of social evolution in predictable stages. Bandelier took the framework and laid the foundations for the scientific work of the pioneer southwestern scholars who followed him; men such as Fewkes, Hrdlicka, Judd, Kidder, Morris, and Nelson. With them we enter the modern era of American archaeology.

Bandelier himself left the Southwest in 1892 and worked mainly in South America, Mexico, and Spain until his death in 1914. He died with much of his work unpublished, but his novel fostered one of the new popular stereotypes of the southwestern Indian. The public had long been nurtured on a diet of sensational and romantic literature about the mysterious Southwest, a diet eventually modified by *The Delight Makers* and by other much publicized researches. Other scholars had courted publicity both to receive congressional appropriations and to interest wealthy patrons in their expeditions. One such philanthropist was Mary Hemenway of Massachusetts, who agreed to finance the Hemenway Southwestern Archaeological Expedition in 1886. The expedition, which Bandelier joined, became a reality through the smooth talking of Frank Hamilton Cushing, a remarkable traveler cum ethnologist with a flair for the visionary and the dramatic as well as for judicious publicity.

Cushing was born on July 22, 1857, the son of a physician. From his earliest years he was in delicate health, having weighed only one and one-half pounds at birth. At the age of eighteen, in 1875, he was appointed to the Smithsonian as an assistant in ethnology; there he played a major role in the institution's exhibit at the 1876 Centennial Exposition in Philadelphia, where he learned of the Pueblo Indians of New Mexico, whose material culture was a prominent feature of the exposition. He soon resolved to work in this far-off area; his ambition was fulfilled in late September 1879 when he accompanied Colonel James Stevenson on a Smithsonian-sponsored expedition to the Southwest. By this time Cushing, despite his almost complete lack of qualifications, was a curator in Powell's Bureau of American Ethnology. This allowed him considerable latitude in choice of area in which to work and the methods he chose to use.

In late September 1879 Cushing arrived at Zuñi, where he was supposed to remain for only three months, but it was not until four and a half years later that he left, forced to return to his neglected duties in Washington. A government mule brought him to Zuñi just as the sun was setting behind the pueblo. The settlement was covered with a pall of smoke. "But I did not realize that this hill, so strange and picturesque, was a city of the habitations of man, until I saw, on the topmost terrace, little specks of black and red moving about against the sky. It seemed still a little island of mesas, one upon the other, smaller and smaller, reared from a sea of sand, in mock rivalry of the surrounding grander mesas of Nature's rearing." Cushing was deeply impressed. The Indians welcomed him with restrained dignity and gave him and the other members of his party accommodations. After two months the official expedition was ready to move on, its photography and sketching completed. But Cushing had barely started his work. He was fired with a determination to live among the Zuñi, to learn their language, and to

249

record their life in greater detail. So his colleagues left him behind with his notebooks and sketches to fend for himself.

By this time he had picked up the rudiments of Zuñi, which endeared him to some of the Indians. But trouble flared up when he started to record the *Kea-k'ok-shi* ("Sacred Dance"). Two Indians tried to prevent him from witnessing the ceremony. So Cushing pulled a knife from his pouch and brandished it in their faces, daring them to stop him or seize his notebooks. The bluff worked. He managed to see the dance, although the people pressed around him so closely that he could not sketch at all. Unknown to Cushing, a meeting of the council was summoned, and executing the visitor or throwing him off the mesa cliff was seriously debated. Instead a Knife Dance (*Ho-mah-tchi*) was ordered, an ancient war dance of the Zuñis which was a prelude to death.

Cushing ensconced himself on a convenient rooftop, where he sat down to enjoy the ritual. Soon he found himself to be the center of the dancers' attention; he was surrounded by a crowd of Indians brandishing war clubs. Quickly he drew his knife and smiled sweetly, an act of considerable courage that took the dancers aback. After hurried consultation the dancers sacrificed a dog by clubbing it to death amid scenes that Cushing said were "too disgusting for description."

For some reason Cushing's cool demeanor made a deep impression on the Zuñi, for he was never molested again. He was allowed to study the structure of the village society in great detail, was even initiated into the secret Priesthood of the Bow in 1881—at the invitation of the Zuñi themselves. Cushing now dressed in Indian clothes. He had his ears pierced. He began to learn about the thirteen secret societies in Zuñi and spent many hours recording creation myths and folk tales. Soon he became aware of the well-regulated routine of life in the passing seasons at the pueblo and was given the name Tenatsali, "Medicine Flower." So great was the trust that the Zuñi had in this sincere anthro-

pologist that they made him a war chief. With a wry touch of humor Cushing recorded his title—"1st War Chief of Zuñi, U.S. Assistant Ethnologist."

Not that he spent all his time in residence at Zuñi.

The Dance of the Great Knife. From Cushing's *My Adventures in Zuñi*.

Decorating pottery.

A pueblo terrace in midsummer.

Pueblo scene.

Zuñi life: three scenes depicted by F. H. Cushing.

He traveled into Havasupai country, briefly went to Hopi territory, and even accompanied a group of Zuñi leaders to the east coast. The Zuñi were received by President Chester A. Arthur in Washington in 1882 and visited Boston, which they named City of Perpetual Mists. There Cushing took time out to cut his hair, which was an unfashionable eighteen inches long, and to get married. He brought his bride back to Zuñi.

The Cushing study was far from an abstract research project. He did much to protect the pueblos' lands from encroachment by whites and Navaho horsemen. His fight against land grabbing led to his ultimate departure from Zuñi, for he ran afoul of the powerful Senator John Logan of Illinois, who threatened to crush the Bureau of American Ethnology unless Cushing was recalled.

In May 1884 Cushing was back in Washington, where he concentrated on delivering lectures and writing up some of his discoveries. His dramatic personality and vivid imagination made him both friends and enemies, for scholars distrusted many of his theories and some of his data. The rest of his career was dogged by ill health. His leadership of the Hemenway Expedition was abysmal, partly because of his minimal administrative abilities and because illness forced him to withdraw from field work. But much was achieved despite the lack of administrative coordination.

The party carried out archaeological excavations in the Salt River Valley, Arizona, that were widely publicized in the East. Cushing himself lectured throughout the West, describing a cemetery of "skeletons surrounded with paraphernalia according to their rank," a pueblo "overwhelmed by a series of earthquakes. . . . so sudden was the catastrophe that the people had no time to carry away anything."

All this reflected Cushing's belief that archaeology was "ethnology carried back into prehistoric times." And he made his point by his dramatic eccentricity, by his efforts to use the history of Zuñi as a means of easing their transition into the white man's world.

254

Cushing's researches were never fully appreciated by either his contemporaries or his successors. In 1900 Charles Lummis wrote of the Hemenway Expedition as "a scattered and uncoordinated wreckage" of artifacts, excavations, and notes. And Cushing had become a public figure. "Cushing, indeed, was epidemic in the culture of New England," he wrote. His "personal magnetism, his witchcraft of speech, his ardor, his wisdom in the unknowabilities, the undoubted romance of his life of research among 'wild Indians of the frontier,' " all contributed to a colorful and imaginative view of pueblo life that heightened popular demand both for inspiration and for Indian artifacts.

The tragedy was that the pot hunter and antique dealer read the literature and moved in behind the scientist to satisfy popular demand. So the birth of scientific archaeology in the Southwest also dramatically accelerated the destruction of sites and burials. Cushing was sent by the bureau to Florida in the 1890s and died there on April 10, 1900, at the age of forty-three. Although he never witnessed the birth of modern archaeology and anthropology in the Southwest, his work paved the way for the first modern field work in the pueblos.

13 "That These Ruins Represent a Considerable Civilization, I Cannot Doubt"

John Stephens and Frederick Catherwood literally created a whole new generation of travel literature in America by their best-selling books. Soon there were many imitators, most of them volumes of travels about the American West, where travel was becoming easier and white settlement more commonplace. But, although the remarkable sites of Yucatan caused great interest, there were few new attempts to carry out excavations or conduct serious research. The distractions of the Civil War and the greater ease of European travel undoubtedly diverted people's minds away from Mexico. Some diplomats were active, notably Ephraim Squier of Ohio mound fame, who excavated in Nicaragua and Peru. The massive works of W. H. Prescott had also done much to satisfy Americans' interest in Mexico, even if many

256

details of the earlier history of Central America
remained buried in Spanish archives. Prescott and
Stephens had cast a somewhat romantic aura over
the pre-Columbian history of Mexico, a form of
romanticism that was reflected generally in the
literature of the day. It was a long time before serious
archaeological scholarship began in Yucatan.

While he was in Boston in 1846 a French priest
named Brasseur de Bourbourg read Prescott's *Conquest of Mexico* and became convinced that he
should devote his life to research into early America.
Brasseur de Bourbourg was born in the town of that
name in northern France in 1814. Living not far from
the Belgian frontier, he became fluent in French,
Flemish, and English at an early age; these linguistic
abilities enabled him to read widely in the travel
literature of the day and led him to dream of traveling himself. In the early 1830s Brasseur worked as a
journalist in Paris, cultivating an easy writing style
that was to stand him in good stead in future years.
At least nine popular books on a variety of fictional
topics flowed from his pen. But he felt himself
increasingly attracted to the Church and to serious
learning. After a spell at a seminary in Ghent,
Belgium, Brasseur enrolled in Rome to complete his
training for the priesthood, where he came in close
contact with reputable Church scholars and well-
known archaeologists.

After ordination at the age of thirty-one Brasseur
settled in Quebec in 1845, where he became professor of Church history in the seminary. But his
interests centered more and more on America. A sojourn in Boston in 1846 convinced him that he was
born to be an Americanist. Later the same year the
young priest went back to Rome to study in the
American sections of the Vatican library and to
train himself in the academic literature of Central
America. This experience turned Brasseur de
Bourbourg into a serious and extremely dedicated
scholar with an enthusiasm for travel and for all
American Indian history.

In 1848 he visited Mexico, where a chance meeting with the newly appointed French ambassador

Brasseur de Bourbourg.

257

gave him an appointment at his embassy, a unique position for a scholar needing academic contacts. On his way to Mexico Brasseur had traveled overland in North America as far west as the Ohio and downstream to New Orleans. He was now to start traveling again, examining archives, collecting manuscripts and books, wandering throughout central Mexico, and journeying to San Francisco as well. He then learned Nahuatl, the Aztec language, from a descendant of Montezuma's brother before writing his first American monograph, an overview of pre-Columbian history and of some recently discovered historical documents. This superficial survey, however, brought him to the attention of Ephraim Squier and the French scholar J. M. A. Aubin, who had assembled one of the finest private collections of Middle American books and manuscripts over a period of almost twenty years.

Aubin, who was rather miserly with the choice items in his library, befriended Brasseur and gave him the complete run of his papers, enabling the priest to spend four years in detailed contemplation of hitherto almost unknown sources. Then in another prolonged peregrination through Middle America Brasseur wandered as far south as San Salvador and Nicaragua, where he got caught up in civil strife and was imprisoned for a short time. Nevertheless he found time to study Indian customs—and to deplore their idolatries.

Guatemalan scholars welcomed him with open arms, lent him books and manuscripts. The archbishop was a fellow historian. Brasseur was by this time desperate for employment, for his exiguous private means were sorely straitened. So the archbishop appointed him parish priest of Rabinal, a small town sixty-five miles north of Guatemala City, a quiet living that Brasseur held for a year. Rabinal was a place, wrote Brasseur, that "disposes one to absentmindedness and contemplation." He fought off languor to visit archaeological sites and translate manuscripts, compiling a detailed history of the tribes of Middle America. After a year he was reassigned to other villages near Guatemala City and

258

studied the local languages so intensely that his
health broke down. It was time to return to Europe
and write up his original researches of the past
decade.

Two years later the four volumes of Brasseur's *Histoire des nations civilisées du Mexique et de
l'Amérique centrale* appeared, a massive monograph
over twenty-five hundred pages long. The complex
history of the various prehistoric and indigenous
states was laid out in detail, the account based
on both manuscripts and traditional histories.
Brasseur's linguistic abilities led to a comprehensive
history, based on new sources that had not been
available to Prescott. His new books established him
as one of the leaders in Americanist scholarship. He
was now a man for whom long-closed archive doors
were opened, an authority consulted by govern-
ments and private scholars whenever any large-scale
research was contemplated. He was able to travel
with official French government funds and devoted
time to translating some of the manuscripts he had
collected during his earlier sojourn in Middle
America. Then, in 1863, he made the most important
discovery of his career.

Bishop Diego de Landa's *Relación de las Cosas de
Yucatan* had dropped out of sight for centuries, having been consulted only by a few Spanish historians
before vanishing into oblivion. But, while recognized as important, the true significance of the
manuscript did not emerge until Brasseur de Bourbourg came across a transcript in the Academy of
History at Madrid. He published it in Spanish and
French as soon as he could, providing a mass of new
information on Maya life, beliefs, and hieroglyphs
that became a fundamental research tool for later
generations of scholars.

In later life Brasseur taught courses on Middle
America at the Sorbonne, visited the Mexican ruins
as a member of an official French commission appointed to study them, and published further
translations. But his health continued to decline,
and he died in December 1873.

Brasseur de Bourbourg once described himself as a

259

priest "whose ecclesiastical duties have always rested very lightly upon me." A tall, bespectacled man, who looked every inch the scholar he was, Brasseur owed much of his success to his strong ties to the Catholic Church. These enabled him to tap hitherto unknown archival sources jealously protected by their ecclesiastical owners. His charming and easygoing personality opened scholarly and religious contacts that would never have been available to less irresistible visitors. His writing style is uncluttered and flows with an ease that belies the serious scholarship behind it. His gift for describing the complex in easily understandable terms combined with his extraordinary linguistic abilities to produce history that probed far deeper than the pioneer researches of Spanish historians or of the celebrated Prescott.

But Brasseur was a romantic, a scholar of lively imagination, easily fired by the stirring events and surprisingly complex beliefs of the Indians he described. Maya mythology and hieroglyphs fascinated him. The writing would, he claimed, be deciphered by his use of Landa as his Rosetta Stone. His extravagant claims ended in failure, and his claimed translations of the only surviving Maya codex in Madrid failed to make sense of the document. He found the sources that led to the partial decipherment of the hieroglyphs, but his overwhelmed mind failed to take the next complex and vital steps.

It is as a compiler of data and sources that Brasseur is best remembered. His interpretations of Middle American history were dubious and frequently wild. The *Histoire des nations civilisées* is dotted with strange interpretations, most notably the fundamental idea that Middle American civilizations had sprung from the lost continent of Atlantis. He attempted to connect the origin myths of the Indians with the Atlantean legend. The origins of Indian languages were to be found, he argued, in Scandinavian and Mediterranean tongues. Then he related Indian legends to historical events in the Old World in pages and pages of tortuous explanation, reasoned in a diffuse manner that both irritated the reader and

A tribute roll from the Codex Mendoza which tells much about the wealth of the Aztec. The hieroglyphs at the left and bottom list the centers from which the tribute is to be extracted. The top row shows blankets, the symbols above them representing the total of four hundred of each that was required. The remaining symbols represent warriors' armor, headdresses, beads, and bundles of feathers.
Bodleian Library, Oxford

260

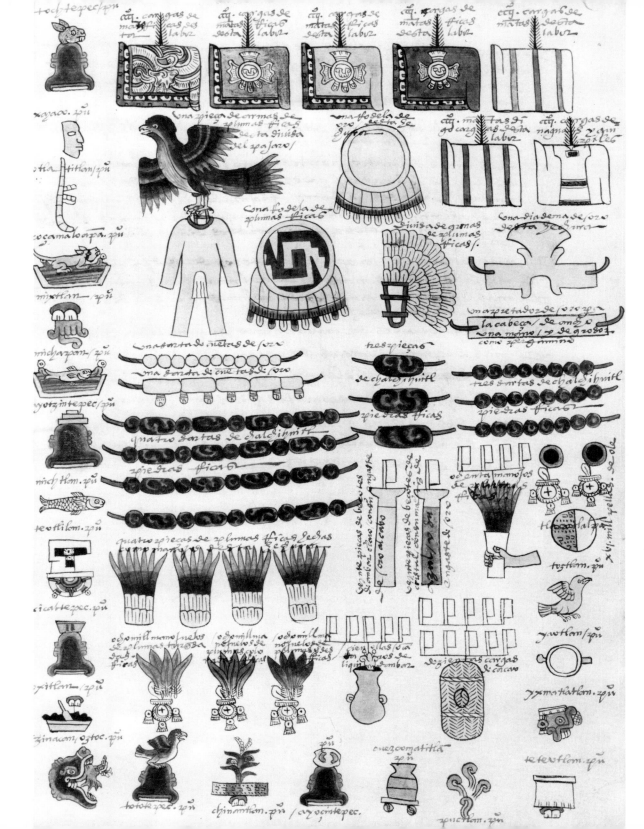

Augustus Le Plongeon.
From his *Queen Moo and
the Egyptian Sphinx* (1896).

obscured the brilliantly acquired historical data that lay behind it. Today, Brasseur de Bourbourg is remembered as the discoverer of Landa and as the man who provided much of the data that led to the partial decipherment of Maya hieroglyphs in the twentieth century.

Brasseur de Bourbourg was a pioneer, working in such a new and hitherto unexplored field of research that it was hardly surprising that he made occasional major mistakes in interpretation. The same could certainly not be said of other workers on the fringe of Mexican archaeology. One was the eccentric and vociferous Augustus Le Plongeon, who came to Yucatan in 1873.

Le Plongeon was born in 1826 on Jersey in the Channel Islands off France. Details of his early life are obscure, but it is known that he came to America in the 1840s in vague search of his fortune. The beginning of the great adventure was hardly auspicious; he was shipwrecked off the coast of Chile, one of only two survivors of the tragedy. After a period teaching in Valparaiso, he joined the California Gold Rush in 1849. Then he became city and county surveyor of San Francisco and helped lay out the streets of Yuba City. Soon he gave up surveying for travel and wandered off to England, Australia, and the South Seas before settling down as a lawyer in San Francisco. Within a few years he surfaced as a practicing physician, having somehow acquired a medical degree and a stream of satisfied patients.

Perennially restless, Le Plongeon was soon off on a new tack. In 1862 he moved to South America, setting up a private hospital in Lima, treating the poor, and spending some time exploring ancient ruins. He wrote a book on the Inca that no one would publish, a manual of photographs, which someone did publish, and translated some religious manuscripts, always with the hope that his contributions would raise him a step above the common man in the public estimation. Le Plongeon now took off for New York, displayed three "veritable old masterpieces," allegedly from a church in Peru, that he tried to sell, and finally decided to become a Maya archaeologist.

262

In 1873 he married a woman of twenty-two named Alice. The two then sailed for Yucatan together, where they were to remain for seven eventful years during which Le Plongeon made frantic efforts to become an authority on Maya ruins. In this he failed dismally.

It took the Le Plongeons, now operating as a husband-wife team, no fewer than two years to do anything. They lived in Merida and familiarized themselves with the country, acquiring influential friends and observing local Indian customs. Finally they made their leisurely way to Chichen Itza through country that was somewhat dangerous in the aftermath of an Indian revolt, a far cry from the feudal estates of Stephens's time. Fortunately Le Plongeon had obtained army protection. Once ensconced at Chichen the Le Plongeons spent three months in productive photography, surveying, and digging. In December 1875 Augustus made his most interesting discovery, a stone figure of a man carved at over life size, posed in an anatomically awkward position. Le Plongeon was transformed with delight, so electrified by his discovery that he compared it favorably with all the sculptured glories of the Near East. In fact it was a far from distinguished piece, surpassed by many others from Chichen and elsewhere. The figure was hastily dug up and levered from the hole in which it was found onto a crude cart.

Triumphantly, Le Plongeon moved his discovery along a specially built track to the village of Piste, where a message from the governor of Yucatan claimed the statue, now named Chacmool, or Tiger King, as state property. The Le Plongeons, who had concocted a grandiose scheme to display their find at the Centennial Exposition in Philadelphia, were appalled. They buried the figure in the undergrowth and hastened to Merida to free their latest pet from bureaucratic red tape. Despite their repeated pleas and a long and wandering appeal to the president of Mexico which claimed that the "greatest discovery ever made in American archaeology" remained "lost and unknown to scientific man," the government

Alice Le Plongeon.
From *Queen Moo and the Egyptian Sphinx*.

263

insisted on retaining the statue. Originally intended for the Merida museum, it was seized for the National Museum in Mexico City, where it remains today. Poor Le Plongeon! He had to be content with sending some photographs and small artifacts to Philadelphia, and even these contributions were lost in transit and ended up in New York.

In the intervals of writing for news of Chacmool, Le Plongeon set down his interpretations of the statue, a strange story of three rulers, all brothers, who had ruled the nations of Middle America many thousands of years before. Chacmool had married a beautiful, aristocratic queen, and both presided over a brilliant civilization at Chichen Itza. They lived together in connubial bliss, loved by their subjects, until Chacmool's younger brother murdered him and fled to Uxmal to found his own city. The grieving queen in the meantime caused the story of the life and death of Chacmool to be commemorated on the walls of Chichen Itza's ball court. This was only one of the strange stories that Le Plongeon wrote in the next few years.

The American Antiquarian Society received a steady stream of reports and descriptions from his field work, mainly on islands off Yucatan and on sites like Uxmal visited by earlier scholars. He soon quarreled with the society, incensed because it refused to buy his photographs or drawings. Le Plongeon simply did not measure up to scholars of the reputation of Brasseur de Bourbourg. He himself was convinced that he was one of the great authorities on Maya archaeology, the man who would decipher the hieroglyphs and solve the problem of Maya origins. He believed, like Brasseur, that the lost continent of Atlantis played a key role in early Maya civilization, but also that the Maya themselves had sailed across the Pacific, and even as far as the Near East, via the Indian Ocean. Vestiges of their "role in the universal history of the world" and of their languages were to be found in "all historical nations of antiquity in Asia, Africa, and Europe." He paraded a strange assemblage of data from Chichen Itza and elsewhere to bolster his theories, dating the

264

Maya to nearly six thousand years before. At one point he blithely stated that Chichen was twelve thousand years old!

The hieroglyphs were easy. "It is said that the deciphering of the American hieroglyphics is a desperate enterprise. . . . I humbly beg to differ from that opinion," he wrote. For years he looked over inscriptions, Landa's work, and earlier efforts, repeatedly announcing that Maya hieroglyphs were picture writing, that he had deciphered the script by drawing the letters of other, deciphered, languages on the hieroglyphs, and by sheer inspiration. There seemed to be some similarity between Maya and practically every known language in Le Plongeon's eyes. They were quite some people, the Maya—clairvoyant, familiar with giants, dwarfs, and the day-to-day uses of the electric telegraph and the metric system.

Eventually the Le Plongeons decided he had acquired enough data. He and his wife returned to Brooklyn, presumably much to the relief of the Meridanos. There they lived for the rest of their lives, surrounded by their artifacts and drawings. Alice Le Plongeon wrote popular articles on Yucatan as well as several more sober papers describing their discoveries in which she played down the fantasies. Meanwhile, Le Plongeon himself worked on his great work, *Queen Moo and the Egyptian Sphinx,* his ultimate statement on Maya archaeology. Published in 1896, this egotistical and tediously written tome was the usual amalgam of speculation and wildly organized facts that proved nothing and made an absurdity of Le Plongeon and his archaeology. A second edition appeared four years later; at least somebody must have read the first, although most serious archaeologists and historians ignored the work. After this final effort Augustus Le Plongeon published no more, partly because no publisher would touch his work. He finally died an embittered man in 1908, probably under conditions of poverty, convinced to the last that he was the unrecognized archaeological genius of his generation. Only a few people, notably James Churchward, the notorious creator of the lost continent of Mu, believed in Le Plongeon or his work.

But Le Plongeon was a phenomenon of his times, the sort of man who sacrificed wealth and personal comfort to study archaeology with a single-minded intensity that amazes. In Le Plongeon's case the goal was fame. A burning ambition fueled by a tragic certainty and self-delusion led him to believe he was the one chosen to reveal the secrets of the Maya. But, unlike many of the self-styled geniuses of archaeology, he never made money from his extravagant writings. All he succeeded in doing was to muddy the academic waters and to help ruin the reputation of legitimate archaeologists in Yucatan.

By the 1890s the professional archaeologist was a more familiar sight in the North American countryside, although not yet the commonplace one it is today. Mexico was less well served by professionals until the twentieth century. Much of the early field work remained in the hands of pioneers like Edward H. Thompson, a self-trained archaeologist whose interest in antiquity was sparked at least in part by the writings of Catherwood and Stephens, which he had read as a young man.

Thompson was the epitome of the pioneer archaeologist—self-trained, tough, and basically an individualist. He was born in Worcester, Massachusetts, in 1856, the son of a railroad station agent. His interest in archaeology began at an early age, in part the result of his mother's influence, for she encouraged him to collect Indian arrowheads. As a young man Thompson studied at Worcester Polytechnic Institute, but engineering did not appeal to him. While contemplating a different career, he learned Japanese with the vague intention of studying the hairy Ainu of Japan. Then he came across the works of Brasseur de Bourbourg. These filled him with an enthusiasm for the Atlantis legend and for the archaeology of Yucatan.

Edward Thompson working at Labna. His office is a room in the Palace there. *Peabody Museum, Harvard University*

An article in *Popular Science Monthly* in 1879 entitled "Atlantis Not a Myth" brought Thompson's name to the attention of a wider audience that included Stephen Salisbury, Jr., the wealthy vice-

president of the American Antiquarian Society. Salisbury had supported archaeological research before. He had given some money to Augustus Le Plongeon, funds for which there had been no return. In a leisured way he was now casting around for a new archaeologist to sponsor and approached Thompson with a proposition. Thompson would be appointed U.S. consul for Yucatan and Campeche with complete freedom to investigate Maya ruins and the modern people in any reasonable way he wished. Salisbury provided a modest subvention; Senator George F. Hoar of Massachusetts, a member of the society, the necessary presidential appointment.

It was in many ways a remarkable situation, for Thompson had never proved his worth as an archaeologist even in North America. Presumably his backers had seen in him qualities that appealed to their long experience in judging people: perhaps a capacity for shrewd observation, hard work, and individual initiative. In these early days of Mexican archaeology so little was known either of the sites or of field conditions that a great deal more depended on the personal qualities of the individual than is the case in these days of closely reviewed and federally supported proposals with tightly drawn and highly specific research objectives.

Thompson immediately set out to prepare for the new task by drawing on the facilities of the Peabody Museum at Harvard, where he studied Maya records and artifacts. He learned the rudiments of photography, some medicine and basic psychology, as well as Spanish grammar and some Maya. Wisely, he left the learning of colloquial Maya until he arrived in Yucatan. In 1885, accompanied by his wife and young daughter, the new consul arrived in Merida, where he established a home base and familiarized himself with the community and local conditions.

Uxmal was close by, and Thompson lost no time before visiting the ruins. Being an acute and energetic observer, he soon rejected the extravagant theories of his predecessors. Like Stephens, he was soon convinced of the indigenous nature of Maya civilization. Atlantis was consigned to oblivion, as he formed a modest general view of the Maya achievement. "That these ruins represent a considerable civilization, I cannot doubt," he wrote. "These ruins tell of a civilization of a state far above the nomads of the West and above the communal pueblos of the Southwest, but not of that advanced state of progress that sends forth a far-reaching influence."

The site of Labna was only seventy-three miles from Merida. Thompson devoted much time to this unspoiled ruin, for it lay off the beaten track, to some extent immune from the depredations of quarrymen and treasure hunters, and in relatively uninhabited country. Indeed, Thompson's Indian helpers had to hack a pathway through the brush to allow the mules and packhorses to reach the ruins on his first visit. Unfortunately Thompson lacked the background to understand the nature of the buildings and vivid inscriptions that he uncovered, beyond realizing that they represented something more than mere art for art's sake. His financial resources were so limited, too, that he could do little more than record the presence of a site and leave it for others to excavate. But he took many photographs and copied murals.

At Chacmultun in 1899 Thompson recorded the structures and frescoes only to return two years later to discover that the site had been ravaged and defaced by treasure hunters. But the very scarcity of funds turned his attention from spectacular finds to the sorts of small details that archaeologists before him had ignored. One good example was the *chultunes*, bottle-shaped cavities in the earth found at every major site. A narrow entrance hid each cavity, a defile that might hide unknown perils. Thompson had himself lowered into over a hundred chultunes, always with elaborate precautions: a rope around his waist, a hat to protect himself from falling stones, and a machete in his teeth. The precautions paid off on one occasion, for a rattlesnake lay at the bottom of a Labna chultune. He managed to kill it before it at-

tacked him. Thompson ultimately concluded that
the pits were for the storage of water and other commodities.

Edward Thompson was not only an excavator and
surveyor, but also an adept technician. When the
American Antiquarian Society requested a plaster
cast of the palace facade at Labna, Thompson devised a formula of plaster, fiber, and paper pulp. His
elegant copies were much admired in Worcester, so
much so that their author was asked to prepare more
molds of Maya ruins for the 1893 World's Fair in
Chicago. The task took forty laborers over a year to
complete. Uxmal was particularly difficult, for the
damp and humid environment sapped the workers'
energy and malaria was rife. Thompson fared little
better than Catherwood and Stephens had. His laborers fell ill, and he himself was temporarily

blinded by fever. But he succeeded in copying several facades, loading the molds on mules, and transporting them to the coast. Once on board ship Thompson collapsed in a state of absolute exhaustion. Ten thousand square feet of his molds from Labna and Uxmal were on display at the fair, a remarkable tour de force that attracted widespread public interest. Thompson was soon in touch with wealthy patrons willing and able to support his future research.

The new patronage enabled Thompson to visit Mitla and Palenque with the noted artist and ethnographer William Holmes, who produced some memorable drawings for the report on the trip. But Thompson's heart was in Yucatan, where he spent more than a decade wandering from site to site combining the duties of U.S. consul with those of an archaeologist. Chichen Itza was his favorite center, one that represented almost unlimited archaeological potential. In Chicago Thompson had been introduced to Allison V. Armour, a wealthy patron of scientific researches. He was able to guide Armour around Yucatan in 1895, taking him to many sites, among them Chichen Itza. Armour had recently given Thompson the necessary funds to buy the hacienda of Chichen Itza and to put it into good order. The notion was to operate the huge ranch on a commercial basis, using the profits to finance a center for scientific research.

When Thompson first arrived the site was overgrown, the seventeenth-century ranch house in ruins, destroyed during the Indian revolt of 1847. Only a small path gave access to the outside world. It took Thompson nearly a year to repair the house, set the ranch in some order, and import good-quality stock. Then he moved into the house, a home he was destined to occupy for thirty years. He commuted by pack mule and train to Merida, where consular duties kept him sporadically busy. Eventually the consular office was moved to the coastal port of Progreso, north of Merida, because of increased sisal exports to the United States.

It was not until 1909 that Thompson resigned his

consular duties. By this time Chichen Itza was taking up all his time. The hacienda never made a large profit, but it gave him the means to carry out a leisured exploration of the ruins he loved. He made no large-scale excavations but merely studied inscriptions and cleared the vegetation off structures and temples. His most spectacular discovery was the pyramid known as the "High Priest's Grave." A shaft led to the interior of the pyramid, a rock-cut chamber, and the graves of five individuals, one of them buried with rich offerings. This interesting discovery was never published in Thompson's lifetime but reached print in the hands of the Field Museum in Chicago three years after his death.

But Thompson's most celebrated, indeed notorious, exploits surrounded the so-called Sacred Cenote, a large natural well at Chichen that Bishop Landa had described as a place of sacrifice and that local Maya had revered for generations. Landa had written of human sacrifices and awful idolatries near the Cenote, stating that a great deal of treasure had been thrown into the pool over the centuries. Thompson had read Landa's account and resolved one day to probe the secrets of the deep water. For years he contemplated the Cenote, an unspectacular, muddy pool about 180 feet in diameter with precipitous cliffs. The calm water lies 65 feet below ground, colored green by algae, itself covering 40 feet of mud at the bottom of the pool. The ruins of a small structure stand at the edge of the Cenote, presumably the platform where the rites and sacrifices were performed.

The first task was to sound the depth and make accurate measurements. These completed, Thompson cast objects into the water from the structure at the edge of the Cenote, plotted where they fell, and decided that the southern side of the pool was the one where most of the sacrificial offerings might lie. The officers of the American Antiquarian Society, among them Charles Bowditch and Stephen Salisbury, were fascinated yet horrified at the danger of the project. Thompson planned to dredge the mud from the bottom of the Cenote and then to examine the

Gold objects from the Sacred Cenote at Chichen Itza.
Peabody Museum, Harvard University

272

crevices under water with the aid of a diving suit. In those days diving was a relatively clumsy art, a far cry from the ingenious scuba techniques of today. There were no facilities for diving at Chichen Itza. Even a minor emergency would probably be fatal. But Thompson exercised his considerable charm and powers of persuasion and his sponsors advanced the funds. He returned to Chichen Itza with an outfit of diving equipment, having taken a course in diving techniques in Boston. There, in February 1904, he erected a derrick and dredge at the edge of the Cenote.

With the aid of thirty locals, the long arm of the derrick was swung out over the calm waters. Dredging began in March, at first with little success. Load after load of stone, mud, and silt were brought to the surface, but only two human bones were found. It was a week before pottery and more bones appeared in the dredge, together with a ball of copal incense. At intervals for the rest of the year Thompson dredged in the Cenote, carefully sifting through bucket after bucket of mud. In December a few gold objects appeared in the dredge, the first of many such finds over the years. In 1909 he began to dive himself, with the aid of a Greek diver from the Bahamas. His assistant devised signals for ascent and descent, built a crude pontoon to float on the surface, and trained the locals in the use of his air pumps. The two men penetrated the darkness of the Cenote and searched the crevices for sacrificial objects. Although they rescued a few items—skulls and long bones—the results were much less spectacular than those from the dredging. Thompson did, however, succeed in rupturing his eardrum.

The material recovered from the mud by the dredge was spectacular. An astonishing variety of ceremonial weapons, masks, weapons, chisels, and copper bells came from the bucket; many had been broken or deliberately mutilated before being thrown into the pool. They were mingled with human bones, a grim reminder of the sacrificial rites at the edge of the Cenote.

No one knows precisely how many objects, or

exactly what, came from the Cenote. Thompson himself kept but a loose rein on his laborers and did little to check his inventories. Numerous tourists, both American and Mexican, visited his dredging operations. Archaeologist Sylvanus Morley saw a fine wooden ceremonial dagger with a copper haft recovered in 1907; others witnessed similar discoveries. Visiting archaeologists were often asked to carry small packages back with them to the Peabody Museum at Harvard, where the artifacts were quietly stored for later examination. There were no public announcements of the finds, nor were they displayed. The Mexican authorities of the time did nothing to control either the work at the Cenote or the obvious export of the finds, despite ministerial visits to the dredging operations. That there was serious pilfering of Thompson's discoveries is beyond doubt. Much of it was probably instigated by an Austrian engineer named Teobert Maler, who had spent many years in Mexico as an explorer of Maya ruins after Maximilian's invasion. For a while the Peabody Museum had retained him to report new sites. He now lived in Merida under conditions of grinding poverty, a bitter and illogical man with a strange idea that the treasures of the Cenote were his, not Thompson's. What came of them we shall never know, for no trace of the looted objects has ever been found.

Thompson now ran into trouble on various fronts. His investigations at the Cenote were drawing to a close, with nearly all his finds either safely in the Peabody Museum, at his ranch, or stolen. As far as can be determined, none were in Mexican museums at this point. A four-hundred-pound statue removed from the mud of the Cenote was dropped on his foot while being moved and crushed the bones. Then the regime of Porfirio Díaz fell, a government that had been indulgent to American archaeologists. The Carranza government which followed it expelled many American residents and businessmen. Thompson rescued some of his friends in a fishing boat and ran a naval blockade to land them in Cuba. Then he returned to his ranch, only to quarrel with some of

275

his tenants over rent. The hacienda was attacked and burned while he was away in Merida. The ranch house and Thompson's priceless archaeological library and collections were reduced to ashes. His plans for a research center were obviously doomed, but, undeterred, he set to work to rebuild the ranch house. This setback would have upset almost anyone else, but Thompson continued to struggle on under conditions of increasing poverty.

The Carnegie Institution of Washington, one of the new institutional backers of archaeological research that were fast replacing the wealthy philanthropists of earlier decades, was now, in 1923, making plans for a huge campaign of excavation and reconstruction at Chichen Itza under Sylvanus Morley. Preliminary plans included some payments to Thompson as the owner of the hacienda. But Thompson nearly wrecked the entire project by choosing the moment when Carnegie officials were fixing up the final details of the project in Mexico City to announce his spectacular Cenote finds in two articles in *The New York Times.* The newspaper quoted Thompson verbatim as exalting the virtues of his finds, details of the great treasures now housed in the Peabody Museum. Fortunately, Sylvanus Morley had done his work well in Mexico City and the Carnegie project was allowed to proceed. But officialdom had received its first inkling of the smuggling that had been going on for decades, in direct and apparently deliberate defiance of Mexico's antiquities law.

But it was not until 1926 that the government took action against Thompson. In that year battery magnate Theodore A. Willard's *City of the Sacred Well* told the full story of the dredging of the Cenote and described the extraordinary richness and variety of the finds from the mud. Writing as he was for the general public, Willard emphasized the gold and silver ornaments, as if a great treasure had been found at Chichen Itza. The Mexican government now took drastic action. Armed with Willard's revelations and a letter written by Maler in 1909 denouncing Thompson's activities, they attached

The sacrifice of a young maiden at the Sacred Cenote, Chichen Itza. A fanciful depiction of the religious rites on the edge of the pool, in Theodore Willard's *City of the Sacred Well* (1926).

276

the ranch for 1,036,410 pesos, charging that the ex-consul had smuggled artifacts for years. A magnificent national treasure was gone forever, claimed the Mexicans. Thompson was forced to return to the United States where he lived in poverty, largely forgotten, until he died at the age of seventy-nine in 1935. He eked out a living from rental on the hacienda paid by the Carnegie Institution and on some royalty income from an autobiography. The lawsuits over the hacienda dragged on until 1944, the Mexican government finally retaining Chichen Itza itself but returning the ranch buildings to Thompson's heirs.

In the furor caused by the Thompson case the Peabody Museum did not escape censure. The Mexicans demanded the return of the Cenote artifacts, a demand that was ignored. The objects were displayed proudly in the galleries, despite a burglary in 1937 in which metal artifacts were stolen from two cases but fortunately recovered. In the meantime the collections were studied and the findings published. Most of what was recovered from the Cenote mud was from the later, Mexican period rather than of the classic Maya. And the popular myth of virgins being sacrificed in the Cenote was disproved by the revelation that most of the remains were those of adults or children, several of them deformed. Only a few were teen-age girls. In the 1950s the Peabody Museum published three lengthy monographs on the Cenote finds. And, in 1958, much of the collection was discreetly sent back to the National Museum in Mexico City, the Harvard authorities claiming that the items had been given to the university on extended loan for study purposes anyhow.

Edward Thompson was one of the last of the great pioneers of Mexican archaeology. From the early twentieth century onward the main thrust of large-scale archaeological research was to be in the hands of academic institutions. Their excavation campaigns and reconstructive efforts placed Maya archaeology on a totally new footing, even if the pace of destruction and treasure hunting accelerated at

278

the same time. The rising tide of Mexican nationalism, the more rigorous training required of young archaeologists, and the higher costs of large-scale excavation have all militated against the lone amateur. But the Catherwoods and Stephenses, Thompsons and others, with their less than adequate training and preoccupation with recording and exploration, had done their work. The foundation had been laid for the less spectacular but more scientific investigations of the twentieth century. Both the academic community and the general public were now familiar with the general achievements of one of the world's most spectacular prehistoric societies.

A photograph of Palenque in the early twentieth century, with much of the clinging vegetation cut away.
Peabody Museum, Harvard University

279

14 "A Demand for the Interpretation of This Mystery"

Harvard University's Peabody Museum came into being at a time when institutional research on the American Indian was passing into more highly qualified and specialized hands. A new interest in archaeology on the part of philanthropists and universities stemmed in part from the new respectability accorded ethnology and geology from surveys in the American West, and also from the evolutionary controversies of the 1860s. It was fashionable and now respectable to look for early fossils. Why not search for prehistoric humans in North America as well as in Europe? It was against this background of heightened academic and public concern that the Peabody Museum became more active in field work.

The museum itself had developed slowly since its

founding in 1866. Its nucleus was its collection of prehistoric Indian artifacts from the Merrimac Valley, which was soon followed by important specimens from northern Europe: some of the first extensive assemblages of material from the celebrated Stone Age caves of France to reach the New World. The Peabody galleries now included the private collection of the famous prehistorian Gabriel de Mortillet, which gave scholars a chance to examine the earliest-known stone tools of prehistoric humans at first hand as a basis for searching for similar artifacts in the New World. In its early years the Peabody was busy acquiring specimens from

The Peabody Museum at Harvard University in the 1890s.
Peabody Museum, Harvard University

many eastern sites and gradually expanded its efforts into the Midwest. By the time the first Peabody building was erected in 1877 the collections of the museum were enormous, covering not only the archaeology of the mounds, but also many smaller collections of items from other continents and the western United States.

The museum's first curator was Dr. Jeffries Wyman, a natural scientist turned archaeologist who excavated shell mounds on the Atlantic coast and in Florida. The second curator was Frederick W. Putnam, an eminent ichthyologist who had a lifelong interest in archaeology and the American Indian. Putnam took up his post in 1875, when science in general and archaeology in particular were beginning to show signs of greater professionalism. He was to become Harvard's Peabody Professor of American Archaeology and Ethnology a decade later, a year before the University of Pennsylvania created a similiar chair in American archaeology. The new curator was an energetic administrator who laid the foundations of the Peabody's magnificent library and of a publication program that rivaled that of the Bureau of American Ethnology in Washington. The library and publications were the basis for exchanging both publications and specimens with other institutions, a pattern of academic interchange that has developed to enormous proportions in the world of archaeology. Today practically every institution has developed its own publication program for the same purpose.

Putnam was also an active researcher and teacher, who worked both on the mounds of the Ohio Valley and on the controversial problem of human origins in North America. The publication of Charles Lyell's books on uniformitarian geology and of *The Origin of Species*, as well as the startling finds of prehistoric artifacts in the Somme Valley, France, had sparked intense interest in the prospects of finding evidence of really early prehistoric occupation of the New World, possibly even earlier than the celebrated Neanderthal skull, dating from fifty thousand years ago, found in Germany in 1856. Putnam became

282

deeply involved in the search for early stone tools. He looked for early stone artifacts in various gravels and excavated coastal shell middens in search of artifacts similar to those recently discovered in Scandinavian "kitchen middens."

There were already some rumors of very early humans. In 1838 a professional fossil dealer named Albert Koch had discovered the burned bones of a mastodon in association with allegedly humanly made stone implements at a site in Missouri. But Koch was a notorious showman and no one took

Frederick Putnam at one of his excavation sites in the Miami Valley, Ohio, 1890. *Peabody Museum, Harvard University*

283

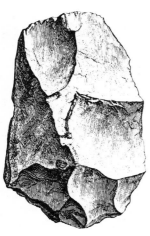

Two stone implements from the Trenton gravels, once claimed to be as old as ancient Stone Age tools found in Europe. The Trenton area received early attention as a possible campsite of early humans in the Americas. Illustration from an article in Winsor's *Narrative and Critical History of America* (1889).

very seriously his discoveries or those of Dr. Dickenson, of panorama fame, who reported finding a human pelvis with some mastodon bones near Natchez eight years later. The bones of mastodons were relatively commonplace, but few scientists believed they had been hunted by humans. But those who thought of the Mound Builders as peoples of great antiquity were enthusiastic in their advocacy of a long period of "barbarism" before the "great civilization" began. The idea of a high antiquity for humankind was supported by many popular writers about North American archaeology, including Sir John Lubbock, whose *Prehistoric Times* was the authoritative account of world prehistory for many years from its first edition in 1865.

A year later, in 1866, a miner named James Watson found a skull 130 feet deep in a mine shaft in Calaveras County, California, a discovery that was brought to the attention of the California Geological Survey and was subsequently claimed to be the fossil of a man who lived in California "before the mastodon was known to exist." As the geologists pointed out, the skull came from a geological stratum dated to the very end of the Pliocene era, a geological period that immediately preceded the celebrated Ice Age in which the earliest European humans flourished. Calaveras Man enjoyed wide fame for half a century until the anthropologist Ales Hrdlicka dismissed it as a successful prank.

By the time Putnam set to work there was quite a catalog of finds of mastodon bones and human remains, but none of the crude flaked stone axes found so often in the Somme Valley and other locations in Europe. The new curator of the Peabody examined an Indian campsite found in the Trenton gravels in New Jersey and claimed it to be twenty to thirty thousand years old. He also supported research in peats and gravels in Pennsylvania, Ohio, and Indiana. Peabody had originally charged his museum with special responsibility for the discovery of "human remains or implements of an earlier geological period than the present." Putnam now assumed this responsibility himself, flying in

284

the face of established academic opinion by recognizing the possibility of very early settlement. This meant he looked closely at the evidence from Calaveras and elsewhere that the California geologist J. D. Whitney, in his *Auriferous Gravels of the Sierra Nevada of California* (1879), had claimed was a sign that Tertiary man had lived in North America. "The archaeologist has no right to be governed by any preconceived theories," Putnam wrote, "but must take the facts as he finds them." The debate surrounding the first human settlement of the Americas raged for decades after Putnam wrote these words. Only when J. D. Figgins found Indian arrowheads with the bones of an extinct bison at Folsom, New Mexico, in 1926 did people finally believe in a really early date for the first native Americans.

A new era in American archaeology, one that was based on sober observations rather than wild speculation, was just beginning. Many more archaeologists went into the field, collecting enormous numbers of artifacts and describing them in proliferating publications. Typical of these archaeologists was Paul Schumacher, who worked in the Santa Barbara Channel region of California in the mid-1870s. "My attention was especially given to the finding and exhuming of the old cemeteries, which, as my experience taught me, promised the richest rewards," he wrote. "The principal aim of the expedition to this region was the collection of implements left by the former inhabitants. . . ." At their worst this generation of archaeologists was little better than a group of collectors; at their best their researches were the prototypes for the careful stratigraphic excavations of later years.

But the major controversy about the prehistoric Indians still surrounded the great and mysterious mounds of the Midwest and South. Squier and Davis's report had added a huge corpus of new information to that of the pioneers. As institutional involvement in academic research became more commonplace, there came into being new organizations designed to carry out such work. The great private surveys of the West were gradually replaced by official expeditions headed by individuals who had once operated on their own. No one was more influential in accelerating this trend than John Wesley Powell, explorer, anthropologist, and administrator.

John Wesley Powell was born in Mount Morris, New York, in 1834. The son of a Wesleyan preacher, his early life was spent in Jackson, Ohio, where the prospects for his father's ministry were more promising than in country that had seen the birth of Mormonism. A close family friend was George Crookham, a successful farmer and fervent abolitionist who acted as unofficial schoolteacher for the community. It was Crookham who introduced John Powell to the earthworks of Ohio and to the strange relics found in them. The small group of boys who came under Crookham's influence wandered all over the countryside with him, digging in mounds for Indian arrowheads, collecting plants and animals, and learning some rudiments of geology. These interests remained with Powell for the rest of his life. His family moved to Wisconsin and then to northern Illinois. In both places Powell continued to dig into mound sites and to spend time in the backwoods. In the late 1840s he came into contact with Winnebago Indians and learned something of their traditional ways, developing a passionate sympathy for Indian life that remained with him for the rest of his life.

At the age of seventeen Powell took a post as a schoolteacher for the princely wage of fourteen dollars a month. He taught arithmetic, geology, and geography, finding it difficult to discover a college where he could obtain the proper scientific training he craved. He did enroll at Illinois College in Jacksonville in 1855 but left after a year to go on a mollusk-collecting trip in Wisconsin. He ended up traveling practically the whole length of the Mississippi in a small rowboat. Both this experience and his constant reading gave him a professional training in geology that more than adequately substituted for the scientific schooling he never received.

The young Powell in 1857–58 was hard at work and walking from mound to mound in Ohio, then westward to Missouri. His objective was to produce

a "catalog of mound-builders' arts," a monograph he
never completed, for the work was interrupted by
the outbreak of the Civil War. Powell enlisted in the
Union army as a private and rose through the ranks
to become a major by the end of hostilities. He
retained the courtesy rank for the rest of his life.
Powell's military experience culminated in the loss
of his right arm at the battle of Shiloh in 1862. Army
life did not prevent him from digging into mounds
in Missouri, Tennessee, and Mississippi, or from
investigating cemeteries near the Shiloh battlefield
as the army waited for fighting to begin. He became
recognized as an authority on mound archaeology, a
man whose cataloging efforts had contributed much
to the actual information available on the mounds.
But his interpretations differed little from the exotic
popular views of the day.

After the Civil War Powell returned to academic
life. He became a geology instructor at Illinois
Wesleyan University at the salary of one thousand
dollars a year. A popular instructor, he took his
students on long summer field trips as far west as the
Rocky Mountains. His first expedition to Colorado in
1867–68 was conducted under the protection of
United States troops, but later trips were far more ad-
venturous. The Indian artifacts he brought back for
Illinois museums were almost the first of their kind
to be displayed in these institutions and caused great
interest. By 1869 Powell was in contact with the
Smithsonian Institution, at whose suggestion he
collected vocabularies and linguistic information
from the Indian tribes of the Colorado River area.

Congress authorized, and the Smithsonian Institution financed, Powell's subsequent famous and astonishing journey down the Colorado where he shot
the rapids of the Grand Canyon accompanied by a
motley band of students and mountain men. Powell
emerged from this experience a national celebrity,
not only as an explorer and geologist of note, but as a
famous anthropologist as well. He was appointed director of the U.S. Geographical and Geological
Survey of the Rocky Mountain Region for his pains
and studied the Hopi and later the Ute, Paiute, and

John Wesley Powell with an Indian near the Grand Canyon
in northern Arizona. A picture taken in the early 1870s.
Smithsonian Institution National Anthropological Archives

Shoshone people. His survey parties ranged widely over Colorado and adjoining states, engaged not only in geology but in ethnological research as well. With his characteristic vision John Wesley Powell realized that an enormous quantity of unique information on Indian languages, culture, and social and religious usages was rapidly becoming extinct. He spearheaded a drive to collect as many data as possible before it was too late, a task that he continued to direct for the remainder of his life.

Physicist Joseph Henry, the longtime secretary of the Smithsonian Institution, initially had been more concerned with science than with archaeology or Indian life. But his institution had become the national repository for the many collections of Indian artifacts and the bulky files of data that flowed into Washington from government officials in the field. Fortunately Henry had realized early that this information would be of more use if it were collected systematically. So his staff prepared and distributed questionnaires that sought information on many different aspects of Indian life—language, habitat, houses, burial practices, population densities, social and religious usages, and so on. The results of the survey were astonishing. Army officers, missionaries, and traders from the distant West responded with an extraordinary miscellany of information that kept the Smithsonian's staff busy for years. Many of the reports were of high quality; some were published in the Smithsonian's *Contributions to Knowledge*. Others were put out as popular news releases or kept on file. By 1875 a huge array of unclassified data lay in the files of the institution.

Powell had become involved with the affairs of the Smithsonian in both an official and an unofficial capacity, playing a major role in the staging of the Indian handicraft display at the Centennial Exposition in Philadelphia in 1876. This gave him an insight into the extraordinary information in the Smithsonian's files, data to which he soon gained free access. There were 670 linguistic studies alone. Given permission to publish from the Smithsonian's data, Powell boldly started a series of *Contributions*

Major John Wesley Powell (1834–1902) in his Washington office. Photography by DeLancey Gill of Washington. Date not recorded. *Smithsonian Institution National Anthropological Archives*

to North American Ethnology, the first volume appearing under the auspices of his Rocky Mountain survey. Eight volumes eventually appeared, studies of the greatest value and importance. But only two were in print by the time Major Powell himself had moved to Washington to head up a new government body attached to the Smithsonian Institution: the Bureau of Ethnology.

The bureau was Powell's brainchild, set up as a result of a major report he had written to the secretary of the Interior after two years of study of the Smithsonian archives. His eloquent plea for a special agency to study the North American Indians was a masterpiece of bureaucratic argument. "The work is of great magnitude," he wrote, "more than four hundred languages belonging to about sixty different stocks having been found within the territory of the United States. . . . the field of research is narrowing because of the rapid change in the Indian population now in progress. . . . in a very few years it will be impossible to study our North American Indians in their primitive condition, except from recorded history." Then he added: "The rapid spread of civilization since 1849 has placed the white man and the Indian in direct conflict throughout the whole area, and the 'Indian problem' is thus thrust upon us and it *must* be solved, wisely or unwisely. Many of the difficulties are inherent and cannot be avoided, but an equal number are unnecessary and are caused by the lack of our knowledge relating to the Indians themselves. Savagery is not inchoate civilization; it is a distinct status of society. . . . the blunders we have made, and the wrongs we have inflicted upon the Indians . . . have been cruel and inexcusable, except on the ground of our ignorance."

Powell filed his report in November 1878, a document that carried the full weight of his powerful authority as a courageous explorer, a war hero, and a respected field researcher and Indian expert. It arrived in Washington at a time when politicians were just beginning to worry about the Indian in more concrete terms. Only four months later, on March 3, 1879, Congress passed an appropriations bill that brought into being not only the U.S. Geological Survey, but also the Smithsonian Institution's Bureau of Ethnology. The appropriation provided two thousand dollars "for completing and preparing for publication the Contributions to North American Ethnology." John Wesley Powell was appointed director of the bureau. Three years later he took over the Geological Survey as well, an act that made him one of the busiest men in Washington.

John Wesley Powell was a man of vast energy and magnetic personality. He could charm congressmen and attracted talented subordinates, whose contributions placed the bureau on the path to greatness. For eighty-five years, until it merged with the Smithsonian's Office of Anthropology in 1964, the Bureau of American Ethnology—the word *American* was added in 1894—continued in the tradition of Powell's leadership. From the beginning Powell believed that the bureau was his personal organization, to be run as he wanted. But the Smithsonian, to which his office was firmly attached, felt otherwise. The secretary of the Smithsonian repeatedly placed liens on bureau accounts for expenditures to collect specimens in the Sandwich Islands or "Alaska and elsewhere," areas where foreign scientists were acquiring excellent artifacts.

The problem was the National Museum within the Smithsonian, set up at the same time as the Smithsonian as a separate body but amalgamated with it a decade later. The collections of the museum had grown enormously, swelled by the acquisitions of government expeditions in the Far West and by gifts from all over the world, often rewarded by gifts of publications, most of them those of the Bureau of Ethnology. While this was gratifying to its staff and good for archaeology, Powell was indignant, for his annual subvention often became a mockery, hampering the research of his staff. In fact, Congress had merely intended the funds to be used for the publication of ethnographic data acquired by geological expeditions, not as a means of supporting a new research organization. Furthermore, Powell in his Annual Reports emphasized the importance of linguistic research, for through languages one could achieve a proper understanding of Indian society. But members of Congress cared little about Indian languages or customs, considering the acquisition of specimens for the National Museum that visitors to Washington could admire at their leisure to be of the highest priority.

Matters came to a head in 1881, when a group of archaeologists persuaded Congress to add a rider to the following year's appropriations that would allocate 20 percent of the bureau funds to be "expended in continuing archaeological investigations relating to mound builders and prehistoric mounds." Powell himself was taken by surprise and disconcerted by the strings attached to his latest appropriation. His ethnographic projects were inadequately funded as it was, but in any case his primary interests were now not in archaeology at all. He had confined himself to a single paragraph in an early Annual Report: "Mound building tribes were known in the early history of discovery of this continent. . . . there is . . . no reason for us to search for an extralimital origin through lost tribes for the arts discovered in the mounds of North America."

Although it is difficult to establish the exact motives of those who lobbied for, and passed, the celebrated appropriation, one cannot help suspecting that some of them hoped that the bureau would disagree with Powell and find evidence of exotic civilizations in North America. Fortunately, subsequent political interference in archaeological research was minimal, and the bureau's new Division of Mound Exploration soon ended the myth of the Mound Builders.

Late in 1881 Powell recruited Professor Cyrus Thomas to head the bureau's new archaeology program. Thomas was born in Cairo, Illinois, and had spent his early career as an entomologist and later a botanist in the Geological Survey of the Territories, now part of the Geological Survey. He came to the bureau as a "pronounced believer in the existence of a race of Mound Builders, distinct from the American Indians." Quite how he had acquired the title Professor is a secret of history; it certainly was not for archaeology.

Within a few months Thomas and eight assistants were working all over mound country, especially in the Mississippi Valley where the destruction of mounds by commercially minded individuals was at fever pitch. The popular interest in the myths and fantasies surrounding the earthworks had caused the farmers who owned mounds to dig into their

Professor Cyrus Thomas.
A portrait in old age.
Photographer and date not recorded.
Smithsonian Institution National Anthropological Archives

293

property in search of the fine, carved tobacco pipes that Squier and Davis had illustrated in their report.

The situation in Thomas's time can be exemplified by the more recent tragedy of the Spiro Mounds in Oklahoma. This fine and elaborate mound complex had been known for years, yet it excited little interest except among occasional pot hunters. Then, in 1933, six relic hunters leased the site and started extensive tunneling operations. Thousands of fine pipes, copper objects, magnificent pots, and other treasures came from the trenches. The market was flooded with fine antiquities—so many, indeed, that a glut ensued. Textiles, pots, ornaments were trampled underfoot, the appeals of archaeologists ignored. The relic hunters boldly turned themselves into the

Pocola Mining Company to head off University of Oklahoma archaeologists. When the state legislature finally acted, law enforcement officials simply looked the other way. Dynamite tore the mounds apart when shovels proved insufficient. Contemporary observers wrote that the excavations were literally paved in broken artifacts. Priceless archaeological information about the burial chambers in the mounds was lost forever, for the university archaeologists who finally gained access to the site in 1936 had only shattered mounds to excavate. Local museums spent years tracking down the finest Spiro artifacts and buying them back from their owners. Thousands of smaller and less important sites suffered the same fate long before the Spiro tragedy. Nor were some self-styled archaeologists much better. Cotton magnate Cyrus Moore spent his summers on specially constructed houseboats on the Mississippi and Ohio rivers. As he floated along with his gang of laborers, he would stop at a suitable mound and dig into it. Thousands of artifacts were loaded on board, and the party then moved on to the next site. Moore did contribute some descriptions of his finds to the archaeological literature but seems to have been little more than a large-scale collector.

Having been forced into the mound business, John Wesley Powell now sounded a clarion call for action. In successive Annual Reports he hit hard at the destruction of mounds and at the myths surrounding their origins. There had been many false statements about the mounds, fantasies encouraged by "the garbling and perversion of the lower class of writers supplemented by the phantasies of those better intentioned." He pointed out that "those who have hitherto conducted the researches have betrayed a predetermination to find something inexplicable . . . and were swept by blind zeal into serious errors even when they were not imposed upon by frauds and forgeries." These strictures did not make the bureau many friends among the lunatic fringe or the collectors.

Soon Powell hired Henry Henshaw, a naturalist, to study the carvings found in the mounds. He

Warrior effigy pipe
from Spiro Mound,
LeFlore County, Oklahoma.
*Photograph courtesy of
the Museum of the American
Indian, Heye Foundation*

295

Wooden deer-man mask, 11½ inches high, from Spiro Mound, LeFlore County, Oklahoma. The surface was originally painted and the ears were inlaid with shell.
Photograph courtesy of the Museum of the American Indian, Heye Foundation

compiled a lengthy paper on the animal identifications made by Squier, Davis, and others, identifications that included mammoths, manatees, and toucans. Henshaw found that not one animal was of a species found outside the Mississippi Valley, nor were the claims for mastodon carvings from Iowa mounds discovered by the Reverend Jacob Gass based on anything more than what Henshaw plainly regarded as forgeries. The problem of forgery, whether of mastodon carvings, inscribed tablets, or just pipes for gullible and avid collectors, had become serious for the Smithsonian and for other museums, because the demand for Indian artifacts was constantly rising. An official inquiry did little to stop a flourishing industry that continues to the present day.

Cyrus Thomas's plans for mound investigations involved the use of three full-time assistants and five temporary employees. Early experience had shown that the work had to be systemized for any impact to be made at all. In 1882–83 the survey covered wide tracts of the Midwest from Illinois, Iowa, and Missouri to Alabama and North Carolina. Over four thousand artifacts were collected for the National Museum, including "three remarkable winged pipes of green chlorite slate of finest workmanship." Some mounds contained objects of European manufacture, showing that some, at least, of the mounds had been occupied after the arrival of white explorers and settlers. The talented W. H. Holmes had been hard at work writing *Ancient Pottery in the Mississippi Valley*; he was the same Holmes who had been active in the West and worked with Edward Thompson in Mexico. Holmes's fine illustrations provided a comprehensive view of the pottery of the mounds, now firmly aligned with native wares.

The inscriptions alleged to have been found in the mounds were soon debunked as forgeries. Indeed, a correspondent from Newark, Ohio, in *Science* in April 1884 had already warned the editors that "any inscribed stones from that locality may be looked upon as spurious. Years ago certain parties in that place made a business of manufacturing and buying inscribed stones and other objects in the autumn and exhuming them the following spring in the presence of innocent witnesses.''

After these initial debunking efforts the mound project was expanded greatly. Most of the field work was concentrated in the area between Ohio and Wisconsin, although Thomas set his team to work all over mound country. The task was an enormous one, even for the most generously endowed expedition, which the bureau's was not. Thomas had several options. He could concentrate on a single area and excavate and survey it in detail before moving on to another after exhaustive inquiries. If he did this, much of his staff would be idle in the winters, while farmers would be planting the mounds in the summers. Another choice was to attempt a comprehensive survey and mapping project covering the whole of mound country from one end to the other before excavating. This was not only impracticable but, like the first option, would also leave the mounds vulnerable to continued destruction and pillage while the survey was completed. So he decided to spread his team thinly over the area and to attempt to cover as much ground as possible with the resources available, keeping his workers busy all year, even excavating before surveys of site contours were complete. He hoped this would minimize destruction and provide the answer to the question of all questions: Were the mounds built by Indians or by others? If they were the work of Indians, then the study of the sites would simply become an integral part of the whole process of studying the Indian tribes of America. If they were not, then a whole new branch of American science would come into being. The purpose of the field work was to show that there had been continuous mound-building activity from the time of white settlement back into remote, prehistoric times.

For seven years Thomas and his colleagues labored over their sites. By 1887 Thomas was able to write: "Over two thousand mounds have been explored, including almost every known type as to form, from the low, diminutive, circular burial tumulus of the North to the huge truncated earthen pyramid of the South. . . . The number of specimens obtained by the division since its organization is not less than thirty-eight thousand; fully one-half of these were discovered by the assistants during their explorations; the remainder were obtained by donations and purchase, though not more than $500 have been expended by the Bureau for this purpose." A stream of preliminary reports laid out the broad outlines of the huge project and some initial conclusions. As early as 1887 Thomas classified the mounds into eight cultural districts: the Wisconsin effigy mounds, Illinois and Upper Mississippi conical mounds, the Ohio area with its earthworks and enclosures, historical mounds in New York, and several zones in the Southeast and South where truncated earthen pyramids and fine pottery were found. Of the mounds as a whole Thomas flatly wrote that all "which have been examined and carefully studied are to be attributed to the indigenous tribes found inhabiting this region and their ancestors." It was clear that the new survey was going far beyond a simplistic consideration of the Mound Builder civilization. Thomas himself admitted that the notion of a vanished and mighty civilization in the Mississippi Valley was "fascinating and attractive." It was a romantic idea that could "warp and bias all . . . conclusions," the notion of a nation that vanished "before the inroads of savage hordes, leaving behind it no evidence of its existence, its glory, power, and extent save these silent forest-covered remains." But the interesting point was that reality was just as fascinating.

Cyrus Thomas's *Report on the Mound Explorations of the Bureau of Ethnology* finally appeared in the Twelfth Annual Report of Powell's Bureau of American Ethnology in 1894, a massive, 730-page work that ranks as one of the great monographs of nineteenth-century American archaeology. Archaeologists of all persuasions had eagerly awaited its appearance, for everyone, however outlandish his views, realized that it would be a definitive report based on more data than Caleb Atwater or Squier and

298

Davis had ever been able to command. The great report was basically an account of systematic field work covering 500 pages in which thousands of mounds are described with almost stultifying monotony and detail. The descriptions were accompanied by a summary of Thomas's conclusions, already foreshadowed in preliminary reports. He showed that there was essential continuity between the Mound Builders and modern Indians, delineated earlier research and the preposterous and not-so-absurd theories surrounding the mounds, and looked at the dating evidence for the sites. He debunked the alleged inscriptions from Iowa and other sites, rescued from historical oblivion eyewitness accounts of Mound Builders at work, and compared the artifacts found in the mounds to modern artifacts in both specific and general terms.

Thomas's bias in favor of an Indian origin for the mounds shows through the report. It was the sheer volume of carefully observed and dissected evidence that he assembled in support of his thesis that made his arguments in general utterly convincing, even if it were possible to cavil about details. *Report on the Mound Explorations* was a demonstration of the academic impact of institutional and governmental resources on an archaeological problem. In a sense it signaled the demise of the enthusiastic and well-informed amateur archaeologist as a large-scale field worker in North American archaeology, although it was to be many years before the professional archaeologist was to dominate excavations and field work in mound country. It is a sad reflection on the destruction of archaeological sites in North America that Cyrus Thomas's monograph is the only definitive account of most of the sites he cataloged. Nearly all of them, except those preserved in national or state parks, have been at least partially destroyed since his team visited them. Thus, this pioneer work remains a definitive source for the archaeologist of today, as well as the final nail in the myth makers' coffin.

Most important of all, however, Cyrus Thomas and his colleagues were the first archaeologists to challenge the hypothesis of a unified nation of Mound Builders, who had settled over a huge area of North America and enjoyed a uniformity of government, religion, and culture for centuries. "The mound-builders were divided into different tribes and peoples, which, though occupying much the same position in the culture scale, and hence resembling each other in many habits, customs, and modes of life, were as widely separated in regard to their ethnic relations and languages as the Indian tribes when first encountered by the white race," Thomas wrote. In other words, archaeologists should be prepared to find and report on diverse societies, with complex relationships, similarities, and differences among them. Prehistoric American tribes had been fully as complex as the modern Indian peoples, who had turned out to be far more varied in their many cultures than the nomadic braves of frontier legend fame. And it is this diversity and its ordering that has been one of the preoccupations and achievements of twentieth-century American archaeologists.

Cyrus Thomas's contribution was enormous and exhaustive. His report did work out somewhat differently from what some political zealots in Washington, with their grandiose notions of ancient, long-lost civilizations awaiting discovery in the Ohio and Mississippi valleys, might have preferred. The impressive point was that the report was supported by other people's researches. Frederick Putnam and the Peabody Museum had dug into the earthworks of the Ohio Valley, Putnam's conclusions adding to the increasing mass of excavated information that pointed to an indigenous origin for the American mounds. The speculative reports of earlier investigators were now to be replaced by sober descriptions that were soon to become an ever more arid wilderness of descriptions, classifications, and carefully drawn conclusions that were more and more deeply buried in technical journals.

Meanwhile the general public continued to believe in the notion of Mound Builders, their ideas fueled by the writings of such people as

300

Congressman Ignatius Donnelly. A self-educated
politician turned author, Donnelly continued to
propagate the world of Atlantis, a lost civilization
that had populated North and Middle America with
"civilized nations" of which the mounds were tangible relics. The survivors of the Atlantis catastrophe
were part of a "great movement of the brown race,"
who had come from a "beautiful and happy land
where their ancestors had dwelt in peace for many
generations." The Atlanteans had withdrawn to
Mexico when attacked by savages from the north.

Donnelly's *Atlantis: The Antediluvian World* appeared in 1882, just as Thomas was getting into his
stride. The book went through nearly fifty printings,

Grave 19 from Madisonville,
Ohio, uncovered by Putnam
in 1897.
*Peabody Museum,
Harvard University*

A party of archaeologists at the Turner mound in the 1890s. The group includes Putnam (second from right) and C. L. Metz (right). *Peabody Museum, Harvard University*

and it is still in print. William Gladstone, the British prime minister, was convinced of the book's authenticity and asked Parliament for funds to search for Atlantis. The request was promptly turned down by his wiser and more sober colleagues.

But the archaeologists were bewildered by the complexities of the archaeological record and the tens of thousands of artifacts from the mounds. The pace of field work quickened. Pioneer archaeologist Clarence B. Moore of Philadelphia explored the mounds of Florida and traveled along the rivers of Arkansas, Louisiana, Mississippi, and Alabama. Another remarkable character was Gerard Fowke, a cavalry officer during the Civil War, who spent many years traveling through the East on foot, examining mound after mound, not on horseback or by rail, but on foot. He had acquired a dislike of horses in the war, distrusted railroads after having

302

been involved in a minor accident, and so spent his summers tramping through Ohio, Indiana, and Illinois in knee-length cavalry boots. This tall, somewhat eccentric archaeologist published several books on his finds, visiting dozens of private collectors and hundreds of sites. Late nineteenth-century archaeology in North America was an amalgam of collecting, hasty excavation, and description, the pastime of a few professionals and hundreds of serious, not-so-serious, and downright eccentric amateurs. From this amalgam came the complicated patchwork of cultural sequences and artifact types that makes up American archaeology today.

Meanwhile, hundreds of mounds were destroyed by farmers, treasure hunters, and others. But there were some triumphs of conservation. Frederick Putnam was able to save the Great Serpent Mound in Ohio from oblivion. The largest known effigy of a snake in the world, Great Serpent Mound is 1,254 feet long and averages 20 feet across. Squier and Davis had described the effigy in their survey and illustrated it with one of their beautiful survey plans. Putnam himself scrambled up the side of the Serpent on a leisurely day in the summer of 1883. "Reclining on one of the huge folds of this gigantic serpent, as the last rays of the sun, glancing from distant hilltops, cast their long shadows over the valley, I mused on the probabilities of the past; and there seemed to come to me a picture as of a distant time, and with it came a demand for an interpretation of this mystery."

Three years later Putnam returned to the Great Serpent, only to find it ravaged by pot hunters digging for artifacts and much denuded by cattle and erosion. John Lovett, the farmer who owned the Serpent, had avoided plowing the effigy but was about to sell his land. Clearly, the mound was in danger of obliteration. So Putnam obtained a year's option to buy on the property and returned to Boston to campaign for the necessary funds. Impassioned letters to the Boston newspapers had the desired effect. Soon a group of local women had raised nearly six thousand dollars, sufficient both to buy the

Aerial view of the Great
Serpent Mound, Ohio.
*Photograph courtesy of
the Museum of the American
Indian, Heye Foundation*

Serpent and to maintain it in its original condition.
Overjoyed, Putnam spent two months in 1887 restoring the Great Serpent, erecting fences, and preparing the effigy for visitors. The first year of the new century saw this rare example of archaeological conservation become an Ohio state park in perpetuity.

As field work continued on a local scale, it became clear that Powell and Thomas had succeeded in blunting the political impact of the myth of the Mound Builders. With great relief Powell was able to announce that "general exploration of the mound region" was discontinued, even if William Holmes and others continued to work on specific mound groups.

In the eighty years since Cyrus Thomas wrote his monograph thousands more excavations in the eastern United States have been made. Radiocarbon chronology and detailed artifact analysis have given us some insight into the complex Indian cultures that flourished around the earthworks. We now know that by 1000 B.C. the local people were living off an economy based on the cultivation of maize, beans, squash, as well as local plants such as sunflowers. This subsistence base gave the people the economic capacity to engage in major construction activities. These Adena people are known to have lived in small communities of several houses, relying heavily on hunting and plant gathering to amplify their agricultural produce. They built huge burial mounds and earthworks over a vast area centered on southern Ohio. Enclosures, circles, and squares were linked into complexes of earthworks and ditches. Elaborate burials were clustered under earth mounds, with the tumuli often sited near enclosures. Sometimes they were built over structures that may have been dwellings or mortuary houses. The dead were often buried in log chambers that were used again and again. Later the rotting timbers collapsed under the weight of earth, leaving a complicated melange for the archaeologist to sort out in his excavations.

Adena society seems to have been grouped into classes of individuals whose status was reflected in their burial rites. It has been suggested that the Adena villages were linked by lineages that transcended the small groups of families living in their scattered villages. There were no settlements of the size that flourished in later centuries. Although Adena trade contacts and artifacts are to be found on the east coast, the culture never achieved the elaborate social structure of later eastern societies.

About A.D. 200 Adena society underwent a transition. The old burial cults were abandoned, as a new religious cult emerged, perhaps first in Illinois. Archaeologists have termed this the Hopewell development. Many of the most spectacular earthworks belong to the Hopewell, especially in Ohio, where

Hopewellian burials from Dickison Mound, Peoria County, Illinois (Mound 478). The dead were buried with elaborate necklaces.
Courtesy of the Illinois State Museum, Springfield

Adena constructions are overshadowed by such famous monuments as the Great Serpent Mound. Enclosures, circles, even octagonal earthworks are associated with burial mounds. These were often constructed in two stages, the first a low edifice that contained a log tomb or a series of cremated burials. This was later covered with basketloads of earth piled up to as much as one hundred feet. Lavish grave goods, far more elaborate than Adena offerings, usually accompanied Hopewell burials. Hundreds of bodies were placed in some mounds, only a few being reserved for important individuals. Finely hammered copper ornaments, made from metal obtained through trade with people from around Lake Superior, were deposited with the burials. So were mica ornaments, shells, marine fish teeth, and obsidian tools made from raw material im-

306

ported all the way from Wyoming. Fine grave pottery contrasted sharply with the more utilitarian vessels of Adena villages. Carved stone pipes were used throughout the Hopewell area and were common finds in nineteenth-century excavations. Unfortunately, however, the treasure hunts of a century ago destroyed much of Hopewell culture before any systematic investigation was possible. As a result there are huge gaps in our knowledge of these remarkable people.

The Hopewell craftspeople produced a range of specialized objects that are found not only in the mounds and settlements of the Midwest, but also at centers of the Hopewell cult outside the central area. So consistent is the workmanship of some fine artifacts that it may be that only a few craftspeople were making them at well-defined localities both inside and outside the Hopewell area. The specialized manufactures were then distributed widely throughout Hopewell country, exchanged for food, raw materials, and other essentials. This trade was a mainstay of Hopewell society, based as it probably was on thousands of individual gift relationships and formal exchanges. Similar relationships were common among other Indian groups. Like the Adena, Hopewell people lived off subsistence agriculture, but probably with locally adapted maize playing a more important part in the diet. Extended families and major lineage groups probably formed the backbone of society, with burial rites reflecting lineage status and achievement in the community. In many respects Hopewell was a logical continuation of Adena society.

After A.D. 550 the Hopewell trading networks assumed less importance, as local cultures developed their own distinctive artistic traditions. One example was the Effigy Mound culture of Wisconsin and Minnesota, where mounds were constructed in the form of animals. These local manifestations do not represent a disruption of earlier traditions, but rather a modest elaboration of Hopewell culture on a regional basis. Little is known of these regional traditions for the most part, as most

Cahokia during the period A.D.
1250–1500. A reconstruction by
A. M. Hodge.
*Courtesy of the Illinois State
Museum, Springfield*

of the sites were destroyed in the nineteenth century.
Then, around A.D. 700, some Mexican cultural traits
spread into eastern North America. The peoples of
the Mississippi Valley in particular adopted more
public rituals and started to build temple mounds,
often grouped around plazas, like those found in
Mexican ceremonial centers. Instead of burial
mounds, the earthworks became the foundations for
temples and chiefs' dwellings. Public display and
political activity became more important facets of
day-to-day life.

The rich floodplain of the Mississippi was well
suited to simple hoe agriculture, the light soils prov-
ing ideal for maize cultivation. Rapid population
growth ensued, with much greater concentrations of
farmers living in enormous palisaded settlements—a
far cry from the scattered villages of earlier times.
The largest Mississippian site is that of Cahokia, in
East Saint Louis. A complex of over one hundred
mounds is dominated by Monk's Mound, a huge edifice over ninety feet high. It has been estimated that
some fifteen thousand people lived around Cahokia,
an important ceremonial, political, and trading
center in its heyday around A.D. 1100.

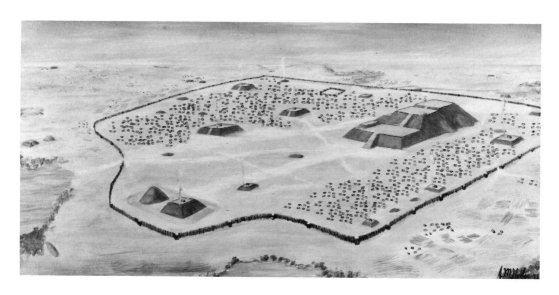

308

The Mississippian tradition spread widely in the Midwest and Southeast; it was a society in which political strength and cohesiveness were based on powerful chiefdoms. The lineage-based societies of Adena and Hopewell were now replaced by a hierarchical society with nobles and commoners, the former a select elite who controlled long-distance trade and ritual life. The Natchez chief befriended by Le Page du Pratz was one such nobleman. His elaborate burial rites reflected the complicated etiquette and strict rules that regulated the smooth course of Mississippian society. And the ritual and political implications of this remarkable culture touched the lives of thousands of American Indians living as far away as Florida and the upper Midwest.

The Mississippian tradition was still in full swing when Hernando de Soto traversed the Southeast in 1540–42. The effects of his journey were devastating. Smallpox and other exotic diseases swept through the South as a result of this and other ventures. Indian populations were decimated and the structure of Mississippian economic and social life collapsed forever. The great earthworks were abandoned. Only a minority escaped extermination from disease, colonization, or European muskets. By the time archaeologists arrived on the scene, little remained but silent earthworks, overgrown mounds, and the makings of a myth.

15 "The Ancient Inhabitants of the Country Must Be Lost"

By the late 1880s the outside world was relatively familiar with the remarkable archaeological riches of the American West, agog at the spectacular discoveries coming from the Four Corners region and elsewhere. The ruined pueblos of the Southwest had been drawn and photographed by trappers and explorers, military and civilian surveyors, and early scientists such as W. H. Holmes. The pioneers were followed by ranchers and settlers who took over the land and staked out a multitude of properties and landholdings. Many of these holdings encroached on archaeological sites. Many of the people who settled in the new land were deeply curious about their surroundings, eager for wealth, hoping for adventure. Many of them turned to treasure hunting as a profitable sideline.

Among these early settlers were five brothers, Quakers and traders, the brothers Wetherill. One of them, Richard, achieved immortality as an amateur archaeologist and collector. For many years a trader in Navaho country, Richard Wetherill spent long days with his brothers exploring the deepest fastnesses of southwestern Colorado. He collected blankets and jewelry, herded cattle, acquired prehistoric pottery and other artifacts from dozens of sites. His collection of antiquities became famous throughout the Southwest. The Wetherill homestead became a mecca for visitors to Mesa Verde and the desert canyons.

Richard Wetherill visited Mesa Verde many times, in search of cattle, or simply to look for artifacts. But no visit was as eventful as the one in late 1888 when Richard and his cousin Charlie Mason came across the Cliff Palace, the greatest of the Mesa Verde ruins.

Cliff Palace, Mesa Verde.
Arizona State Museum

Jackson and his party had missed this huge complex of more than two hundred rooms and twenty-three kivas, semiunderground secret religion assembly places. Nearby lay the Spruce Tree and Square Tower ruins, both structures that had been missed by earlier visitors. The Cliff Palace was obviously a very important site, one that would repay many years of exploration. Although Wetherill had major family responsibilities and a mortgaged ranch, he spent the winters exploring Mesa Verde and accumulating a large collection of pottery and other artifacts.

In spring 1889 the Wetherills exhibited their collection in Durango and Denver, only to find that no one was interested in their finds. Nor would anyone buy them. Bankrupt but wiser, they were about to return to Mesa Verde when Charlie Mason sent a desiccated mummy to Denver, one he had found in the canyon. Immediately public interest rose to fever pitch. Everyone wanted to see this strange curiosity. The new interest carried over to the other finds as well. In a few weeks the Denver Historical Society was bidding for the first Wetherill collection. Apparently the society was afraid that the unique finds would go out of the state. It was not until 1890 that the members could be persuaded to pay three thousand dollars for the artifacts, an enormous sum for the day.

In the following years the Wetherill brothers surveyed and mapped most of the sites in Mancos Canyon and assembled three more collections from Mesa Verde. The first of these was bought by a Chicago entrepreneur and later ended up in the University of Pennsylvania Museum. Another was exhibited at the Chicago World's Fair of 1893 and was acquired by the state of Colorado. A smaller assemblage was accumulated by the Wetherills and a young Swedish archaeologist named Gustav Nordenskjöld. His *Cliff Dwellers of Mesa Verde*, published in 1893, was one of the first descriptions of the cliff dwellings for the scientific community. It was widely read by archaeologists and lay people alike. The influence of Richard Wetherill lurks behind every page; his unparalleled knowledge of

312

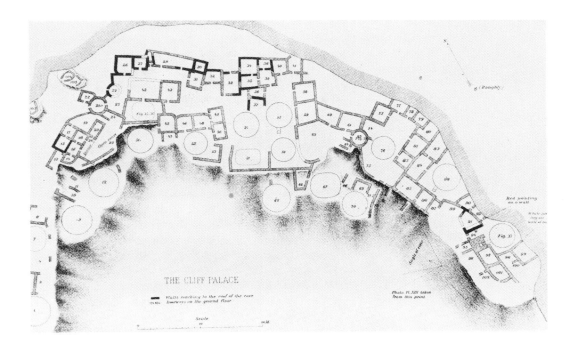

THE CLIFF PALACE

Mesa Verde was freely shared with the young
Swede, as it was with hundreds of visitors to the remote canyon.

Richard Wetherill found collecting so lucrative
that he and Charlie Mason put an advertisement in
the *Mancos Times*. For about a year this appeared in
each issue:

> Mancos Canyon & the Aztec Cliff Dwellings.
> Indian Curios, Aztec Relics, Photographs for
> Sale. Address: Richard Wetherill, Alamo
> Ranch, Mancos, Colo.

A barn at the ranch became a small museum for the
collections, where tourists could buy fine pieces. But
after 1895 Wetherill realized that there was more
profit to be made from larger collections. He stopped
advertising and worked almost exclusively on a
collection that ended up in the American Museum of
Natural History.

Richard Wetherill's collecting activities have been
the subject of controversy. Some regard him as noth-

Gustav Nordenskjöld's plan of
the Cliff Palace at Mesa Verde
was the first accurate plan of this
remarkable site to be published.
He was assisted by Richard
Wetherill.

313

ing more than a pot hunter. Others feel that he worked scientifically by the standards of the day. He was a subscriber and contributor to *The Archaeologist*, a journal whose readers could obtain information on where relics might be purchased or dug up. The editor contented himself with a blast at vandals, but then added that "the sale of a whole collection, or part of it, so long as complete finds are not split is always proper. Single specimens bought of dealers, may be sold with the free conscience, also complete finds." But at least he condemned the destruction of what he called "Scientific Testimony." Richard Wetherill was better than most collectors: at least he kept some sketchy records of his excavations, probably not much worse than those of scientific contemporaries. It should also be noted that both the Peabody Museum and the Smithsonian Institution had refused to sponsor Wetherill's original work at Cliff Palace, although they were prepared to accept donations. And the Wetherills had mortgages to worry about.

Richard Wetherill spent his last years working at Pueblo Bonito on excavations sponsored by the Hyde family. Frederick Putnam was consulted; he sent out George Hubbard Pepper to work alongside Wetherill. Dozens of rooms were cleared, large collections made. The Navaho laborers quietly pocketed some of the finest turquoise pieces, but Wetherill bought them back a few weeks later—the only strategy left for an archaeologist competing with collectors. By 1897 Richard had opened a store near Pueblo Bonito and more or less settled near the site. Not only did this seem a good business investment, but both Hyde and Wetherill were worried about new legislation designed to protect ruins from vandalism and collectors. Squatter's rights would eventually enable the Wetherills to claim the site as their own—and what an investment that would be!

The huge excavations continued until 1900, by which time over 190 rooms had been cleared and over half the site been excavated at a cost of over twenty-five thousand dollars. The vast collections in New York shed a completely new light on the

314

archaeology of the Southwest. But others were
concerned about the quality of the excavations and
allegations of looting. Edgar Hewett, the director of
the School of American Research in Santa Fe and a
well-known archaeologist, alerted federal authorities. He was apparently concerned about the
large collections leaving the state. And stories were
circulating about the profits on antiquities that were
being made through the Wetherill store. A lengthy
investigation by the secretary of the Interior produced a long report that drew attention to the official sponsorship of the Pueblo Bonito excavations
and also to the illegal Wetherill homestead. The excavations were suspended by government order and
Wetherill was told to move. But it was not until
1907 that he finally signed over the title of his land
to the government. By time the 1906 Antiquities
Act was in effect, protecting the sites that Wetherill
loved from vandalism. Three years later Richard

Pueblo Bonito.
Arizona State Museum

Mummy with breech cloth in place, probably collected by Richard Wetherill. From Grand Gulch, Utah.
Photograph courtesy of the Museum of the American Indian, Heye Foundation

Wetherill was murdered by a Navaho gunman as he was rounding up cattle.

The Wetherills were not the only collectors at work. Others advertised their services as relic collectors. But the treasures of Mesa Verde were one of the first inklings of the riches that lay ready for the taking. Soon dozens of avid pot hunters descended on

316

the Southwest, stripping ruins of their contents as quickly as they could. San Juan County was a particular target. The local farmers had already plowed out hundreds of stone house foundations. Their rocky mounds often yielded potsherds, stone tools, and sometimes human bones. Others found that larger mounds were in the way. Some on the banks of the Animas River were simply sluiced into the water. Soon relics from hundreds of sites were being sold by the lot in Denver or Santa Fe. Some localities, like the Aztec ruins, became famous for their many skeletons, buried deep in the rooms of the long-abandoned settlement. For a while the settlers thought little of the many finds they made in the course of exploration or plowing. They simply used the stones from foundation and ruin for building materials. But when the Wetherills started to make a profit from their Mesa Verde finds, Indian artifacts ceased to be curiosities. They became money, another resource to be exploited in times of economic slump.

Typical of these settlers was Scott N. Morris, who arrived in the San Juan area in the early 1890s with the vague intention of starting a freight service. Business was irregular, but it took him all over the San Juan region. Soon Morris heard of the many stone ruins with their hidden riches. The freight service brought contacts with a collector in Colorado Springs who sought first option on any finds Morris could make. This was obviously a lucrative commercial opportunity, so Morris started work in his own backyard. A mound there yielded some pots and a good start. By the end of his first winter in the Southwest, Morris had not only accumulated a large collection of pots but had also acquired many antiquities from ranchers and cowboys scratching around nearby. He sold the lot to his contact, Mr. McClurg of Colorado Springs. A later Morris collection went to the Carnegie Library Association of Pittsburgh. Part of this assemblage came from a trench he dug in the great mound of debris at Pueblo Bonito in 1893. Scott Morris's son Earl was an active participant in these ventures, having acquired, so he claimed, an interest in archaeology at the age of three and a half. Although he was also a sporadic pot hunter, Earl Morris was one of the respected pioneers of southwestern archaeology, among the first to receive formal training in the field. He later cleared and restored the Aztec ruins as well as attracting national attention for his discoveries at Mummy Cave and elsewhere.

Public interest in the Pueblo Indians and their culture was such that a major industry in relic hunting was rapidly developing at the turn of the century. Frantically, professional archaeologists, headed by Edgar Hewett, lobbied for restrictive legislation that would outlaw archaeological excavation on public lands. The Lacey Law of 1906 extended some limited protection to key sites. Mesa Verde and Chaco Canyon were declared national monuments soon afterward. Hewett himself started a southwestern archaeological field school, to train young men in the proper methods of excavation, showing them the difference between pot hunting and serious archaeological research. One of his early pupils was Earl Morris, soon to become a close colleague of Jesse W. Fewkes, N. C. Nelson, A. V. Kidder, and other eastern archaeologists who spent season after season developing a chronological framework for southwestern archaeology. Much of these men's work involved clearing up publicly owned sites after the massive treasure hunts and excavations of the pioneers. Such digs had cleared hundreds of rooms in search of antiquities with scant regard for chronology or architectural detail.

The principle of stratigraphy had been well established in European caves and in the Near East in the mid-nineteenth century. Rudimentary stratigraphic archaeology, based on the principle that the lowest is oldest, had been practiced in the Ohio mounds by Squier and Davis. But much excavation in the Southwest still consisted of clearing out rooms piecemeal to obtain as many finds as possible. Collectors eagerly sought the brightly painted clay vessels from the pueblos, failing to realize that they provided a vital key to the long and complicated history of Indian culture in the Southwest. The complex occupation layers in the pueblos were shoveled away in a frantic search for salable artifacts.

Nils C. Nelson, an archaeologist working with the American Museum of Natural History, was the first person to use the thousands of fragmentary potsherds from the pueblos more exactly. Nelson, a robust and earthy Scandinavian, was an ideal archaeologist for this complex task. His technique was simple, an archaeological extension of Bandelier's historical work in earlier decades. The uppermost levels in the pueblos often yielded artifacts similar to those used by modern Indians as well as Spanish objects. For years it had been assumed that most western sites were occupied for too short a time before the Spanish occupation for there to be any stratigraphic layers in them. Nelson disagreed. He took a cluster of sites in the Galisteo Basin in New Mexico, excavated small stratigraphic columns through their occupation deposits, and built up a chronological sequence of pottery. In doing so, he worked back from the known to the unknown. He found that at least four pottery types preceded the dated vessels associated with the Spanish occupation that came from San Cristobal ruin, built after the foreigners arrived. San Cristobal itself contained broken brass candlesticks and other signs of the Pueblo Revolt of 1680, together with characteristic pottery vessels that bore traces of attempts at Spanish glaze techniques. Horse and other domestic animal bones came from the same historic levels. The earlier horizons contained painted black-and-white vessels rather than the glazed painted pots of historical levels. Other styles with the black-on-white tradition would be traced through the levels of the Galisteo sites.

Nelson's Galisteo work and the publications resulting from it ushered in a new era of archaeology in western America, one that began to remove the chronology of the pueblos from the realm of guesswork to a scientifically based time scale.

It was the Harvard-trained archaeologist Alfred V. Kidder who carried Nelson's work to its triumphant

The East Building at Mummy Cave, Canyon del Muerto. Earl Morris and A. V. Kidder are examining the site.
Courtesy of the American Museum of Natural History

conclusion. Kidder had first visited the Southwest in 1907 as an undergraduate, working on an arduous, summer-long archaeological survey with Hewett. While a student he also had a chance to visit Greece and Egypt, to see the complex stratigraphic excavations being conducted there, an experience that influenced his own thinking about American archaeology. European archaeologists were, by this time, well aware of the importance of the humble potsherd, thanks to the many attempts made to date the prehistoric remains of northern and western Europe by relating them chronologically and stylistically to those from the Mediterranean civilizations.

Kidder now resolved to use potsherds to refine and expand Nelson's work. He began excavating in the deep middens at Pecos, New Mexico. The pueblo had been flourishing at the time of Coronado's expedition in 1540, a critical chronological baseline. There was obviously a long history of prehistoric occupation before the sixteenth century. Deep layers of occupation material lay at the east, southeast, and southwestern corners of the ruin. Kidder proposed to slice through these deposits to obtain a stratigraphic sequence of culture layers based on pottery before tackling the complex problems of

the architecture. He also wanted to obtain as many burials as possible so that the groups of pots buried with the corpses could be studied as sealed dating units.

When he trenched into the middens in 1915, he offered his laborers a bonus of twenty-five cents for each skeleton they found. It was only a few days before the price was lowered to ten cents and then the bonus abandoned altogether, for skeletons piled up by the dozens. Huge trenches yielded over 750 skeletons in the first four seasons alone. Carefully dissected columns of ash and occupation debris were meticulously sifted for small pottery fragments. The finds were classified in the laboratory and compared both with grave lots and with potsherds from Galisteo and other settlements. They provided a long cultural sequence for Kidder to describe. "It is safe enough to postulate," Kidder wrote, "the former presence in the southwest of a more or less nomadic people, thinly scattered over the country, ignorant of agriculture and pottery making." The early people lived off small game and wild vegetable foods. Eventually they acquired the arts of agriculture. But farming did not make much of an impact on their way of life. These "Basket Makers" made no pottery and had not lived in permanent homes. Kidder dated them to about 1500–2000 B.C. They were followed by pre-Pueblo and Pueblo peoples, with more permanent settlements, higher agricultural yields, and the eventual development of pueblo architecture.

In the closing pages of his classic report on the first stages of the Pecos work Kidder traced a broad, sweeping outline of pueblo history, pointing out that "the Southwest owes to outside sources little more than the germs of its culture, and that its development from these germs has been a local and almost wholly an independent one." It was an indigenous but most remarkable cultural development, a great tragedy of native American history, that "so much human effort has come to naught, and that so many hopeful experiments in life and living were cut short by the devastating blight of the white man's arrival."

A desiccated burial unearthed by Earl Morris from Warrior's Cave, Canyon del Muerto, in 1928. *Courtesy of the American Museum of Natural History*

North terrace excavations from the top of the main ruin mound at Pecos during the A. V. Kidder expedition. The remains of the oldest settlement lie just within the later defense wall. These trenches yielded over ninety skeletons. From A. V. Kidder, *An Introduction to the Archaeology of the Southwest* (New Haven: Yale University Press, 1927). *Yale University Press, New Haven*

Pointing out that his sketch was the merest preliminary outline, Kidder had finally placed the legendary Seven Cities of Cibola in their true historical perspective.

From 1915 to 1929, with a three-year gap during the First World War, Kidder labored at Pecos, whose rich and unexploited cemeteries and ash heaps yielded a chronological framework for the prehistory of the Southwest that has survived, with some modification, ever since. Kidder's aim was not only to collect objects, but also to find pottery "so stratified to make clear the development of the various Pueblo arts, and thus enable us to place in their proper chronological order many other Southwestern ruins." He found no fewer than six settlements on top of each other at Pecos, a series of occupations that enabled the Harvard archaeologist to postulate eight major cultural stages that began with John Wetherill's Basket Makers and ended with the Spanish occupation.

But Kidder was not satisfied. So he arranged an informal conference in his excavation camp at Pecos of all those known to be working on southwestern archaeology. Some forty archaeologists sat down in August 1927 to review progress so far and to plot a chronological framework for future study. The idea was "to pool knowledge of facts and techniques, and to lay foundations for a unified system of nomenclature." The Pecos conference postulated three stages of Basket Makers and five stages of Pueblos, providing a framework for the next generation of field work that dissipated much of the chaos that had surrounded the undisciplined archaeology of early years. The Pecos conference has now become an an-

Skeletons in the depths of the Pecos mound. A. V. Kidder excavations. From A. V. Kidder, *An Introduction to the Archaeology of the Southwest* (New Haven: Yale University Press, 1927). *Yale University Press, New Haven*

323

Typical Basket Maker product from Basket Maker's Cave, Cave Lake Canyon, Kane County, Utah.
Photograph courtesy of the Museum of the American Indian, Heye Foundation

nual affair, attended by several hundred people working in the Southwest.

But the Pecos terminology suffered from one major disadvantage, apart from its possible undue rigidity. There was as yet no means of dating the ruins in calendar years, although efforts to achieve this goal had been underway for years. The astronomer A. E. Douglass had been working on climatic changes and their relationships to astronomical phenomena since 1901. Douglass had concentrated on the annual growth rings in southwestern trees, using much more sophisticated counting methods than those of Manasseh Cutler in Ohio in 1788. He found that the thickness of the annual growth rings in his trees fluctuated with the annual rainfall, with thinner rings growing in dry years, and wider rings in wetter seasons. Initial experiments with fir and pine trees took him back about two hundred years. Soon he was able to date segments of trees by comparing the inside sections of logs and the sets of rings on them without reference to the outermost rings of the tree.

From the oldest living firs and pines Douglass extended the technique to dead trees, using beams from old Spanish churches of the colonial period and then from prehispanic ruins to take him back further and further into prehistory. In 1918 he examined some beams from Aztec ruins and from Pueblo Bonito, devising an ingenious tool that enabled him to bore into the cores of prehistoric beams without disturbing the structure they still supported. With the aid of Earl Morris and other archaeologists the Arizona astronomer was soon able to show that the timbers from Aztec ruins covered only an eight-year span. The Pueblo Bonito beams were different and generally older than Aztec. But these were only relative dates, for the sets of tree rings from Aztec, Pueblo Bonito, and other sites were not as yet tied to the chronology from living trees. It took Douglass another ten years to bridge the gap between history and "floating chronology of the prehistoric ruins. The search for the missing beams gradually narrowed until 1928 when Douglass started to look closely at sections from timbers in Hopi villages in

northern Arizona. He persuaded the Hopi with rich
gifts—bolts of purple velvet and turtle shells—to
allow him to bore into the age-old wooden beams of
their homes. But the earliest date was about A.D.
1400, too late to connect with sets of rings from the
prehistoric sites. The Gap, as it came to be known,
was finally bridged a year later at a sizable ruin lying
under a Mormon barnyard at Show Low, Arizona,
where a charred log bore rings that dated back to A.D.
1237, an overlap of twenty-six years with the relative
chronologies of the prehistoric ruins.

Within a few weeks Douglass could provide an accurate chronological framework for the Pecos horizons that dated Pueblo Bonito to the tenth to
twelfth centuries A.D., Mesa Verde and Aztec ruins
to a more recent period. There had been a great
flowering of Pueblo culture in the San Juan region
culminating in the twelfth century, with Mesa Verde
coming to a climax in the thirteenth century. Pecos,

Aztec ruins.
Arizona State Museum

the Galisteo cultures, and the Kayenta region of Arizona enjoyed an even later efflorescence. The new science of dendrochronology with its correlated tree rings had given archaeologists the first accurate time scale for pre-Columbian Indian history, one that has stood the test of time and now been extended back into the first century B.C.

All modern archaeology in the American Southwest has sprung from the research of the archaeologists who collaborated to produce the original Pecos terminological framework and from the findings of the tree ring specialists that bridged the gap between the historic and the prehistoric pueblos. The innovations of southwestern archaeology spread into other regions of North America. Potsherd archaeology was successfully applied in the Mississippi Valley and eastern North America in the 1930s. But, despite the early efforts of Manasseh Cutler and others, tree ring dating has remained largely a southwestern phenomenon, because of the markedly seasonal growth of trees in the desert and the excellent preservation conditions for prehistoric beams in its dry environment.

The Bureau of American Ethnology had been only one of several organizations that had studied the habits of the Indians of the West. John Wesley Powell had been a fearless campaigner for Indian rights, fighting venality in the Indian Bureau and the cynical attitudes of settlers and big business interests. In the late nineteenth century the noose of civilization began to tighten around the Indian. Petitions were circulated calling on the army to round up the "savages" and feed them like penned cattle on desert reservations. One western newspaper editor called them "a set of miserable, dirty, lousy blanketed, thieving, lying, sneaking, murdering, graceless, faithless gut-eating skunks as the Lord ever permitted to infest the earth, and whose immediate and final extermination all men should pray for." This type of attitude was commonplace. Others contended they should be deprived of legal rights and social freedom. It was felt that good money would be wasted on helping such worthless people.

326

Powell recommended setting up reservations where Indians could live in peace, rather than being shot on sight, extinguished by disease, or hunted by troops. Prophetically, he wrote of the prejudices against the Indian, of people who "can see in the Indian race only hordes of demons who stand in the way of progress of civilization, and who must, and ought to be destroyed." Others, he continued in a famous article in *Scribner's Magazine,* who know the Indian better wonder "that a morally degenerate, but powerful civilization, should destroy their primitive life." Then he added, prophetically, "Whether we desire it or not, the ancient inhabitants of the country must be lost."

But the efforts of Powell and other reformers were buried, for the most part, in the files of the government bureaucracy in Washington, while the decimation of the western Indians continued apace. The records of the Bureau of American Ethnology contain a mine of information about the western Indian, but only a fraction of what was lost with the disruptions and chaos of the last two centuries. Along with the genocide of the Indian went the destruction of their age-long ways of life and the ravaging of their archaeological sites.

The California Indians were a case in point. When the Spanish explorer Juan Cabrillo passed through the Santa Barbara Channel in 1542 his sailors counted numerous Chumash Indian villages and recorded names of no fewer than twenty-five of them. By the mid-nineteenth century barely a Chumash Indian still existed, for the dense population of the mainland and offshore islands had been decimated by disease, ruthless exploitation, and other causes. By 1880 virtually no California Indians survived in their native state, except in remote valleys of the Sierra, whereas the original aboriginal population of California may have been as high as 150,000 souls.

The most northerly Spanish mission had been established at Sonoma, far from the remote valleys of the Mount Lassen region where Indian groups continued to live in peace until the 1840s. In 1844

327

the Mexican government granted tracts of land in the Sacramento Valley that encroached on the Sierra foothills and the territory of the wild Indians. The decimation and tragedy that had struck Indians near the missions had so far left the Yana and other mountain tribes untouched. Few white people lived in the northern vastness of California before the Gold Rush brought prospectors by the thousands to the Sierra foothills. Busy trails crisscrossed hitherto sacrosanct Indian hunting territories. In 1850 the Yana tribe, for example, occupied a territory of two thousand square miles or more. There were between two and three thousand of these Indians. Twenty-two years later only twenty or thirty Yana remained in the same area.

Unlike the Spanish colonists of the coast, the Americans and northern Europeans of the Gold Rush arrived in much larger numbers, convinced of their right to new land and eager to grab all they could. There were few governmental restraints in the early days. Many of the frontier people were misfits at home, contemptuous of restrictions and discipline. Most of these settlers agreed that the Indian was an inferior being, of use only as a laborer, a slave, or a concubine. Any troublesome Indians were simply exterminated. New diseases brought by the settlers, forced migrations, and revenge for sporadic Indian cattle raids decimated the mountain tribes. So did the despoiling of their land by mining, water pollution, and all the phenomena of the industrial society. It has been estimated that between three and four thousand mountain Indian children were kidnapped for slavery between 1852 and 1867.

The Indians fought back with ferocity, exchanging murder for murder. The violence reached its height during the Civil War years. But the Indians were doomed to extinction by the sheer weight of white numbers. Vigilante patrols tracked them down in their own country, supported by a wave of popular feeling against the Indians. An agent of the Indian Bureau appealed to the army to "protect and remove the Indians" in July 1863, for the local whites were threatening to exterminate all Indians. A year later the vigilantes massacred three-quarters of the remaining Yana, even farmhands. The scalps of the slaughtered Indians were dangled from the hunters' belts. Mopping-up operations continued into the early 1870s, directed at small groups of Indians such as the Yahi, a tiny subgroup of the Yana. In 1867 or 1868 a party of four cattlemen were rounding up cattle in Yana country when they came across traces of a steer that had been killed and butchered by Indians. They picked up the hunters' trail with dogs, followed the unsuspecting Indians to a remote cave, where more than thirty Yahi, including infants, were quickly slaughtered by the four men's rifles and revolvers. One of the men, Norman Kingsley, preferred a revolver, for the rifle "tore up" the bodies so badly. Kingsley's name now commemorates the cave where the massacre probably occurred.

The Yahi were soon almost extinct. The few remaining tribe members withdrew into their own remote world, simply vanishing into the wilderness. There were no raids, no traces of fire. The Yahi went completely underground, living in utter concealment, hunting small game and gathering acorns in season. But they watched the ever encroaching white settlers and engaged in some sporadic raiding after 1884. By the 1890s there were only five Yahi Indians left, among them a young man who was to achieve immortality for being the last surviving "wild" California Indian.

Even at this late date there were occasional glimpses of the Indians' presence. A surveying party disturbed their camp in November 1908. The Indians quickly melted into the brush just in time. But they left an old woman behind under some blankets. The surveyors looted the camp. The young hunter managed to rescue his mother after the men left but his sister and an old man with her vanished forever. It seems probable that the old woman died within a few days, leaving her son on his own to live the way he always had—in absolute solitude—an existence he kept up for three years.

The California newspapers were full of the surveyors' story. It excited the interest of two anthropologists at the University of California. Berkeley had acquired a Department of Anthropology in 1901, founded with the financial assistance of Phoebe Apperson Hearst, a passionate collector and the widow of a mining magnate. Her collecting activities centered around the classical civilizations and Peru until the president of the university suggested she support some research nearer her home. The first anthropologists appointed to the new department were led by F. W. Putnam of the Peabody Museum at Harvard, who conducted the affairs of the Berkeley museum at long distance, spending only the summers in California. Under him was Alfred Kroeber, destined to become one of the leading American anthropologists of the twentieth century. In 1906 Thomas T. Waterman, a linguist and ethnographer, was added to the group.

Both Kroeber and Waterman were in the field for much of the year, the former gathering data for his monumental *Handbook of the Indians of California,* the classic description of the tribes of California that was published in 1925 and has remained the definitive source of information on the subject. Waterman had spent some time in Yahi country when the surveyors' story had first appeared in the newspapers. In October 1909 he spent a month in the Deer Creek area where the Indian camp had been found the year before. The camp looked the same as it did when looted by the surveyors. There were no signs of more recent Indian activity.

Yahi country appeared deserted until April 13, 1911, when a surveyor found a cache of hunters' possessions in an oak tree, which had obviously not been there for long. Four months later, watchdogs at a slaughterhouse near Oroville cornered a man in a corral. The butcher called J. B. Webster, the town sheriff, who realized that the prisoner was an Indian in an extreme state of exhaustion and fear. His captive surrendered without resistance, a pitiable sight, naked and almost starved. Webster housed the shivering Indian in the local jail, while he debated what to do with him. The newspapers were soon on to the story, for the incident had aroused intense

Ishi at the time of his capture.
Lowie Museum of Anthropology, University of California, Berkeley

curiosity in the community. The jail was crowded with sightseers until Webster locked them out. No one could understand the captive, not even other Indians or half breeds. But when the story—and a photograph—reached the San Francisco papers, Kroeber and Waterman immediately realized the significance of the unintelligible language. The sheriff's prisoner might well be the sole survivor of the practically extinct Yana Indians.

Waterman hastened to Oroville, armed with such Yana vocabularies as were available, all from areas to the north of Oroville. After some frustrating hours, a few common words were found, enough to enable Waterman to communicate with the prisoner and to establish that he truly was "wild," in the sense that he had no experience of white society. A temporary interpreter assisted the flow of communication for a while, as Waterman debated the captive's future with the sheriff, then with the University of California at Berkeley and authorities in Washington. Soon agreement was reached. The stranger was released to the staff of the University Museum, at least temporarily. He was escorted to San Francisco by Waterman himself and given a room in the museum, which remained his home for the remaining four years and seven months of his life. It was there he met Alfred Kroeber, curator of the museum and on the threshold of a great career as an anthropolgist.

The newcomer caused a sensation in San Francisco. Reporters flocked to the museum, impresarios tried to acquire the "wild Indian" for their shows. Kroeber turned down all offers and kept them all at a distance. In response to constant requests he named the museum's guest *Ishi,* a Yahi word for "man," and Ishi was the name that stuck to the last Yahi for the rest of his life. Ishi arrived at the museum two months before it opened its doors for the first time. He became one of its star attractions, occupying a room long used for Indian visitors brought to the city by anthropologists for linguistic researches or as guests. The museum was a cozy place, at that time a place of residence for the jani-

331

Alfred Kroeber at the time
of the Ishi expedition.
*Lowie Museum of Anthropology,
University of California, Berkeley*

tors, too. So Ishi was comfortably housed and soon
became a regular feature of the museum for visitors.
Thousands of people met Ishi, shook his hand, and
enjoyed the sight of him making bows and arrows,
practicing the age-old crafts of the Yahi hunter.

But Ishi was far more than a living museum
exhibit. He was a source of unique information about
a vanished way of life. Kroeber and Waterman spent
many hours studying the Yahi language and observing Ishi at work making weapons and other tools.
The museum collections were enriched with his
products. Supplies of obsidian, juniper, wood, and
other materials were constantly being sought,
commodities often in short supply, for Ishi insisted
on precisely the correct materials. People going into
the field from the museum were given exact
instructions about what to collect and how. So hard
did Ishi work that the supply sometimes failed to
keep up with the demand. The museum became a
living laboratory for Stone Age life, where Ishi made
not only craft tools for himself, but also arrowheads
and other implements for exchange with other
institutions. Time and time again he would
demonstrate the making of stone tools, removing
delicate slivers of obsidian from larger lumps of raw
material and shaping them into fine arrowheads.

In May 1914 a unique expedition set out for Deer
Creek. It consisted of Ishi, the two anthropologists,
and Dr. Pope from the hospital near the museum,
who had formed a close friendship with Ishi and an
understanding of his emotional attitudes. By train
and pack mule the expedition returned to Ishi's old
haunts and visited his old camps. The anthropologists were shown how to stalk with a simple
bow and to decoy game to close quarters so no
quarry was wasted. They saw him choose the trees
and the actual boughs from which the bow and arrow came, shredding deer sinews for the bow-
string, fashioning a bow to the style of the person
who used it. For weeks the new bow was seasoned
carefully, to create an accurate and deadly weapon.

Kroeber had obtained a permit to hunt for scientific purposes "one male deer at any time and in

332

such manner as the gentleman mentioned above may select.'' Ishi took his colleagues on a hunt. The first day was a failure, for they bagged nothing. Ishi promptly imposed a ban on smoking, for, he said, the smell of tobacco clung to the hunters' skins. Two days later, Ishi bagged a deer, stalking his quarry noiselessly through the brush. Always staying downwind of his victim, Ishi would wait for hours, decoy the deer, haunting the places he knew they visited. The bow shot itself was fired from a crouched position, the entire deer hunt set up according to carefully prescribed rituals that reduced the odors carried by the hunter and focused his attention on the hunt.

The expedition lived off meat and fish taken by Ishi and others with Yahi weapons. They learned the songs of the chase and covered a large part of Yahi ancestral territory. Village sites and trails, hiding places and caves, were plotted on a map. Hunting grounds and burial sites were chronicled, place names and terms for over two hundred native plants and herbs written down. Photographs of Ishi and his territory enlivened the account and provided a check on accuracy. But the most important result of the expedition was not in the form of a tangible account of Yahi life. Kroeber and Waterman were able to obtain a unique and intangible ''feel'' for Ishi's territory, for the extraordinarily close relationship between a Stone Age hunter and his environment. Every yard of territory had significance, perhaps as the site of a hidden trail, a burial ground, or a source of seasonal food. It was a different kind of hunting from that of the white man, with its senseless destruction of herds of buffalo and killing for the pleasure of it. Kroeber observed a living relationship with a living environment, where animals were as much entitled to life as humans. The Yahi had a relationship with the animals, one in which animals were hunted not only for their meat but for the by-products—pelt, bones, horns—as well. The Yahi made deliberately economic use of resources. Humans were an integral part of the territory they occupied. Every person or thing, animal, human, or

Ishi hunting in Deer Creek, California, 1914.
Lowie Museum of Anthropology, University of California, Berkeley

333

plant, was concerned with the business of equilibrium and survival.

The results of Ishi's work with the anthropologists form an impressive bibliography of books and articles, among them major descriptions of the Yana by both Kroeber and Waterman. There were many gaps, especially in tribal folklore and language. Through force of circumstance these were never filled, partly because recording technology was barely in existence, and also because Ishi himself did not live to share all his tales and beliefs with his friends. The last "wild" California Indian died on March 25, 1916, having contracted tuberculosis a year before. His last days were spent in the museum where he had worked for over four years. Ishi was cremated in a coffin which contained a bow, five arrows, a basket of acorn meal, and some other possessions. His ashes, deposited in a small, black Pueblo jar, were placed in a niche at the Mount Olivet Cemetery, inscribed simply, "Ishi, the last Yana Indian, 1916."

Ishi's public was sorry when he died, for the last "wild Indian" had found his way into many peoples' affections, especially those who visited the museum regularly. Young children were fascinated by him, especially those who had read stories of the American West and had learned how to use a bow. Others were impressed by his craftsmanship, by the living insight he gave into the lost world of the Stone Age hunter. Perhaps a few people realized, too, what the relentless expansion of the American West had taken from them, an insight into a wilderness and a world the pioneers had torn apart forever. Others had a romantic view of Ishi, a simple, untutored savage who had lived like a child of nature and been cruelly wrenched from his pastoral homeland. A few worried over his moral state or the likelihood he would take to drink. Some people were concerned lest Kroeber send Ishi back to the wilderness to starve. But it was the humanity of Ishi that left the most lasting impression on the public, for this gentle and quiet man directly contradicted the common view of the Indian as a wild and bloodthirsty savage.

The tragedy of Ishi is not the man himself, for

334

he left a wonderful legacy to anthropology and American history, but the realization he gave so many people of the magnitude of the genocide that had occurred. Perhaps the most telling legacy of the whole affair is correspondence quoted by Theodora Kroeber, Ishi's latter-day biographer. An assistant commissioner in the office of Indian Affairs in Washington wrote to inquire what "capacity" and "intelligence" Ishi had for "civilization." Could he be tamed for "simple manual labor"? Kroeber succinctly replied: "I beg to state that from the outset Ishi has conformed very willingly and to the full extent of his understanding, to the customs of civilized life." Officialdom soon gave up and closed its Ishi file. As far as Washington was concerned, Stone Age Californians had ceased to exist, even as a curiosity.

16 Conclusion

Maya standing pottery figurine representing a nobleman or a warrior-priest. He holds a knife and a staff and wears a conical hat. From the island of Jaina, Campeche.
Photograph courtesy of the Museum of the American Indian, Heye Foundation

The early development of archaeology in the New World was closely tied to evolving European attitudes toward the American Indian. It all began with the conquistadores' unquenchable lust for gold and precious stones, a lust fueled by the apparent wealth of the Aztec and Inca states. Nothing was sacred to the treasure hunters—temples and palaces were looted, graves robbed, native priests tortured for information about gold. Hundreds of Spaniards died on abortive expeditions in search of the legendary Fountain of Youth and the Seven Cities of Cibola. Within a few generations most of the gold artifacts and artistic achievements of the Aztec and Inca had passed into private hands, been traded against gambling debts, or been melted down for the royal treasuries of Europe. Missionaries wrought

336

further destruction. In their zeal to bring the Indians into the Christian fold they wrecked temples for building stone, burned codices, and broke up innumerable figurines and fine art objects. We will never be able to study the full spectrum of Aztec or Maya technological and artistic achievement as a result. The damage to American archaeology is simply incalculable.

Hand in hand with conquistadorial destruction went a sporadic intellectual curiosity about the Indians themselves. It was a curiosity that led some Spaniards to wonder whether the native Americans were human at all. But to Franciscans like Diego de Landa the Maya were only too human—people whom he tortured on one hand while he studied them avidly on the other. Spanish historians were conscious of the need for justification of colonization, exploitation, missionizing. They looked to Mediterranean lands for the ancestors of the Aztec and Maya, ignoring the evidence of the great temples themselves. They were allowed to pass into complete oblivion, to be swallowed up by the dense rain forest in which they nestled. Centuries were to pass before a delighted world was able to contemplate the incredible achievements of the prehistoric Mexicans afresh. Perhaps it was as well for archaeology that this oblivion ensued before everything was destroyed.

Intellectual attitudes toward the North American Indian were slow in forming. The northern peoples lacked the spectacular wealth and elaborate social organization of their southern neighbors. There were no high temples reeking of human sacrifice, nor could caches of gold be carried across the Atlantic for display in European capitals. Some tantalizing narratives, a few delightful drawings, and a scattering of artifacts formed the average Englishman's view of the American Indian four hundred years ago. From these scattered impressions and occasional glimpses of captive Indians came a romantic view of the native Americans that was to persist for many generations. The simple Indians of Virginia seemed to be living in an idyllic environment, one that was

337

exotic and kindly, plentiful and leisured. The impact was akin to that generated by the South Sea islanders in the eighteenth century. It was reflected in art and literature and bore no resemblance to the disillusionment that soon characterized the colonists' day-to-day dealings with the Indians. The tribesmen seemed to be the very embodiment of the Garden of Eden, the veritable heirs of Adam and Eve.

The speculations about the origins of the Indians that emerged from the first intellectual shock of their discovery were, of course, centered around theological dogma. That the Indians were descended from Adam and Eve was accepted as a basic proposition. What was at issue was the means by which they had arrived in the New World. Were they the descendants of the Ten Lost Tribes of Israel? Had bold voyagers crossed the Atlantic in search of a new homeland thousands of years before Columbus? Were the Indians Jews or Asians, Phoenicians or Chinese? There were no ready answers to be found, especially since the Indians themselves were at a loss to explain their history. In time all kinds of special-interest groups espoused pet theories about the Indians. These they laid before the public bolstered by a curious variety of data gleaned from many and varied sources. With the notable exception of Thomas Jefferson and a few other pioneers who dug carefully into ancient Indian mounds, no one thought of digging in search of information about the early Americans.

This was hardly surprising, for the science of archaeology was very much in its infancy in the eighteenth century. Antiquarians on both sides of the Atlantic were preoccupied with the great classical civilizations of Greece and Rome. After Napoleon's abortive campaigns in Egypt they turned their attention to the Nile as well. The Mediterranean lands were richly endowed with fine temples and spectacular art objects. These could be looted and excavated with ease, to the gratification of the collector and the enrichment of private and public museums. No one knew of any spectacular monuments or fine temples far away across the Atlantic in the New World, for the Maya ruins of Yucatan had been forgotten. The North American colonies were devoid of any dramatic archaeological sites. So the great acquisitors and dealers went elsewhere. The artifacts of the ancient Americans were ignored except by a minority of collectors who coveted Indian artifacts for their ethnographic museums. The American Indians simply appeared irrelevant to the great antiquarian concerns of the eighteenth century.

A new era in American archaeology began with the expansion of the colonies to the west. The colonial intellectuals were deeply curious about their homeland. A few, like Jefferson, had already researched some aspects of Indian life, stimulated in part by the travels of William Bartram and other pioneers. But as the deserted earthworks of the Ohio and Mississippi valleys came into public consciousness, curiosity about the early inhabitants of the new territories reached fever pitch.

This curiosity was many-faceted. Hundreds of poor farmers eking out a bare living from newly cleared lands plowed away Indian mounds to plant crops. Many dug for treasure in their local earthworks. The mounds were found to contain thousands of burials and elaborate artifacts. The farmers sometimes made a profit. Even if there was no gold, many east coast collectors were very happy to buy up the finds for their cabinets of curiosities or for friends or clients in Europe. Cities like Marietta and Columbus were sited in the middle of abandoned Indian earthworks, to the detriment of the archaeological sites. Many mounds and fortifications were obliterated as gridirons of streets and new houses were laid out in serried lines. Few people paused to study the former inhabitants of the mounds that were coming under the plow. Their curiosity was centered around treasure, land, and wealth rather than prehistory.

But an inevitable myth arose, that of a formerly great and prosperous race of Mound Builders, who had inhabited the Ohio Valley and the Midwest long ago. How could the modern Indians, who were so primitive, possibly have built the vast earthworks that dotted the American landscape? people argued.

339

Even respectable scholars turned to more exotic explanations, of vanished civilizations that had landed in the New World and created a vast empire there long before Columbus arrived. Legend and fantasy, romance and epic narrative soon surrounded the myth of the Mound Builders. The myth became theological canon, part of Mormon faith, an often repeated theme of the popular and romantic literature in the nineteenth century. To a great extent the Mound Builders became the historical justification for American colonization, for the settlement of Indian lands. There was a complete historical vacuum surrounding both the Indians and the mysterious earthworks. Like the unknown vastness of space, the empty spaces of American history had to be filled with something, a convenient explanation for mysterious phenomena had to be created. The myth of the Mound Builders provided a fruitful field for unscrupulous pseudo-anthropologists whose researches provided "explanations" and "ancient traditions" from Indian informants. It was all wonderful escapism from the realities of a harsh life and people lapped it up. Many authors made fortunes from the Mound Builders. But, as author Samuel Drake once remarked, the story "gained much of its Wildness and Improbability in its passage through a wild and savage country."

Fortunately for American archaeology, a few pioneer researchers attempted to record details of mounds and earthworks before it was too late. The names of Caleb Atwater, Ephraim Squier, and Edwin Davis are deeply respected in archaeological circles. They were pioneers who worked in the Midwest before the days of official archaeological expeditions and research institutes in east coast universities. These pioneer researches and those of the Mound Division of the Bureau of American Ethnology finally laid the great myth to rest, at least in the scientific mind. But the popular image of mound archaeology long revolved around exotic civilization and foreign settlers. Eventually, as a greater awareness of Indian cultural achievements percolated into the popular imagination, so did the myths retreat to the lunatic fringes of archaeology. But the banishment of the myths did not result in any slowing of the inexorable destruction of the earthworks themselves. Today, few undisturbed mounds exist outside the confines of national or state parks.

The rapid expansion of scientific research in the nineteenth century coincided with the opening up of the Far West. This was the territory of the Seven Lost Cities of Cibola, of the mysterious pueblos of the Southwest. The military expeditions of the 1850s and 1860s were soon replaced by official surveys and by scientists working with the support of private philanthropists or of government. Gradually the mysteries of the pueblos were revealed to an excited world. The Philadelphia Exposition of 1876 was a turning point, when the public was able to view a comprehensive display of Indian life in the Southwest and see some of the artifacts from the pueblos themselves. From that moment on the pace of archaeological research and pot hunting accelerated, as both scholars and treasure hunters dug into the abandoned ruins of Aztec and Pueblo Bonito, emptying the Mesa Verde ruins with breathtaking ruthlessness and speed. North America had finally discovered its own spectacular archaeological treasures. Apparently they were there for the collecting. It was not until the early twentieth century that some southwestern pueblos were placed under official protection and treasure hunting halted in their shattered precincts.

But by this time the damage done to archaeological sites in North America was already serious. Antique dealers from Boston, New York, Philadelphia, and other eastern cities had long been buying collections from the mounds and earthworks of the Midwest. Private collectors ranged far and wide, digging into mounds on Sunday afternoons and collecting large pottery caches from burials in the Southwest. Some of the "relic collections" accumulated during the 1870s and 1880s were enormous. Even the unspectacular Indian coastal shell mounds of the southern California coast were raided for their artifacts. In January 1876, for example, a Connecticut

341

Working drawings of wall paintings at Chichen Itza prepared and published by the Stephens party.

collector whose name is not recorded visited the Reverend Bowers of Santa Barbara, California. After a prospecting visit of several weeks and numerous purchases, the gentleman "collected and shipped to his Eastern home over two tons of implements, utensils, weapons, etc. pertaining to the stone age." The local newspaper noted approvingly that visitors found Santa Barbara a "rich field for the recovery of the buried treasures they so highly prize." Archaeology was certainly a boost to the local tourist industry. Doubtless there are thousands of similar stories buried in the archives of local newspapers in other cities, too.

The accelerating pace of collecting and site destruction stemmed not only from the rapid settlement of the West, but also from a much more intense interest in archaeology in general and in the collection of everything, from Indian artifacts to geological specimens, from birds to model railroads. By now the cultural achievements of the native Americans had been in the public eye for several generations. The stereotyped image of the American brave and the Wild West were part of this consciousness. So were the spectacular discoveries of Frederick Catherwood and John Lloyd Stephens. Their revelations about Maya archaeology sparked a wave of interest in ancient American civilization. Stephens wove a brilliant synthesis of travelogue, entertaining peoples, and exotic ancient civilizations into a coherent and human narrative that brought American archaeology into everyone's household. Above all, Catherwood's artistry captured the environment of the Maya sites, entwined as many of them were in dense, humid rain forests. Catherwood portrays the entanglement and the intricate carvings so vividly that one almost expects Maya priests to emerge from the forest and resume their sacrifices at the foot of the carved idols that remain. "Many later artists were to draw and paint . . . ," wrote Hugh Honour recently, "but none more effectively stamped on the European imagination the image of these strange civilizations which seem . . . to emerge like natural forces out of the dark jungle that will once

342

again reclaim them." The historian W. H. Prescott's great volumes of Mexican history were as widely read in Europe as in the Americas, Thomas Macaulay noting that "every schoolboy knows who imprisoned Montezuma."

Yet, remarkably, archaeologists and collectors were slow to emulate Catherwood and Stephens. It was to be nearly half a century before serious foreign investigators revisited the Maya. The Central American countries were better known during the nineteenth century for their exotic products and constant revolutions than they were for their monuments. The 1851 London Exhibition at the Crystal Palace mirrored the current European view of the world. Mexico was represented by a few wax models and an exhibit of woods that "may prove of value to the naturalist." Sixteen years later the Mexicans pro-

The Mexican Exhibition in London, 1825. A lithograph by A. Aglio.

343

vided a replica of the temple of Xochicalco, complete with a row of skulls and exotic carvings. Of original artifacts there were none at either exposition. Unlike the Egyptians, whose antiquities featured prominently in Paris, the Maya remained an exotic and savage civilization at the edge of the known world.

People were reminded of the bloodthirsty Aztec by novel and popular history, by the writings of the famous schoolboy storyteller G. A. Henty. In 1891 one of Henty's boy heroes fought alongside the Spaniards in Mexico. *By Right of Conquest* was a stirring tale of a young Englishman's adventures in remote Central America and of his narrow escape from an Aztec sacrifice. Of course the hero and the conquerors prevailed. It could not be otherwise in Victorian England. So the exotic and bloody popular stereotypes of the Central Americans were perpetuated to become part of European culture a century ago.

Our story ends with the beginnings of scientific archaeology itself. With the Bureau of American Ethnology in the East, Frederick Cushing, Adolph Bandelier, and Alfred Kidder in the Southwest, North American archaeology slowly moved, at least partially, from treasure hunting and uncritical digging to careful classification and meticulous analysis of thousands of finds. The Southwest in particular became a veritable laboratory of archaeological experimentation, in tree ring chronology and stratigraphic ordering of pottery, in restoration of pueblos and antiquities legislation. Mexican archaeology was placed on new footing at the end of the nineteenth century with the careful researches of Edward Thompson, A. P. Maudslay, and others. Detailed descriptions of temple and inscription replaced the casual investigations of yesteryear. Pottery styles and minute chronological changes were analyzed in the first systematic attempts to understand the prehistory of Yucatan and the Valley of Mexico. Much of this most serious and systematic research coincided with the first institutionally sponsored research in Central America, by the Carnegie Institution of Washington, the Peabody Museum, and others.

The story of archaeology told in these pages is but the beginning of an exciting narrative of fascinating discovery and dedicated research. The twentieth century has seen the emergence of archaeology as a viable and respected academic discipline, a means for hundreds of people to make a living. Thousands of sites have been dissected and surveyed. Enormous collections of artifacts from mound, shell midden, and pueblo fill the museums of North America. Among them the National Museum of Anthropology in Mexico City takes its place as one of the great public institutions of the world, designed to preserve the past, to study it, and to foster a sense of national identity among the diverse peoples of Mexico. Elaborate chronologies and detailed classifications of artifacts of all types have proliferated in the archaeological literature of the past seventy years, replacing the simplistic reports of earlier years.

Today we know a great deal about the outlines of New World prehistory. The first Americans are thought to have crossed the Bering Strait at least twenty thousand years ago, perhaps even earlier. Frederick Putnam has been vindicated, for the native Americans have lived in North America far longer than the Victorians envisaged. Agriculture and domestic animals were the subject of intense experimentation in Mexico by 6000 B.C. Maize was favored in the Southwest after 2000 B.C. and even earlier. Twenty-five hundred years ago the great indigenous states of Mesoamerica were emerging to take their place on the world stage. They are known to have reached their apogee in the Christian era, only to be destroyed within a few years by the ravages of the conquistadores. The closing centuries of prehistory in the Americas brought the gradual extinction of long-established adaptations and indigenous lifeways in the face of inexorable European settlement. It is, indeed, a miracle that any traces of traditional American Indian life have survived at all.

For all the detailed chronologies and sophisti-

345

cated ecological studies made by archaeologists, enormous gaps still exist in our knowledge of the history of the native Americans. Tribal histories, handed down from generation to generation by word of mouth, are in danger of extinction before they are recorded for posterity, a task that was begun by Powell and his successors and that is still incomplete. Thousands of Indian settlements have been excavated in the name of science. The artifacts from them have been dumped in museum storage warehouses and then forgotten, lying on shelves without associated notes or records of cultural association. An enormous backlog of museum study and publication of old excavated collections exists, an untapped archive of American history. Many worthwhile and profitable archaeological careers await those who are prepared to forgo excavation for museum analysis. The trouble is that a museum study career does not hold the glamour and appeal of archaeological excavation. Academic prestige, a cachet of "respectability" won through that mystical archaeological rite of passage, "field work," the assumption that experience running a dig means that one's archaeological judgments are sound, all militate against this choice of career for the fledgling archaeologist. Many chapters of American history are as deeply buried in museum collections as they once were in the ground.

One can understand archaeologists' preoccupation with excavation. The basic archives of native American history lie in the ground, in all types of archaeological sites, from shell middens to caves, from pueblos to temple mounds. These vital and irreplaceable archives are being destroyed with breathtaking speed, not by archaeologists but by Americans as a whole. There is now a real danger that no prehistoric Indian sites will remain for archaeologists to study within one or two centuries. The story of the native Americans is about to be obliterated by pot hunters and treasure seekers, developers, government projects, and industrial activity.

The twentieth century has brought not only scientific archaeology but an upsurge in public interest in

346

artifacts and sites as well. Hundreds of amateur archaeological societies have proliferated in the Americas in the past half century. Many of them are respected and hard-working bodies, worthy colleagues of such long-established organizations as the Society for American Archaeology. A minority are thinly disguised covers for treasure-hunting and pot-collecting clubs. Their members meet for surreptitious expeditions in search of arrowheads and undisturbed sites. These they ravage, pockmarking their quarry with burrows that bear no resemblance to archaeological excavations. The artifacts from their diggings are wrenched from cultural context, displayed, sold, or traded for similar specimens. An entire industry surrounds the pot hunter, that of the collector of objects. The fact that devotion is lavished on Indian artifacts is merely grist to the mill. It could equally well be beer can openers, barbed wire, or matchbox labels.

Americans have long cherished the dream of buried treasure, of a crock of gold at the end of the rainbow. The dream is reflected in the farmer—treasure hunter of a century and a half ago, and in the pot hunter of today. Unfortunately, Indian artifacts have acquired a steadily increasing value over the years, one now exacerbated by inflation, increased demand for a diminishing resource, and the high prestige attached to the collection of antiquities and fine art objects. The victim has been national history. Thousands of sites have been ravaged for personal gain and for sport. Whole chapters of American Indian history have been lost forever. The beautiful Mimbres vase displayed in a New Mexican home is valueless to American history; it is merely a fine bauble that titillates the artistic fancy. In this sense the goals of collectors and archaeologists are in collision, with tragic consequences for American history.

The damage wrought to our historical archives by developers, road engineering works, flood control schemes, and strip mining, to say nothing of deep plowing and forestry, is even more devastating. The government flood control schemes of the 1930s destroyed hundreds of sites in the South. Accelerated freeway construction and house building in Florida, California, and all parts of North America have taken a devastating toll of prehistoric sites. Thousands of Indian burials have been bulldozed into oblivion. Deep plowing in Arkansas has raped hundreds of sites, to the extent that archaeologist Patrick McGimsey estimates that at least 25 percent of the prehistoric settlements in that state have been destroyed in the past decade. At this rate Arkansas will have no undisturbed sites left in another generation. The toll of mounds in the Midwest and of Indian settlements in California has been just as bad. Virtually the only undisturbed and protected archaeological sites in Los Angeles County, as an example, are in federal and state parks.

There are no easy solutions to this critical problem. Legislation to protect archaeological sites is impossibly expensive to enforce. In any case, the federal and state legislation that currently exists is ineffective, or not nearly comprehensive enough, especially insofar as it affects private lands. There are no licensing procedures for archaeologists. Practically anybody can set himself up as an archaeologist and go ahead and excavate, although this is becoming harder in some parts of the country. Although environmental impact reports are now required of many development projects, there are not enough trained archaeologists around to handle the work. Thus, many such documents are ineffective and inadequate, and they fail to do justice to the sites they describe. Many archaeologists are so occupied with teaching and urgent rescue excavations that they have no time to carry out such work as well. At the practical level archaeology itself is in a crisis of manpower, legislation, and available resources to carry out the massive and urgent rescue operation that is in prospect.

Archaeology is divided within itself. The past seventy years have seen a revolution in archaeological methods. Complex descriptive and classification schemes have been erected, new digging methods introduced. Radiocarbon dating and

348

tree ring chronologies have changed the face of prehistoric time scales. The advent of the digital com-
puter and systems approaches to the social sciences
in the 1960s have taken archaeologists to the brink of
another quantum jump in theoretical and analytical
approaches. The world of academic archaeology, as
opposed to rescue excavation and environmental impact reporting, is in turmoil. It is deeply concerned
with the body of archaeological method and theory,
with establishing truly scientific approaches to the
study of New World prehistory. Since the days of
Adolph Bandelier, American archaeology has
thought of itself as part of anthropology, as a means
of studying humans in the past, a way of giving
anthropology some time dimension. This approach
is a natural one, since American archaeologists have
always been studying a society other than their own.
There is no historical identity with Indian society on
the part of white archaeologists.

The sense of American nationalism so carefully
fostered by the Bicentennial and other such displays
of patriotic fervor does not generally embrace
the achievements and cultural traditions of the
American Indian, for all the protestations to the
contrary. There is no public, and little professional,
sense of urgency about archaeology being a unique
source of native American history, with its own archives and story to tell. The study of prehistory in
North America appears to be largely an academic
discipline concerned with anthropological abstracts
and artifact descriptions, and more recently with
ecological studies. And the public still regards archaeological sites as curiosities and sources of
treasure, its imagination titillated by the modern versions of the Mound Builder hypothesis that speak of
Ancient Astronauts and Egyptian voyages rather
than the Ten Lost Tribes of Israel.

Yet, ironically, the great achievements of the
American Indian are available for thousands to appreciate and enjoy, at Mesa Verde and Cahokia,
Teotihuacan and Uxmal. Thousands have visited
these spectacular sites, yet few think of them as part
of our common American heritage, in a world where

349

the human diversities of the past are rapidly becoming irrelevant in the face of accelerating cultural change. Many different cultural traditions are slowly being forged into a common national heritage culled from many ethnic sources.

The fostering of national unity is a task for politicians and not for archaeologists. But the task of saving the history of the native Americans for posterity is one both for archaeologists and for the public. The federal government has made a start in refining its methods of encouraging salvage, rescue work, and environmental impact reporting, through changes in its contract system to stimulate what it, rather inappropriately, calls the research market. It remains for archaeologists to concentrate their efforts on the delicate strategies needed for preserving what remains of the American past before it is gone forever. But the public has the ultimate responsibility. Archaeological sites are a finite resource in the Americas. No longer, like Thomas Jefferson, Earl Morris, or John Lloyd Stephens, can we afford to dig and study them without a thought for conservation

and preservation. A change in social values and an acceptance of responsibility for the American past must come soon if anything is to survive for our descendants to appreciate and enjoy. One can be certain that those who placed American archaeology on a scientific basis would approve.

Palenque: shell plaque, 2¾ inches high, representing a Maya nobleman, or a priest, seated on a low throne, once entirely inlaid with precious stones. Inlaid pearl ear ornament.
Photograph courtesy of the Museum of the American Indian, Heye Foundation

Sources

Writing this book involved reading a huge and diffuse body of literature. The sources given here are ones that I found particularly useful. Length restrictions forced me to neglect many fascinating byways of American archaeology, which the reader can explore through these basic sources.

To my knowledge there is only one summary of the history of American archaeology as a whole: Gordon R. Willey and Jeremy Sabloff's *A History of American Archaeology* (San Francisco: W. H. Freeman, 1974), written for an academic audience. A factual narrative, it possesses a most useful and comprehensive bibliography. C. W. Ceram, *The First American* (New York: Harcourt, Brace, 1971), contains much popular information.

Chapter One

The discovery of the Americas is amply documented in a shoal of both good and dreadful books. Samuel Eliot Morison's two-volume *The Discovery of America* (New York: Oxford University Press, 1971 and 1974) has no peer. No one interested in the early voyagers can do without it. A. L. Rowse, *The Elizabethans and America* (New York: Harper, 1959), is a summary of the conflicts and intellectual debates caused by the discovery of the New World. G. R. Crone, *The Discovery of America* (New York: Weybright and Talley, 1969), deals with geography. Lee Eldridge Huddleston, *Origins of the American Indians* (Austin: University of Texas Press, 1967), studies the intellectual arguments.

Hernando Cortés is immortalized in W. H. Prescott's *Conquest of Mexico* (New York: Harper, 1843). Bernal Díaz, *The History of the Conquest of New Spain,* translated by J. M. Cohen (Baltimore: Pelican Books, 1963), is a first-hand account. So are Cortés's own *Five Letters to the Emperor, 1519–26,* translated by J. Bayard Morris (New York: Norton, 1962).

Chapter Two

Diego de Landa's *Relación de las Cosas de Yucatan* has been translated several times. An easily accessible and extensively indexed version is that edited by Alfred M. Tozzer in the *Papers of the Peabody Museum of American Archaeology and Ethnology* (Harvard University, no. 18, 1941). Robert Brunhouse's *In Search of the Maya* (Albuquerque: University of New Mexico Press, 1973) is a mine of information on del Río. The latter's *Description of the Ruins of an Ancient City* . . . can be found in most major university libraries. A good background account of Mesoamerican archaeology to accompany the Middle American chapters of this book is Muriel Porter Weaver, *The Aztecs, Maya, and Their Predecessors* (New York: Seminar Press, 1972).

Chapters Three and Four

There is an enormous literature on the early explorers of the southern United States, including several authoritative translations. Samuel Eliot Morison's second volume is informative, while de Soto and Cabeza de Vaca receive attention in F. W. Hodge's edited translations: *Spanish Explorers in the Southern United States* (New York: Scribners, 1907). The Natchez funeral ceremonies are described in John R. Swanton's translation of Le Page du Pratz, *Histoire de la Louisiane* (Paris, 1858), published by the Bureau of American Ethnology in 1911. A. Grove Day, *Coronado's Quest* (Berkeley and Los Angeles: University of California Press, 1940), is a thorough account of the events leading up to Coronado's expedition and of the adventure itself. Translations of the journals and reports of the expedition can be read in George P. Hammond (ed.), *Narrations of the Coronado Expedition* (Albuquerque: University of New Mexico Press, 1940).

Chapters Five and Six

The fundamental source on mounds and the mound controversies is Robert Silverberg, *The Mound Builders of Ancient America* (New York: New York Graphic Society, 1968). Like anyone writing on this complex subject, I owe Silverberg an enormous debt. Thomas Jefferson's archaeological investigations have been widely quoted and can be read in his *Notes on the State of Virginia* (1784) or in Glyn Daniel, *Origins and Growth of Archaeology* (Baltimore: Pelican Books, 1967). Fawn Brodie, *Thomas Jefferson: An Intimate Biography* (New York: Norton, 1974), has few rivals. Bartram's book can be found in most larger libraries and has been reprinted frequently. Caleb Atwater, "Description of the Antiquities Discovered in the State of Ohio and Other Western States," *Transactions of the American Antiquarian Society,* vol. 1 (1820), is another reprinted classic (New York: Johnson Reprint Corporation, 1970). Fawn Brodie, *No Man Knows My History* (New York: Knopf, 1945), is a mine of information on Mormon treasure hunting.

Chapters Seven to Ten

These four chapters follow well-trod ground. Robert Brunhouse, in *In Search of the Maya* (Albuquerque: University of New Mexico Press, 1973), has written of the personalities described in these chapters. A later volume by the same author, *Pursuit of the Ancient Maya* (Albuquerque: University of New Mexico Press, 1975), deals with early twentieth-century workers. But the writings of the pioneers themselves are fascinating. Jean Frédéric Waldeck's *Voyage pittoresque et archéologique dans . . . Yucatan* (Paris, 1838) is remarkable for its fine and highly characteristic art. The Walker-Caddy expedition is well described by David M. Prendergast, *Palenque* (Norman: University of Oklahoma Press, 1967).

Catherwood and Stephens have received praise from many archaeological writers, notably C. W. Ceram, *Gods, Graves, and Scholars* (New York: Knopf, 1953). Victor von Hagen's *Maya Explorer* (Norman: University of Oklahoma Press, 1947) and *Frederick Catherwood, Architect* (New York: Oxford University Press, 1950) are the definitive biographies of both men. I have used them extensively here. But the real fascination of Catherwood and Stephens lies in their own work, in their extraordinary gifts of communication. No one should miss John Lloyd Stephens, *Incidents of Travel in Central America, Chiapas and Yucatan* and *Incidents of Travel in Yucatan* (New York: Harper, 1841 and 1843, respectively). Both are still available in paperback through Dover Press, New York. These books have been my primary sources for these chapters, as well as Frederick Catherwood's rare folio, *Views of Ancient Monuments in Central America, Chiapas and Yucatan* (London, 1844).

Chapter Eleven

Robert Silverberg on the Mound Builders was one of the major sources here, for he is the only person to have sifted through the enormous literature in depth. No one seems to plow through Schoolcraft's book, but E. G. Squier and E. H. Davis, *Ancient Monuments of the Mississippi Valley*, is a much consulted classic (New York: Johnson Reprint Corporation, 1965). William Pidgeon, *Traditions of De-coodah and Antiquarian Researches* (New York, 1852), is worth a quiet laugh. In sharp contrast is Samuel Haven, *The Archaeology of the United States* (Washington, D.C.: Smithsonian Institution, 1856), a sober assessment of the state of American archaeology in the mid-nineteenth century.

Chapter Twelve

Two outstanding books provided the foundations of this chapter. William H. Goetzmann's *Exploration and Empire*

(New York: Knopf, 1966) and *Army Exploration in the American West* (New Haven, 1959) are the fundamental sources on early western exploration. They include some archaeological endeavors. The military reports of the 1840s make fascinating reading; a good example is William Hemsley Emory, *Notes on a Military Reconnaissance from Fort Leavenworth in Missouri to San Diego in California*, 30th Cong., 1st Sess., Senate Executive Document 7 (1848). Senate Executive Document 64 (1850) contains the James Harvey Simpson report referred to in the chapter. The Hayden reports can be found in the National Archives, while W. H. Jackson, *Time Exposure: Autobiography of W. H. Jackson* (New York: G. P. Putnam, 1940), is an interesting piece of western history. Adolph Bandelier is well described by Leslie A. White, *Pioneers in American Anthropology: The Bandelier-Morgan Letters, 1873–1883*, Coronado Cuarto Centennial Publications, 1540–1940 (Albuquerque: University of New Mexico Press, 1940). Bandelier's *Delight Makers* (New York: Dodd, Mead, 1890) is a fascinating example of the novelist's craft.

Frank H. Cushing, *My Adventures in Zuñi* (New York, 1882–83), originally appeared as a series of articles in *The Century Magazine* in those years. The book has been reprinted at least three times, one of the best known by American West Publishing Company (Palo Alto, 1970).

Chapter Thirteen

The best account of this fascinating period of archaeological history has been compiled by Robert Wauchaupe, *Lost Tribes and Sunken Continents* (Chicago: University of Chicago Press, 1962), who deals with Brasseur de Bourbourg and Auguste Le Plongeon. Edward Thompson is well served by his autobiography: *People of the Serpent* (Boston: Little Brown, 1932), but this has to be amplified from other sources. Robert Brunhouse's *In Search of the Maya* (Albuquerque: University of New Mexico Press, 1973) provides a summary account, while the same author's *Pursuit of the Ancient Maya* (Albuquerque: University of New Mexico Press, 1975) gives background on some of Edward Thompson's contemporaries. Theodore A. Willard wrote two books that deal with Thompson and his discoveries: both *City of the Sacred Well* and *Kukulcan the Bearded Conqueror* . . . should be read with a critical eye.

Chapter Fourteen

The early history of the Peabody was described by J. O. Brew (ed.), *A Hundred Years of Anthropology* (Cambridge, Mass.: Harvard University Press, 1968). John Wesley Powell has many biographers. I drew on W. C. Darrah, *Powell of the Colorado* (Princeton: Princeton University Press, 1951). The history of the Bureau of American Ethnology is well described by Neil M. Judd, *The Bureau of American Ethnology: A Partial History* (Norman: University of Oklahoma Press, 1967), where details of its early publications will be found. No archaeologist should miss Cyrus Thomas, *Report on the Mound Explorations of the Bureau of Ethnology*, Twelfth Annual Report of the Bureau of American Ethnology (1894). Robert Silverberg described the effigy mounds, while Robert Wauchope, *Lost Tribes and Sunken Continents* (Chicago: University of Chicago Press, 1962), is both vastly entertaining and highly informative. Henry C. Shetrone's *The Mound Builders* (New York: Kennikat Press, 1930) completes a basic reading list on mound sites. Gordon R. Willey, *An Introduction to American Archaeology*, vol. 1: North and Middle America (Englewood Cliffs, N.J.: Prentice-Hall, 1967), is the definitive modern account.

Chapter Fifteen

Frank McNitt, *Richard Wetherill: Anasazi* (Albuquerque: University of New Mexico Press, 1967), describes this fascinating pioneer archaeologist and collector. Earl H. Morris is chronicled by F. C. and R. H. Lister, *Earl Morris and Southwestern Archaeology* (Albuquerque: University of New Mexico Press, 1968). This account can be supplemented by Ann Axtell Morris, *Digging in the Southwest* (New York: Doubleday, Doran, 1933), a wife's account of the same events. A. V. Kidder, *An Introduction to the Study of Southwestern Archaeology*, 2nd ed. (New Haven: Yale University Press, 1963), is still a fundamental source on Pecos and the early classification systems. And Theodora Kroeber's *Ishi in Two Worlds* (Berkeley: University of California Press, 1965) reduces many readers to tears.

Chapter Sixteen

Hugh Honour, *The New Golden Land* (New York: Pantheon Books, 1975), is a recent and fascinating account of Europe and the Indians. Its illustrations are particularly fine. No one seriously interested in American archaeology should miss Patrick McGimsey, *Public Archaeology* (New York: Seminar Press, 1972), a devastating account of the destruction and legislation involved in contemporary archaeology. Carl Meyer's *The Plundered Past* (New York: Atheneum, 1973) is also required reading for all archaeologists and would-be collectors.

INDEX

Page numbers in boldface refer to illustrations.

362